365 Meditations for Teachers by Teachers

365 Meditations for TEACHERS by TEACHERS

Sally D. Sharpe, Editor; Angela M. Bailey, Cindy M. Bradley
Danny Hill, Cathy Howard, Amy Maze, Kellen Beck Mills

DIMENSIONS
FOR LIVING
NASHVILLE

365 MEDITATIONS FOR TEACHERS BY TEACHERS

Copyright 2005 by Dimensions for Living.

All rights reserved.

This book is printed on acid-free paper.

Library of Congress Cataloging-in-Publication Data

365 meditations for teachers by teachers / Sally D. Sharpe, editor; [contributors], Angela M. Bailey . . . [et al.].
    p. cm.
  ISBN 0-687-49681-0 (alk. paper)
    1. Teachers—Prayer-books and devotions—English. 2. Teaching—Religious aspects—Christianity. 3. Devotional calendars. I. Sharpe, Sally D., 1964- II. Bailey, Angela M.
  BV4596.T43T47 2005
  242'.68—dc22

2005004615

05 06 07 08 09 10 11 12 13 14—10 9 8 7 6 5 4 3 2 1
MANUFACTURED IN THE UNITED STATES OF AMERICA

CONTENTS

INTRODUCTION
Touching Hearts, Changing Lives

BESIDES PARENTS AND GRANDPARENTS, PERHAPS NO ONE HAS greater influence in our lives than teachers. No doubt, most of us can think of at least one teacher who touched our heart or changed our life in some way. Sometimes even the most seemingly insignificant "touches" have a tremendous impact. I think of my first-grade teacher, Mrs. Pennycost. She would jokingly say that she "cost a penny," but she had a million-dollar smile that made you feel special and loved. She genuinely cared about each and every student, and she showed it in so many ways. Perhaps most memorable was being invited to her home for a special "one-on-one" afternoon with the teacher. She extended this invitation to every student in her class during the course of the year. Mrs. Pennycost taught us much more than reading, writing, and arithmetic; she also taught us to believe in ourselves and to appreciate our unique personalities and abilities. She truly touched our hearts and changed our lives.

Touching hearts and changing lives—that, in a nutshell, is the high calling of teaching. It is a sacred and noble calling, yet one that is demanding and draining and often disappointing. That's why six Christian writers who share a love for teaching have come together in this book to offer biblical guidance, practical insights, personal stories, and words of encouragement for the daily challenges of teaching. Though they write in a variety of styles and draw from a multitude of experiences, they have a common purpose: to remind you that your efforts each day truly do make a difference—for your students, for the future of our country and world, and for God's kingdom. The writers include four classroom teachers and two principals, but all know firsthand both the difficulties and blessings of answering God's call to touch hearts and change lives through the vocation of teaching.

Regardless of what or where you teach—whether it be elementary, middle, or high school—you will find that these devotions "ring true" because they are written by teachers who have experienced similar challenges, struggles, needs, and joys. Although the book begins with the month of August—the first month of the school year in most school systems—you may begin using the book at any time of the year, making your way through the months until you've completed a year's cycle. It is my prayer that, in the process, you will come to have an even deeper appreciation for your God-given calling and your incredible potential to touch hearts and change lives. May God bless you as you bless our children.

Sally D. Sharpe, Editor

ABOUT THE WRITERS

Angela M. Bailey (AUGUST-SEPTEMBER) spent most of her childhood years in Nashville, Tennessee, and later moved to Atlanta, Georgia, to attend college and graduate school. She is currently in her twenty-first year in education, serving as an elementary principal in the Cobb County school system in Marietta, Georgia. Angela enjoys reading, speaking, and writing. She has two children who reside with her in Stone Mountain, Georgia.

Cindy M. Bradley (APRIL-MAY) has served as Director of Christian Education in two churches, one in Danville, Virginia, and the other in Fort Myers, Florida. Currently she is a media assistant at Riviera Elementary School in Palm Bay, Florida. She has led several seminars for teachers and organized a youth mission trip to the Bahamas. Cindy continues to have a heart for missions and has participated in a missions team to Chile and assisted Samaritan's Purse in hurricane disaster relief in southwest Florida. She enjoys music, reading, cooking, laughing, walking on the beach, and spending time with friends.

Danny Hill (OCTOBER-NOVEMBER) has taught and coached at the middle-school level, has been an assistant principal at the high-school level, and has served as principal of Southside Elementary, a K-8 school in Lebanon, Tennessee, for thirteen years. He has taught adult Sunday school for more than ten years and has coached several youth basketball and baseball teams. He also serves on the board of directors of a community bank. Danny and his wife, Debbie, a high school guidance counselor, have three children who enjoy sports—especially golf—and traveling together.

Cathy Howard (JUNE-JULY), a native of Denver, lived in Montana, Washington, North Dakota, and Wyoming before settling in Imperial, a small town in southwestern Nebraska, twenty-five years ago. She is still in love with her job: teaching high-school English, speech, and drama in Imperial's K-12 580-student district. Her grown children, two daughters and two sons, live in or near Imperial, so five of her seven grandchildren attend school in the same building where she teaches. She plays various stringed and keyboard instruments and is an organist and youth-group coordinator for her church. Her work has appeared in various local publications and in *Chicken Soup for the Single Soul*. She also has published a children's play, *The Frog Princess*.

Amy Maze (DECEMBER-JANUARY) is an elementary public school teacher in Nashville, Tennessee. She has a master's degree in elementary education and is a National Board certified teacher. In addition to teaching children, she has taught adult education courses. She also has worked with and taught children ranging from preschool through high school at her church in Nashville. When she is not teaching, she enjoys traveling, shopping, scrapbooking, and learning new things.

Kellen Beck Mills (FEBRUARY-MARCH) is a middle-school art teacher, artist, and mother of two teenage boys. She specializes in the mediums of paint and collage and also designs greeting cards. Kellen writes essays and poetry, and she journals on a regular basis. She feels that work, family, and personal interests all interconnect for her in the creative process of living and growing closer to the Lord in faith each day. She lives in Fort Myers, Florida.

AUGUST
Less Stress!

Angela M. Bailey

AUGUST 1
GOD'S PROMISE OF PEACE—READ MATTHEW 6:25-34 AND JOHN 14:27.

BEFORE EACH NEW SCHOOL YEAR, WE ARE PRESENTED WITH new strategies, materials, team members, students and parents, and sometimes administrators. These changes often require shifts in thinking, teaching styles, and even preparation. Then, as the first day of school draws near and more of our time is devoted to decorating classrooms, reviewing class lists, meeting with grade-level teams, and participating in staff development and in-service, stress begins to build!

In the midst of the preparation and planning, we must remember that our heavenly Father is always with us, guiding us and giving us his peace. We must concentrate on what is truly important and do a good job for the Lord.

When you feel stress building, focus on "resting in the Lord." In the morning, pray about the day and turn it over to the Lord. You will experience better days filled with peace.

This month we will consider ways to reduce our stress and keep our focus on the Lord, remembering that he will give us his perfect peace as we trust in him. And that's a promise we can count on!

Father, each day help me let go of my stress and focus on the peace you have promised me. Amen.

August 2

Keep Your Joy—Read Nehemiah 8:10 and Psalm 30:5.

As summer draws to a close, we begin to plan all the lessons we're going to teach in the coming year. We think about field trips, centers, gifts for students, and room decorations. Then, suddenly, we realize that school is upon us and we have so much to do—including all the meetings that the administration has arranged! Stress builds, panic sets in, and we get heated and agitated. Just a few days ago we were happy, thinking of all the wonderful activities we would do with our students. What happened to our joy? Why are we now short-tempered with a sour look on our faces?

The students and parents need and deserve to see our joy, not our frustration. Our job is to assure them that we are ready for this exciting job and are confident we will have a successful year. If we allow ourselves to get stressed out, we will have no patience for Evan who needs an extra push, no encouragement for Brandy who needs to do a little better, no pat on the back for Lauren after she finally learns her multiplication facts.

If we remember that the Lord is the source of our joy and we stay close to him, then we will be able to keep the joy in the classroom and school and continuously make learning pleasant!

Lord, restore the joy in my heart no matter what situation arises or what I'm faced with. Amen.

August 3

Good Relationships—Read Ephesians 4:32a.

When my son's first-grade teacher took the time to eat dinner with us because my son had made progress in school, it was the highlight of my son's year. Personal touches such as that make an impression on the student as well as the entire family.

As educators, we need to be intentional about developing good relationships with our students and parents. Working on this at the *beginning* of the year goes a long way toward preventing unnecessary conflict later on. Then, if there should be something negative that needs to be discussed later in the year, there will be goodwill to cushion the conversation and help everyone communicate better.

I always make it a practice to call parents at the beginning of the year and welcome their children to my class. I let each parent know how proud and privileged I am to have the opportunity to teach his or her child for the year. Sending notes is fine, too, but there is nothing like personal contact.

What can you do to strengthen your relationships with your students and parents?

Lord, show me ways I can develop good relationships with my students and parents this year. May my love for you overflow into every other relationship in my life. Amen.

AUGUST 4

DO WHAT IS RIGHT—READ GALATIANS 6:9.

I remember my mother telling me when I was a little girl, "Always do what is right and you will never have to worry about being wrong." She was right. Doing the right thing eliminates a lot of worry!

I remember a student who always was teased by the other students because she wore glasses and was very skinny. Many times the students would blame her for devious tricks they had played on others. Often she would take the blame, refusing to tell the teacher the truth. After a period of time, however, the little girl began to get tired of the children blaming her and picking on her, and she began to bully others.

As teachers, we need to recognize the signs indicating that students are being teased or bullied and do what is right to protect and help those children. Children should always know that when they enter our schools, they are safe. When expectations regarding teasing and bullying are given and are followed consistently, students usually will comply.

This year, focus on having a classroom where students *always* feel comfortable to learn and grow.

Lord, thank you for telling us in your word not to grow weary in doing right. Guide me each day in leading your children. Amen.

AUGUST 5

POSITIVE THOUGHTS—READ JAMES 1:22.

When I was offered my first teaching job, I asked my mother, who was teaching in middle school, for advice. She said, "I have one piece of advice that will carry you through your entire tenure of education: Don't spend the majority of your time in the teachers' lounge!" I wouldn't understand that until I actually began teaching. She also told me to think positive thoughts instead of focusing on the negative communication I would hear.

In education, it almost seems natural to complain because everything is constantly changing. However, our thoughts always should reflect what we can do to move with the change and work for good.

During my first year as a teacher, I worked with a teacher who said she would never make the changes that were being demanded of us. She did not return the following year! Well, that eye-opening experience taught me to have a positive attitude and do my best to do whatever was required or requested.

As educators, it is our job to do all we can to meet the expectations not only of our students and parents but also of our administrators. Rather than getting "hung up" on a request, spend your energy on how you can make the change work in a positive way for you and your students.

Father, help me be not only a hearer of your word, but also a doer. May I not question what is asked of me but respond with optimism and enthusiasm. Amen.

AUGUST 6

NO MORE COMPLAINING—READ EXODUS 16:3.

As I've mentioned, change is inevitable in the field of education. Curricula change, assessments change, students change, expectations change—*everything* changes. Along with these changes, we have to adjust and start over. Sometimes this can be especially difficult if we've made up our minds that we are not going to change!

When the Israelites were traveling with Moses, they complained because Moses had taken them out of Egypt into the wilderness where they were not guaranteed food each day or a comfortable place to sleep each night. They complained consistently to Moses, and he told the Lord that the people were hungry. So, the Lord sent manna from heaven each morning for them to eat. After receiving the bread, however, they still weren't happy; they continued to complain about everything.

As educators, we have to be willing to make changes if we want to continue growing in this ever-changing field. When curricula change, there are reasons; when assessments change, there are reasons. Instead of worrying so much about the change, let's consider how we can truly affect the lives of children with this change. Instead of complaining about it, let's consider the positive effects that this change can bring upon our students and our schools.

Father in heaven, I will not complain but will accept the task you have given me and wait for your direction to complete it. Amen.

AUGUST 7

IMAGINE AND BELIEVE—READ GENESIS 15:5-6.

Before I became a school administrator, it seemed that every year I was assigned the students with behavior problems. My colleagues would tease me and say, "Oh, you can handle them; that's why you get them each year." Then they would share their "war stories" about their experiences with these students when they were in their classrooms.

Usually I found that when I didn't begin the year with my mind already made up about these challenging students, they would surprise me every time. I often reminded myself that the Lord told Abraham to count the stars, saying that he would make Abraham father of as many children as the stars he could count. Though it was difficult at first for Abraham to believe this promise because of his age, he began to believe what seemed impossible, and the Lord "reckoned it to him as righteousness (Genesis 15:6 NRSV)." God was, indeed, faithful to his promise.

Students need to know that we love them. We must focus on the end results instead of what we see now, imagining that we can achieve success. If we communicate our goals for our students, the majority of them *will* follow through. It's when they sense that we don't care about them that they become discipline problems.

Make it a practice to remind yourself daily that what seems impossible *is possible* with faith!

Father, thank you for our jobs and for the children I teach and lead. May I, like Abraham, imagine and believe, trusting you to make the impossible possible. Amen.

AUGUST 8

BE STEADFAST—READ 1 CORINTHIANS 15:58.

As teachers, we have the awesome job of influencing lives forever. When students enter our classrooms, they generally view us as the authority figure. (Though some students see us differently, the majority hold this view.) If we want to be successful, we must realize how much power we possess and determine to remain steadfast or consistent in our expectations; we must remember that the tone we set at the beginning of the school year continues throughout the year; and we must acknowledge that, even though they may never admit it, students want parameters.

One year when I was teaching third grade, many of my students had been labeled by previous teachers as "the worst students in the school." Nevertheless, I decided that I would treat them just as I had treated all of my previous classes. I came in the first day with my usual high expectations, and I proceeded to model these expectations and allow the students to practice them. I was consistent with every expectation, never wavering.

After a few months, teachers were commenting, "How did you get them to act that way?" I told them that I had remained consistent and steadfast in what I wanted to accomplish, and I had set high expectations for all the students, regardless of how they had been labeled in the past.

Father, help me be steadfast and consistent in the parameters and expectations I set for my students, remaining confident that my efforts are not in vain. Amen.

AUGUST 9

HIGH EXPECTATIONS—READ 1 TIMOTHY 4:11-12.

I have always had high expectations of students. The question I have to ask myself is this: Am I modeling the same kind of behavior I expect of them? There is an old saying: "Practice what you preach." In other words, if I say it, then I must do it as well!

When I was in elementary school, there was a teacher who most students did not like at the beginning of the year. This teacher was "mean" because she expected every child to follow her rules. Actually, she was an awesome teacher who used creativity, taught every child, and worked well with parents. But when it came to discipline in her classroom, everyone had to follow her rules.

Whenever students saw her, she consistently modeled the same behavior she expected of them. By the year's end, everyone loved this lady because she had enough guts to set limits and never lowered them. Even though they didn't like the rules at the beginning of the year, by the end she was their favorite teacher.

Since becoming a teacher, I have tried to model the same expectations for my students. I have found that all students want teachers to set parameters and, more important, to be consistent with them. It's when we waver back and forth that students find an open space and "fill it."

Lord, help me stay strong and consistent as I model the behavior I expect of my students. Amen.

AUGUST 10

TRAIN UP A CHILD—READ PROVERBS 22:6.

Once I had to attend a meeting in the media center at my school. One of the paraprofessionals would be assigned to cover my third-grade class, which was located in a trailer in the back parking lot.

After the meeting, I went to my classroom and found my students sitting quietly, completing the work I'd written on the board. The strange thing about this peaceful scene was that there was *no* adult in the classroom! My students said that they had been alone the entire time and had assumed I was in the front office listening to them over the intercom, just as I had told them I would do someday. In my absence, they had taken the attendance and lunch count and sent someone to turn those counts in to the front office. They also had started their work, which was written on the board. I found out later that no one had informed the paraprofessional to come to my room.

As I've said, my expectations of my students have always been clear and consistent. So, they thought that this was a test, and they wanted to prove to me how responsible they could be.

High expectations communicated in love can dramatically influence the atmosphere of our classrooms as well as the achievements of our students.

Lord, help me "train" my students in such a way that they will not only meet my expectations but also exceed them. Amen.

August 11

Working for God—Read Ephesians 6:7.

In every school where I've worked, I have worked with teachers who went far beyond what was expected of them, as well as those who did only the bare minimum. On individual teams, colleagues know which teachers they can go to for sharing new ideas, discussing classroom achievements, and asking for help in particular areas. Administrators also know which teachers are committed and which ones are less enthused.

In teaching, as in any job, we need to continually realize that we are working first and foremost for God. Every lesson we teach and every skill we present should be done in a way that pleases and honors God. You see, we often lose sight of who is really in charge. We think we're working for the system, but we're not. We're working for God. Students are the first ones to know when we don't want to teach, and when they realize this, they stop working to their full potential.

Once we "get" this revelation, we will be more enthusiastic about our position and our purpose. Administrators and other colleagues also will begin to notice when we change our outlook. Most important, *God* will notice!

Lord, help me eliminate much of my stress and worry by remembering that I am working for you, not the system. Amen.

August 12

Are You Complacent?—Read Colossians 3:23.

Schools have different academic levels. There are high-, low-, and average-achieving schools. Some teachers have a passion for a certain level and will teach only at a school that is at that level. Whatever our preferences may be, we need to be sure we never become complacent. The students at each of the levels need our dedication each and every day.

I once taught at a high-achieving school where the administrator, who felt that we had become too comfortable and complacent, wanted us to improve our test scores. One staff member commented, "We're already number twenty in the state! What do you want—number one?" The response was, "Yes! We set the expectation, and students will rise to meet it."

When I taught in the classroom, sometimes I was tired and didn't think I could accomplish any more; but when I would go that extra mile, the students would always "move" with me. Students are waiting for our direction. If we know where we are going, it's easy for them to follow, move ahead, and excel.

No matter what level of school we work in, let us continuously encourage our students to excel!

Lord, keep me strong—physically, mentally, emotionally, and spiritually—so I can give it my "all" each and every day, remembering that I am working for you. Amen.

AUGUST 13

A POSITIVE INFLUENCE—READ MATTHEW 5:13-16.

One year I received a call to leave my third-grade classroom and become an assistant principal. It was only the sixth week of school. My students were sad and their parents were disappointed. They decided to give me a farewell celebration, which was very humbling because I didn't realize how much I had influenced their lives in such a short time. One little girl I had taught how to read recorded and played the song "Wind Beneath My Wings," explaining that she felt I was her hero.

Later that same afternoon, the principal and staff of our school gave me a good-bye celebration where I was showered with gifts, funny stories, and acclamations of the job I had done. I gave thanks that day for the opportunity to have an impact in the lives of my students and colleagues.

Jesus said we are to be salt and light—to influence others for good. As teachers, we all influence the lives of our students. The question we need to ask ourselves is this: Will I have a positive or negative influence? May this question help us block out all the distractions that threaten to sidetrack us so that we may stay focused on being salt and light.

Thank you, Father, for giving me the job of educator. Help me be a positive influence in my classroom each day. Amen.

AUGUST 14
"WHY, LORD?"—READ 1 THESSALONIANS 5:17.

Lord, each day you give me these students to serve. Sometimes it's difficult because they are on different levels. Sometimes the parents dismiss information I give them as if I don't know what I'm talking about. I know that you have given me this job for a reason. I know there is a season for everything. But, I have to ask you, Lord, why are the students not more enthusiastic about learning new and won-derful skills? Why do they sometimes come to school hungry and wearing the same clothes they had on the day before? Why are they sleepy during the day? Why, when it is time to go home for the summer, do some of the children begin to cry?

It is not meant for me to know the answers to all of these questions. You have given me this assignment because you know I can handle it; you know I'm the person for the job because you have chosen me. It is not my place to question but to be obedient and do the job that you have given me.

Lord, help me remember that you will never give me more than I can handle, and that you will never leave or forsake me. I'm thankful that I can lift my prayers to you continu-ally, "without ceasing," and you always hear me and give me just what I need. Amen.

AUGUST 15
PARENT-TEACHER CONFERENCES—
READ 2 TIMOTHY 2:24-25.

Each year we have parent-teacher conferences, which allow us to share the "whole picture" of the child. This is also an opportunity for us to offer suggestions for remedying weaknesses we have observed.

I once held a conference where the parents were obviously not happy with the report I was presenting. During the months preceding the conference, I had sent home weekly updates and had made several telephone calls to express concern for the student's performance. The student also had received additional support after school. Still, the parents questioned *everything*—from the grades to the computation of the grades to the number of graded assignments given.

That kind of response can truly "stress out" a well-intentioned teacher. Thankfully, I had gathered all of the necessary information prior to the conference. So I was able to answer all of the parents' questions and go beyond what was asked to substantiate the grades given—all in a positive, gentle tone. By the end of the conference, the parents apologized for their behavior and asked for additional suggestions.

My father used to always tell me, "You can kill people with kindness." What he meant was that you can change people's negative attitude toward you by treating them with kindness. Once again I discovered that he was right.

Lord, when difficult situations arise, help me be gentle and kind. Amen.

AUGUST 16

"HIGH STAKES" TESTS—READ 1 CORINTHIANS 13:7.

I used to work in a school that was always in the newspaper because of the poor performance of the students on statewide tests. No matter how much we wanted to improve our test scores, each year the scores would not be high enough according to state guidelines to make the cut. The teachers were hardworking and had a passion for teaching. They regularly attended staff development training and tried new strategies. Yet, because it was a very transient school with students of many languages, the challenge to raise the scores was daunting.

Even so, there were many positive things about the school, including the amount of learning that was actually taking place and the passion of the teachers and administration for the students. Our students would hug us each morning and greet us with a smile. Similarly, parents appreciated us because they knew we cared about their children.

Although a school may not be performing well on a "high stakes" test, this does not necessarily mean that the school is not performing in other areas. We need to be proud of *every* accomplishment we make with our students, remembering that our hard work and hope *will* bring results down the road—perhaps when one of our students becomes a teacher, a doctor, or even president of the United States.

Lord, every gain I make is a step toward accomplishment. Help me have the kind of love for my students that always hopes and perseveres. Amen.

AUGUST 17

SMALL ACTS OF LOVE—READ JOHN 13:34.

I was summoned from the office to work with a kindergartner who had been kicking children at his table and had been rude to the paraprofessional assigned to his classroom. When I got to him, I saw that he had been crying.

After I asked why he was having such a bad morning, he shared with me that he had not had any breakfast and that he had had to get himself ready for school. When I told him I could have gotten him breakfast in the cafeteria that morning, he said, "No, when I go in the cafeteria, the children laugh at me and call me names because I don't dress like they do."

He also shared that his parents had left last night and had said they would be back but had not returned. Knowing that he would have to get to school the next morning, he had not slept all night so that he would not be tardy.

His comments explained why he had had such an outburst. Now with understanding, I asked him, "What can I do to make your day better?" His response was simply, "Can you wipe the tears off of my glasses?"

With our overcrowded days, it's reassuring to know that love is as simple as wiping away tears or giving a pat on the back.

Lord, help me remember that even the smallest acts of love make a big difference. Amen.

AUGUST 18
GETTING "OFF TRACK"—READ MATTHEW 19:13-14.

One day while teaching a lesson on the solar system, one of my students suddenly interjected, "Wouldn't it be great to speak to the officials at NASA and ask them to give us a tour and tell us about one of their shuttle missions?" I thought to myself, *Yes, that would be a superb idea, but I don't know if NASA will agree to it.*

Well, wouldn't you know, one of the parents knew someone who worked there, and we were later able to have a virtual tour of NASA as well as get information on one of the shuttle missions. That lesson became real to my students because I allowed them to get me "off track" and, eventually, to learn far more than what was originally anticipated.

Despite our desire to remain in control and on task, sometimes we need to welcome interruptions and turn our attention to what may *appear* to be off track or less important. That's exactly what the best teacher of all time, Jesus, did. May we follow his example.

Lord, help me seize, not squelch, teachable moments, always affirming my students' questions and ideas. Amen.

AUGUST 19
GOSSIP—READ JAMES 3:6.

As an educator, I am always surrounded by teachers and administrators. One day I had lunch with one of my colleagues in the teachers' lounge, and she began to tell me about one of her students. She told me about his parents' divorce, his test scores, his behavior, and his academic struggles. Neither of us realized that in the lounge with us was a substitute teacher who happened to be a parent at the school. Well, this parent decided to share what she had overheard with other parents, and eventually the information got back to one of the student's parents.

The teacher who had shared the information with me was well-intentioned. She was not bad-mouthing the child or wishing the child were out of her room; she was just gossiping. Unfortunately, her tongue created quite a "blaze."

The same kind of scenario has happened as parents have noticed different behaviors of students while visiting or substituting in classrooms and, later, have begun to gossip. Many times I, too, have been tempted to discuss situations regarding my students; I know, however, that such talk would not solve any problems or relieve any concerns but would make things worse. The best practice is to talk about our students with parents only, refraining from gossip completely. A closed mouth is good "fire insurance."

Lord, you gave me two ears and one mouth for a reason. Help me close my mouth and open my heart. Amen.

AUGUST 20

RECOGNIZING DIFFERENCES—ROMANS 12:6A.

During my commute to school one morning, I noticed all the speed limit signs: 35 mph on the back streets, 45 mph on the major streets. Similarly, movie theaters have limits in the form of ratings: G, PG, PG-13, and R. Streets and highways have speed limits and movies have ratings because they are not all the same. This makes me think of the students I work with each year.

God makes every child unique, with specific gifts, abilities, and talents. Some we are able to teach at an accelerated rate, whereas others we must spend a little more time with. Some excel in one area, whereas others excel in another. Because each child is different, our expectations must also be different. We need to adapt to students and their individual needs rather than teach according to what makes *us* comfortable.

What if we were to give each child an individual plan and teach each day according to that child's specific needs? We would have more students succeeding than failing, more students excited to come to school each day. Of course, this would require more work on our part; but, ironically, more work in this case would actually decrease negative stress because our students would be happier and more productive. The benefits for the students would far outweigh any inconveniences for us.

Lord, help me see the differences in my students, recognizing their particular strengths and abilities, and continually making accommodations to meet their needs. Amen.

AUGUST 21

FEARFULLY AND WONDERFULLY MADE—
READ PSALM 139:14.

"That is not true! If you don't stop saying that, I'm going to hit you!"

A girl in my classroom had said something about another girl that was untrue, and the other student was mad and ready to fight. It's a common scene in our classrooms—one that can lead to increasing disruption, conflict, and stress.

Children are often mean to one another, making cruel remarks that have long-lasting effects. I remember being teased as a child because I was skinny and wore glasses. I never let these statements bother me, however, because my parents taught me to have confidence in myself. Unfortunately, many children don't get that kind of instruction at home, and they are ready to argue and fight when hurtful words are spoken.

At the beginning of each year, we should discuss with our students what it means to hurt someone else's feelings, and we should model daily what respectful behavior looks like. Then, when we see a behavior that is contrary to the expectations we have set, we must respond immediately by correcting the students involved and giving them an example of the model behavior. Rather than simply penalizing our students in some way for hurtful words or actions, let us teach them the worth of every individual and the power of loving and respecting others.

Lord, help me teach my students that each person is "fearfully and wonderfully made," deserving to be treated with love and respect. Amen.

AUGUST 22
TIMES OF LOSS—READ 2 CORINTHIANS 1:3-4 AND PHILIPPIANS 1:21.

As teachers, we often get to experience personal events with our students. They invite us to birthday parties, baseball games, graduations, weddings, ballets, and other events. One year I received an invitation to the funeral of the father of one of my students, who had died early one Easter Sunday morning.

This student was always a very happy little boy, but this unexpected tragedy was something he could not truly comprehend. His father was in his early forties and had not been sick. As his teacher, I felt that I needed to attend.

As I sat next to the boy at the funeral, he asked when we could leave and if his father was going to come out of the casket. These were questions I was not prepared to answer. It was heartbreaking. This little boy had had only six years with his father. They had not had time to do so many things together. How would he learn all the things a father teaches his son? I knew that my job was not to try to answer all of his questions but to comfort him and be available to him.

When tragedy strikes in the lives of one of our students, we never know how we will touch that child's life by simply being kind, loving, and available.

Lord, remind me that you are always creating something new. Keep me alert so I may follow your plan and share your love. Amen.

AUGUST 23
SUPPORTING ADMINISTRATORS—
READ TITUS 3:1-2 AND 1 THESSALONIANS 5:11.

School systems usually experience continual turnover. On the local level, you might have as many as two principals within four years—and the same holds true for superintendents. Common remarks made by staff are, "I will outlast this principal, too," or "I'll still be here after he or she is gone!"

Some new administrators change the structure of the school to fit their personality, not taking into account what has been done previously. Many administrators, however, come in and observe the culture of the school before making changes as needed. Even so, it seems that whenever a change is made, we are quick to judge the administrator in charge. If we don't like the change, we tend to become frustrated or angry with the individual. The truth is, many times a change will actually benefit us if we will simply "hold on" and wait.

As educators, we don't like it when students or parents judge us before they even experience us as their teacher. Likewise, it is unfair for us to prematurely judge the administrator. Instead of participating in negative conversations about the administration, find out what you can do to offer your support. Be a problem solver rather than a problem maker. Use your energy for building up rather than tearing down.

Father, your word instructs us to build up rather than tear down. Help me always to be respectful and supportive of those who lead. Amen.

AUGUST 24

HURTFUL COLLEAGUES—READ JAMES 1:5.

Have you ever worked with team members who shared your ideas as if they were their own? Or have you worked with those who always are trying to overshadow you or make themselves look good? For example, in front of parents do they talk about all the great things that are going on in their rooms?

At school we experience many personalities that are not reflective of the manners our parents taught us! Still, I'm always taken by surprise when I see others doing things to deliberately hurt another so that they can shine and overshadow. Hurtful colleagues cause conflict and magnify tension and stress.

As Christians, we need to remember that God will always take care of us and give us the wisdom we need. Many times when we are in situations with difficult or hurtful colleagues, we want to give them a piece of our mind—even though we know that won't accomplish anything productive. Instead, we should pray and ask God how to respond. God will give us the wisdom we seek and, in the end, we will truly shine.

Lord, you always give me the wisdom I need. Remind me to seek you first instead of taking matters into my own hands. Amen.

AUGUST 25

WHO WILL COUNSEL?—READ PSALM 33:11.

My father was a pastor. One afternoon, my aunt shared with me that he had called her and commented, "Who counsels the counselor?" Ministers are always counseling their church members in marriage, divorce, finances, work, and other areas; but when they need someone to talk to, where can they turn? After all, they are the counselor!

In a way, we teachers are seen as "counselors" in the classroom. So, when we don't know how to reach a particular child or have some other problem or concern involving a student or parent, where can we turn? After all, we're known as the "expert."

We have to be careful because we truly don't know who will keep our comments confidential. As teachers, we simply cannot afford to trust everyone we come into contact with at school. My mother used to say, "You can count your real friends on one hand, and you will not use all of your fingers."

When you need counsel or advice, have an initial counseling session with the Father, seeking wisdom through the word and prayer. Turn the problem over to God, and he will show you what to do or where to seek further help.

Lord, whenever I need help or advice, you are there to guide me. Thank you for being the ultimate counselor. Amen.

August 26

Leave It "Outside"—Read 1 Peter 5:7.

As human beings, we experience all the difficulties of life—financial problems, relationship problems, health issues, and so forth. These situations cause stress, which can be hurtful to our minds or our bodies.

Once when I was going through a hard time, I found it difficult to focus each day on what my task was with the children. I realized that if I wasn't careful, I could become consumed by the problem. So, I decided that I would leave any personal concern that did not deal with school outside the building each morning. After all, my students had situations of their own that I needed to handle. I had to make sure that my students were my number one priority while I was at school.

As difficult as it may be, we can learn to leave our personal problems and issues "outside." Otherwise, they will disrupt our concentration, cloud our thinking, and interfere with the important job we've been given to do. Of course, this does not mean that you cannot speak personally with one of your colleagues; rather, be careful not to let the issue consume your entire day.

Learn to leave your troubles outside the building. You will be happier, and your students and colleagues will, too!

Lord, help me cast my burdens on you each morning as I enter school, trusting you to meet all my needs. Amen.

AUGUST 27
PUNCHING HOLES IN THE DARKNESS—
READ MATTHEW 5:16.

My father once preached a sermon entitled "Punching Holes in the Darkness." He said that sometimes it seems we are not accomplishing all we would like to accomplish. We try to help and encourage others, and we see them making the same mistakes.

As teachers, sometimes we teach a skill over and over only to have the child make the same mistake on a test. Other times we review vocabulary words again and again, only to see the child miss several of the words on an assessment. All of this leads us to believe that we are "punching holes in the darkness." We begin to doubt our ability to do the job.

The truth is, if we will keep on punching holes, eventually the light will shine through! If we keep on doing what we know is right and keep on shining our light, we will reap the benefits.

I was reminded of this when I attended the graduation ceremony of a former student. She had had great difficulty learning to read, yet she stood at the podium eloquently reading a beautiful piece she had written. I had flashbacks of us reading together in the classroom, reviewing every word. I cried as I received the revelation that what I had done for her had not been in vain.

May we continue to shine our lights into the darkness!

Father, help me persevere as I continue to punch holes in the darkness and let my light shine through. Amen.

AUGUST 28

GOD IS IN CONTROL—READ PHILIPPIANS 3:3.

I had been a teacher for twenty years and, overall, my experiences had been positive. I had been able to help my students accomplish great strides. Then, one year I was given a group of students I couldn't seem to reach—a first for me. Talk about stress!

At midyear, a student teacher was assigned to me, and I began to work with her just as I had worked with other student teachers in the past. I shared strategies I had used with the students, candidly mentioning that the strategies had not worked. The next day she began meeting with students to find out information that would help her design lessons. After a while, the students began to respond to her. What's more, they began to respond to me better, as well!

Even though I had been very effective in years past, God showed me that I didn't have control; he did. I realized that I needed to listen to him more and that, rather than being the director, I needed to be directed. That school year was a turning point in my career.

As teachers, we need to put our confidence in God, not in the flesh—in our own abilities. Only God has the power to change lives. Will we let him take control and allow him to work through us?

Lord, you are in control, not me. I humbly ask you to direct me and use me each day for my students' good. Amen.

AUGUST 29

WISDOM—READ PROVERBS 1:7 AND PROVERBS 12:15.

One day while working with one of my students, I noticed that he continued to make mistakes on the playground. The students were playing a game, and when it was this student's turn, they wouldn't play with him. He became angry and began shouting bad names at the other students. Well, the students didn't like that, and they chose not to play with him.

I tried to counsel the student and tell him what he could do to correct the problem, but he did not want to hear what I had to say. After being ignored for the entire playtime, he gave up and sat out. The next day when I brought the class out for playtime, he was more cooperative with the other students, and they included him in their games for the entire play period. On our way back into the building, he said that he was sorry he had not listened to my guidance. He said that after he had used some of the techniques I had suggested, the other children had been more willing to play with him.

We, too, can benefit from wise counsel—if we will listen.

Father, give us wisdom through your word and through godly people who can help steer us down the right road. Amen.

AUGUST 30

LISTEN FIRST—READ JAMES 1:19 AND PROVERBS 17:27.

A colleague was preparing for a parent conference about a struggling student. She had mounds of documentation. The conference had been rescheduled twice to accommodate the parents' schedule.

When the parents arrived, they looked as if they had not eaten in a few days. After apologizing for having to reschedule the conference, they listened as the teacher told them that their daughter was lacking in her studies and seemed uninterested in her work. They were polite, listening to every comment and studying the documentation.

After the teacher finished speaking, she noticed that a tear was rolling down the father's cheek. He said that he had been out of work for four months and they had been living from shelter to shelter.

The teacher understood what her role with this family needed to be. She arranged for the father to get a job as the school custodian for the remainder of the year and for the family to move into a new apartment. Soon she saw a smile on the little girl's face once again, and eventually the girl brought her grades up to all A's.

We will never know what's really going on in a child's life if we don't take time to listen. Spending some quality time with a struggling child and his or her parents is always time well spent.

Father, create in us a listening spirit and close our thoughts and mouths until we have heard the full story. Amen.

AUGUST 31

WHAT KIND OF TEACHER ARE YOU?
—READ EPHESIANS 4:15.

If someone were to ask you what kind of teacher you are, how would you respond? Are you critical, cranky, cute, convinced? If your students were asked this question, which of the preceding adjectives would they choose?

Many of us might hope that our students would say we're a little of all of them—critical because we are critical of the work that is turned in and we try to get students to produce more; cranky because we might not be in the best mood when we don't have students' full attention during lessons; cute because we dress comfortably to handle whatever situation the day might bring; and—my favorite description—convinced because we know the job we do is important. But perhaps the most important description of all is Christlike—striving to become more and more like Jesus every day.

What kind of teacher are you? May we always be the role models that our students deserve.

Lord, I want to be more like Jesus every day. Amen.

SEPTEMBER
Let God Guide You

Angela M. Bailey

SEPTEMBER 1
SEEK GOD'S GUIDANCE—READ PSALM 32:8.

WHEN I TAUGHT FIRST GRADE, THERE WAS A TWENTY-SIX-YEAR VET-eran teacher on our team. When she spoke, everyone listened. The children all respected her, and parents adored her. Often when I walked my students in the halls, she was in the hall with her students, too. I always heard her saying, "Shh, shh, shh," as her students walked to lunch, the playground, or the bathrooms. Her consistent reminders to her students affected all the other students in the halls. Her hallway routines were a great lesson for the teachers as well, because she always expected excellence from each of her students.

During the hustle and bustle of our busy days, God is try-ing to get our attention. We need to be like this teacher and remind ourselves to hush and wait for God to direct us. God wants to be the guide in everything we do each day. If we will spend time with God each day and allow God to direct us, we will relieve our shoulders of the heavy burdens we are carry-ing. There simply is no substitute for regular quiet time with our heavenly Father.

This month we will explore some of the ways we can let God guide us each and every day, helping us be the best teachers we can be.

Father, thank you for always being available when I seek you. Your direction is beyond what I could ever dream. Amen.

September 2

Thinking "Outside the Box"—Read Galatians 5:14.

I once taught in a school that was very transient and had many languages and countries represented among the students. One year many of the parents would not attend parent conferences, PTA meetings, or any other events offered at the school. We got together as a staff to try to determine why parents were not attending school events. The students always seemed enthusiastic about upcoming activities, but the parents would not bring them.

We finally realized that we were not speaking the same language as the parents, and they were not comfortable with us. So, we hired a parent facilitator to be our connection with the parents. She explained to them the importance of attending such events to ultimately help their children. We also began to have mini meetings at various apartment clubhouses so that parents would not have to bring all their children to the school. Some of the teachers coaxed their teenagers to baby-sit during PTA and parent conferences. The county also helped us by providing interpreters during parent conferences to make sure that everyone was on the same page.

These few changes turned the school around, making it a community school where everyone felt accepted and appreciated. We learned that sometimes loving our neighbors as ourselves requires thinking "outside the box"!

Father, help me make love my aim and find ways to express this love to all of my students. Amen.

September 3

"Angels" Watching—Read Psalm 91:11.

On my first day as a teacher, I was thrilled to meet my new students. By the second day, I was feeling hot and sweaty, and my right arm began to feel numb. So my principal took me to a nearby medical center. When the doctor took my temperature, it was 104 and my right arm had grown about five times its normal size.

The doctor informed me that I had gangrene, and that he would have to amputate my arm. I was delirious because of my temperature, but I was coherent enough to ask for a second opinion. I wondered about the impression I was making on my new principal, colleagues, and students.

Eventually, I received a second opinion from a specialist and was diagnosed with cellulitus, which required me to be treated in a hospital for one week. During that week, the first-grade team took care of my lesson plans and students. The teachers and administration didn't even know me well, yet they took care of everything so that I could rest easy.

During my first week of school, "angels" were there to assist me. The scout motto "Always be prepared" is a good one. We never know when we will be able to help others.

Lord, thank you for the "angels" you send to care for us when we are in need. Amen.

SEPTEMBER 4

NEW STUDENTS—READ MATTHEW 25:40.

One year a Hispanic student joined our classroom after the start of the year. This was his first time in our country, and he did not speak English. Over the course of that semester, I began to teach my students conversational Spanish so that they could speak to him and he would feel comfortable speaking to us.

After a few months, this student developed head lice. I called his parents to explain what they needed to do for treatment. The next day the boy came to school with a tube hat on his head. When I asked him to remove his hat, he looked at me with his big beautiful eyes and didn't say a word. I asked him to step outside the room and asked him what was wrong. As he began to cry, he took off his hat and showed me that his head had been shaved.

His parents did not understand what they were supposed to do, so they had shaved his head. I told him that he could wear his hat until his hair grew back if he wanted. I also informed the principal what had taken place so that the boy would not get in trouble when he walked through the halls with a hat on his head. Sometimes bending the rules is the best way to show love.

Father, help me know when to bend the rules or create new guidelines when a child needs loving understanding. Amen.

SEPTEMBER 5

A TIME FOR EVERYTHING—READ ECCLESIASTES 3:1, 4A.

It was time for my formal observation by an administrator—an annual practice for all teachers. This observation was to be thirty minutes long, and if I was successful, I would go up one level on the pay scale and become a tenured teacher. I prepped my students for the observation by talking about what an observation was and having them practice appropriate behavior. My students were ready, and so was I.

When my observer walked in, she was dressed as a witch—green face and all. You see, it was Halloween. As she walked in, she was saying silly statements to get my students to laugh. I was so proud of my students, though, because they maintained their composure and did not laugh. Throughout the entire lesson they kept their eyes on me and followed directions. We got through the lesson without any disruptions.

When I talked with the observer later, she asked how the students were able to suppress their laughter. I told her that we had discussed what to do when things happen that make you want to laugh in a serious situation; you try to hold yourself together and get through it, saving your laughter for later. I also told her that after she left, I let them laugh for a full five minutes!

Lord, thank you for teaching me that there is a time and a place for everything—a time to weep and a time to laugh. Amen.

September 6

Venturing Out—Read Colossians 3:1.

One of the units I taught in third grade was "communities." When I got to the section that discussed skyscrapers, my students became very curious. Most of them lived in a small rural city and had never ventured out. I decided to take the students on a field trip through downtown Atlanta so that they could see the skyscrapers.

As we approached Atlanta, the children were amazed at how tall the buildings were—how they touched the sky. I could not believe the excitement I saw in their eyes. Taking them to the city, rather than simply reading about skyscrapers, was "real life" and sparked their interest.

Sometimes we are like that in our relationship with God. We stay closed up in our routine because we don't want to leave our comfort zone. We don't venture out to experience more of God and learn all God wants us to learn. We get comfortable with what we know of God and God's Word, and we don't take the time to become more intimate with God. But when we open ourselves up—when we venture out with God—we experience the same excitement my third graders experienced when they saw real skyscrapers. We, too, can discover new excitement and enthusiasm when we "seek the things that are above."

Lord, the more time I spend with you, the more my mind and soul are renewed. Fill me with an eager desire to seek the things that are above. Amen.

September 7

A Gentle Answer—Read Proverbs 15:1.

A staff member came running, saying, "Mrs. Bailey, there is a man rambling through our recycling bin without permission!"

When I arrived outside, I observed a man with rain boots up to his knees and gloves covering his lower arms, rambling through the cans and throwing out the trash.

I smiled and introduced myself to him, and he smiled and told me his name. As we began to talk, he said that each time he had passed our recycling bin he had noticed the out-of-place trash and had wanted to do something about it. So he had spoken to the company in charge of the bins, and they had agreed to allow him to take a few of the cans if he would pick up the trash. He explained that he was a retired fire chief and that one of his hobbies was to design soda cans into cars, airplanes, trains, and other vehicles. He showed me some of his samples and told me to pick one out for ourselves.

I could have approached this man in a very negative tone and questioned why he was on school property, but I thought that kindness would be a better approach. As a result, I received a gift and a friend.

Lord, thank you for teaching me that a gentle answer turns away wrath. May I always be kind and gentle when I speak. Amen.

SEPTEMBER 8

SEASONING STUDENTS—READ MATTHEW 5:13.

For some of us, cooking is fun; for others, it is a chore. Personally, when I have time, I like to experiment to see what new recipes I can create. Seasonings are always crucial to boost the flavor. If one seasoning doesn't give the desired taste, I choose another to create what I want. Even after the food is cooked, I still may add salt or pepper according to my taste.

Teaching students is like seasoning food. We experiment with students to see how they learn and what the best method for instruction is. Also, when one strategy doesn't work well, we switch to another. Sometimes students have a difficult time meeting the goals we have set for them, and we have to take time to allow them to "simmer in the pot" while we reflect on the best technique to use. Once we add that personal touch to our teaching, our students will follow us every time, making learning fun for all involved.

When we cook with love, all who partake of the delicacy will be happy; the same is true of teaching.

Father, you have given us the assignment to teach one of your best gifts to us: children. Guide our plans for each lesson we prepare and "serve." Amen.

SEPTEMBER 9
"READ IT AGAIN!"—READ 2 TIMOTHY 2:15.

Whenever I read aloud to students, I like to sit on the floor with them. While I am reading, their eyes are filled with excitement and their imaginations are running wild with varied interpretations. Many times, if the story is exciting, students will say, "Read it again!" I usually find a lot of joy in this because it lets me know that I'm making reading fun for them, and it makes me think that maybe one day they will love reading and make it a part of their everyday lives.

Once I started reading the Bible seriously and reflecting on the scriptures, I began to say down in my spirit, "Read it again!" I was amazed at how the scriptures truly reflect "real life" experiences. The fact that something written so long ago relates to what goes on in the world today is amazing.

How many books have you read that will answer every question you have? The Bible will never be outdated. It's the best guidebook I could ever have; I use it for every situation that arises. I have found that when I let the Word rule, every situation comes out better than expected.

Like my students, I like interesting material that keeps my attention and makes me want to "read it again"!

Father, thank you for the Bible, which inspires all who take the time to read it. Give me a continual hunger for your word. Amen.

SEPTEMBER 10
LOVE ENDURES ALL—READ 1 CORINTHIANS 13:7 AND 1 JOHN 4:7.

Today I attended the funeral of one of my colleagues who lost her battle with cancer. Also attending were former team members and various staff members. It appeared as though half the church was filled with educators who had known and worked with this teacher.

During the eulogy, the minister shared how this teacher was always a bright light for parents, students, staff, and personal friends. She always had a kind word for everyone. She loved her students, and they loved her. The ultimate expression of love during her five-year battle with cancer was that one of her former students took this teacher into her own home and allowed her to live with her family as she went through chemotherapy. What an awesome testimony of love shared and given.

God's Word tells us to love everyone. Wouldn't it be a tremendous testimony if all of us could share the level of love this teacher and former student shared? Her life can be an example for us in how we go about our day-to-day routines.

Look people in the eye, give them your full attention, laugh often, and say "I love you" each time you feel you should. Maybe if we start showing more love, others will follow.

Lord, thank you for growing me up to be an educator full of love and hope, so that I can reap what I've sown. Amen.

SEPTEMBER 11

A LESSON IN FRIENDSHIP—READ PROVERBS 17:17.

As teachers, our job involves much more than academics. Daily we have opportunities to emphasize character and teach life skills.

One day I asked two little girls in my classroom, "What kind of friends are you?" These girls had been friends for a while, but something had torn them apart. They began to separate from each other in the cafeteria and on the playground. They also had gossiped about each other with other students. It's normal to have students that will not get along, but these two girls had been good friends. I knew that we had to get to the root of the problem and solve their differences.

After the other students had gone to lunch, I asked the two girls to stay and eat lunch in the classroom with me. As we sat and ate together, I said that I knew they used to be good friends and asked what had happened to change their closeness. During a brief conversation of "she did this" and "she did that," we were able to get to the root of the problem. The girls decided that they would work on developing their friendship instead of destroying it. I was proud that these students were able to make this decision and learn an important lesson in friendship.

Father, may I follow your lead and take advantage of every opportunity today to teach love, which endures forever. Amen.

SEPTEMBER 12
CHILDLIKE FAITH—READ MARK 10:15.

One day a student said that her doctor had diagnosed her with scoliosis. The doctor reported to her parents that with surgery there could be a chance of total healing—or total paralysis. Without the surgery, her spinal column would eventually curve completely and she would not be able to walk straight. She was a tall, beautiful young lady. Though I was worried about the diagnosis, she seemed to be at peace.

That evening I thought about what I could do to help the family. The following day, she told me that she had prayed and she knew God was going to give her total healing after the surgery. When she said that to me, I thought, *If this child can have faith like that, why can't I?*

In the coming weeks, family and friends donated blood, the student's pastor and intercessory prayer team prayed for healing, and close friends and family went to the hospital for the surgery. The surgery took six hours, and she was in the hospital a total of four days. On the first day, she was able to sit up in the bed. By the second day, she was taking small steps. Today, she walks around tall and beautiful just as she said she would. Like this student, we should always have total faith in what God can do.

Dear Lord, forgive us when our faith is lacking. Help us have the faith of children, remembering that you are in charge. Amen.

SEPTEMBER 13
ALL EYES—READ PROVERBS 15:3.

I remember walking home from school with my brother when I was a little girl. As we approached our neighborhood, the front porches were filled with people watching the children play outside. If we had been in trouble at school, somehow the neighbors always knew it by the time we reached our yard! They would chastise us, and then our parents would provide further embarrassment once we entered our home. It truly seemed that God's "eyes" were everywhere!

Times have changed. More parents work outside the home than ever before, and many children simply don't have a "village" of family and neighbors watching over them and helping instill in them values such as respect for teachers and school. As a result, many children come to school without having any parameters for their behavior.

Instead of being disappointed in these students, it is our job to teach them proper behavior. Students are smart and they will "act out" even more if they realize that we are frustrated. We must keep our cool and create a safe and stable environment where they can learn and grow. Our classrooms must be places where students can express themselves, find high expectations for behavior and academics, and be encouraged. The best solution we can offer is to guide and direct them, stimulate them, and most of all, love them!

Father, help us create a "village" of love, encouragement, and support within our schools, reassuring our students that we are watching and that we care. Amen.

SEPTEMBER 14

AFFIRMATIONS—READ 1 THESSALONIANS 1:4.

A teacher's job was highly respected within the community in which I was reared. My parents always told me to follow the teacher's directions. There was never a time when I heard either of them say that the teacher was wrong and I was right. Whatever the teacher said was the gospel.

In today's world, some people don't have that same level of respect for teachers. Grades are questioned and teachers are held accountable for almost everything. This kind of attitude can make teachers feel their job is not important. Yet, the majority of teachers I have worked with have been wonderful teachers—teachers who have a lot of passion for their job.

So, the next time someone says something about you, your classroom, or your teaching style, continue to say to yourself that you are a great teacher. Walk into the building each morning reciting affirmations such as 1 Thessalonians 1:4, remembering that God loves you and has chosen you. You have to feel good about yourself before someone else can see the greatness in you. Smile and keep doing a great job every day. Don't let outside influences interfere with the job God has given you to do with his children. After a period of time, those who criticize will begin to see the light that is shining around you.

Father, help me keep my joy when others try to destroy it. Amen.

SEPTEMBER 15

RENEWAL—READ PSALM 37:7A.

As teachers, we often find ourselves planning and working before, during, and after school, as well as on weekends.

Sometimes it seems as though our days and nights never end. We take work home and forfeit time with our families. We are always taking care of others and forgetting about tending to our own needs. However, when we fail to spend adequate time renewing ourselves, both our students and we suffer the consequences.

Begin to set aside time to regularly renew your mind, body, and spirit. Take a long walk and a long hot bath. Drink a cup of hot tea and reflect on your life. Write in a journal each day about your experiences with students and parents, staff, and family members. Look to see how much time you spend developing your relationship with the Father. Tell yourself that you are going to get closer to God, plan how you will do it, and stick to it! Remember, many outside influences can creep in to shift your focus, so remain faithful to the plan you've made.

You will find that when you make renewal a priority, you will be at peace and your days will be better directed.

Lord, we always feel pressure to complete our tasks, and we need your help in balancing our lives. Amen.

SEPTEMBER 16

DATA DRIVEN—READ JOSHUA 1:8.

At a summer teacher's conference, the speaker was discussing the importance of collecting data for instruction. He said that, as educators, we don't know what to teach if we don't constantly assess the strengths and weaknesses of our students. Data helps guide our instruction so that we know where we're going and when we need to stop. Once students have mastered a particular skill or assessment, then we can move on to the next level. Studying the data and using it as our guide enables us to individualize lessons and units and begin to have more personable relationships with our students.

In a similar way, we should allow the Word of God to be the "data" that guides our daily walk in this world. Studying the word equips us to handle the inevitable storms of life; helps us to know how to handle problems with students, parents, or colleagues in a way that is pleasing to God; and gives us a more peaceful life. May the word be our all-in-one data resource for daily living.

Lord, may I always look to your word for the guidance and direction I need every day. Amen.

SEPTEMBER 17

PATIENCE—READ ECCLESIASTES 7:8B AND 1 JOHN 4:7.

Mary was an eighth-grade middle-school student who enjoyed all of her subjects except for one: math. She didn't like math because she didn't feel competent to understand it. Sometimes when she would ask for help in class, the teacher would say that it had already been explained once. The teacher would let the entire class know that Mary had asked for help again before explaining the problem to her.

Now, Mary wasn't always the "perfect student" in class. Oftentimes she would laugh and talk with others during class. However, many of these off-task behaviors were a cover-up because she didn't want to be embarrassed for continually asking for help. You see, Mary had lost interest in math because her teacher had made her feel inadequate for not "getting it" the first time.

Even if we must explain the same skill over and over again, we owe it to our students to make sure that they are grasping the material. We need to realize that many times a student acts out because of something he or she is lacking—such as Mary's inability to understand a math skill the first time. Patience is a virtue that can help us show God's love to all our students, especially those who are struggling.

Lord, help me show your love by being more patient with all of my students. Amen.

SEPTEMBER 18
WISE INSTRUCTION—READ PROVERBS 16:20A
AND PROVERBS 19:20.

Marie had to take a remedial writing class her freshman year because she had not learned the proper mechanics of drafting a paper with a clear beginning, middle, and end. This embarrassed Marie, but she knew she needed the class. Surprisingly, when she began class the first day, it was packed with many other freshmen who also needed the class.

Mrs. Smith knew that teaching freshmen how to write would be a difficult task, so she set to work immediately. The first day of class she assigned a topic for the students to write about, and the next day she held individual conferences with them to review their papers. When Marie met with Mrs. Smith, she read her paper aloud as instructed; and as she read, she noticed many grammatical errors she had made.

During the following weeks, Mrs. Smith used those initial papers to teach her students how to write. Knowing what each student's weaknesses were, she was able to design her lessons to meet those deficiencies.

Her plan worked. Marie actually began to enjoy writing and sharing her work in class. Eventually she completed the class with an A! Mrs. Smith's wise teaching method produced a great writer in Marie. And because Marie was willing to learn and accepted the instruction of her teacher, she truly accomplished an important life skill.

Lord, help me teach in such a way that is truly beneficial to my students. Amen.

SEPTEMBER 19

CLAY IN THE POTTER'S HAND—READ JEREMIAH 18:6.

A colleague was bitter because she felt the "needs improvement" mark she had on her evaluation was invalid. I suggested that she reflect on the year and see if there might be any validity to the evaluation. After a few months and some deep thought, she began to see evidence of some areas that needed correction.

None of us is perfect; we all need help in various areas. Often we feel embarrassed and don't want others to know that we need assistance. God is always available to us during those times. He sees us broken into pieces and wants to put us back together. We don't have to "fight our own battles" or carry the stress by ourselves. All we have to do is turn to God. If we will prayerfully look at ourselves and remain open to God's direction, we will recognize what we must do. Then, once we begin to make changes, an amazing thing happens: Our attitude changes, too.

My colleague realized she needed to revise her lesson plans and make many other changes as well. As a result, she ended the year by receiving an excellent evaluation. She also gained a great deal of respect for her administrator. Rather than give up, she put herself into God's hands; and when she did, God changed her attitude regarding the entire situation.

Lord, when I allow you to mold and shape me, everything changes for the better, including my attitude. Thank you for giving me hope. Amen.

SEPTEMBER 20

LYING LIPS AND RUMORS—READ PROVERBS 10:18-20.

Emma was always socializing with her friends. One day a boy at school spread a rumor that Emma had made negative statements about her girlfriends. Once Emma found out, she tried to convince her friends that the rumor wasn't true; but no one believed her.

Some other girls in the school threatened to beat Emma up because of the rumor, and she was scared. She began to wait until everyone had been dismissed in the afternoons and then she would sneak out the side door. One day a concerned parent called Emma's mother and told her that Emma had told her son she wanted to commit suicide. Noticing that her whole demeanor had changed, one of Emma's favorite teachers also alerted her mother that something was wrong.

Devastated by the news, Emma's mother took her for counseling and alerted the administration of the school. The teachers and administrators adjusted schedules, changed dismissal procedures, and spoke privately with all the students who were involved in the threats. In time, Emma's outlook improved and she returned to her old self.

Rumors can be extremely damaging and destructive to a student's self-esteem and well-being. Our students need us not only to help teach them the destruction of slander and rumors but also to listen and provide help when others hurt them with lies.

Father, may I help protect my students from "lying lips." Amen.

SEPTEMBER 21

BEING TRANSFORMED—READ ROMANS 12:2
AND 2 CORINTHIANS 3:18.

While driving down the street, I noticed a car with a spare tire. The driver didn't look too happy about having a temporary tire on his car. I thought about the time it takes to remove a flat tire and put on a spare, and how a spare is essentially a bandage until a new tire can be purchased.

Sometimes students can be like flat tires that need to be replaced. They need new strategies when the old ones aren't working. Every student learns differently, and a teacher's job is to determine the best method of learning for each student. Like changing a tire, changing a strategy involves making needed adjustments until the child's thinking begins to change and learning improves. You see, the process of transformation always begins in the mind.

Many children have some kind of skill deficiency that keeps them from reaching their full level of achievement. Our job is to teach them in such a way that we get them where they need to be. The sooner we make assessments, determining where they are, the sooner we can begin making the needed changes.

Father, may the process of transformation continue in my students until they reach their full potential and become all you would have them be. Amen.

SEPTEMBER 22
HAPPINESS—PSALM 86:4.

Gwen's school year was not off to a good start. Her students were not following the class rules she had established, and parents were dissatisfied and complaining. Gwen entered the building each day not wanting to be at work, and her teammates felt her dissatisfaction.

Finally, one afternoon, the principal asked Gwen to meet with her after school. During their conversation, Gwen shared that she was unhappy, and the principal inquired about the reasons. Gwen explained that this class was a little more challenging than any class she had experienced before, and that she also had too much going on in her personal life.

Gwen finally realized that she was looking for happiness in all the wrong places. She knew that before anything could change in her classroom, she had to look at her situation differently. She needed the inner peace that comes from knowing that God can take care of any problem we will ever encounter. Once she changed her thoughts, she was much happier—and so were the students and parents.

Lord, continue to draw us nearer to you. Amen.

SEPTEMBER 23
MODELING FAITH—READ HEBREWS 11:1.

Each time Sammy's teacher asked him to read, he stumbled over his words. The other students were used to Sammy having difficulty, and they never laughed at him. Those who sat near Sammy assisted him whenever he had difficulty. Sammy enjoyed this, but he longed for the day when he could be independent of his classmates.

Sammy's teacher worked with him before and after school twice a week, and his parents were appreciative because they were not readers themselves and wanted their son to have more instruction than they had received.

Sammy began each day determined that this would be the day he would read without help. With all the assistance he received, Sammy read his first paragraph without help by the middle of the year. He was so proud of himself. He began to help with the announcements each morning, and he also became a peer tutor with the kindergarten students.

As teachers, we have the opportunity each day to instruct and encourage our students so they may overcome their weaknesses and experience success. We have the opportunity to teach them that faith is "the assurance of things hoped for, the conviction of things not seen." May they learn from our example that when we put our faith in God, God can pull us through any difficulty we will ever face in life.

Lord, thank you for the faith you give us, enabling us to become all we can be. Amen.

SEPTEMBER 24
RESPECT—READ ROMANS 13:7.

When I was growing up, the two professions that received the most respect were teaching and preaching. We were taught to respect the minister of our church and the teachers assigned to us. It never occurred to us that our parents would ever take our side over our teachers' side on any given issue.

Today I see a different view of teachers. Many parents tend to question teachers and the decisions they make. They forget that they would not be where they are today if it weren't for the teachers in their own lives.

I am grateful for the teachers who worked with me to make sure that I knew my multiplication tables and could read a paragraph with excitement and confidence. Other teachers had me memorize poems that served as lessons for me to live by. All of my teachers cared about me, and I knew it.

The teachers I work with and observe today have the same characteristics that my teachers had thirty-five years ago. They want their students to succeed.

As educators, we deserve to be respected, for ours is a challenging and often difficult job. May we always live in such a way that is worthy of that respect.

Father, thank you for the privilege of being a teacher. Help me always be worthy of respect. Amen.

SEPTEMBER 25
FEAR—READ 2 TIMOTHY 1:7.

One year my principal said that she was going to place a child with disabilities in my classroom. I was honored that she thought I was capable of handling such a challenge, but I also was scared to death because I had never taught any children with disabilities before. Would I have the strategies needed, and would I be sympathetic and patient enough for this child to be successful? These were the questions that continued to run through my mind before the first day of school. In the meantime, I organized my classroom for my students. I decided that I would not separate this child when she entered but would place her with all the other students.

The first day of school came, and I met my new students. The last student to enter the classroom was my special-needs student. She had the prettiest smile, and I could tell that she was a little frightened. I welcomed all the students and talked about how each of us is different and how we must work together as a team and not discriminate because of our differences.

I continued to recite that same message throughout the year. It wasn't long before my fear and my special-needs student's fear disappeared. That year turned out to be one of my best years in teaching!

Lord, teach us not to be fearful, reminding us that you have given us a spirit of power and love and self-discipline. Amen.

SEPTEMBER 26

ENDURANCE—READ COLOSSIANS 1:11-12.

This was Martha's first year of teaching, and she had been assigned to teach in an alternative school—a school for students who have had discipline problems. Martha wasn't sure what to expect, so she prepared for the worst and prayed.

After introducing herself to her students, she proceeded with the lesson. Immediately the students began talking among themselves, not paying her any attention. Martha quickly understood why these students had been placed there.

As the days passed, the same scenario occurred again and again, with the students showing disrespect toward Martha. Although she was discouraged, she continued to pray and ask for guidance.

After about two weeks, Martha entered the classroom one morning and instructed the students to listen. Then she began to lay out her expectations, including what the students needed to do each day if they wanted to make their way back to their home schools. She told them that she cared about them and that she held each student accountable for his or her learning.

The following days and weeks were much better for Martha; and with continued prayer, she was able not only to practice endurance but also to have a spirit of joy despite the challenges she faced each day.

Father, help me patiently endure challenges and maintain a spirit of joy and thankfulness throughout the day. Amen.

September 27

Anger—Read Psalm 14:29.

Anger is destructive. It can lead us to do things that we later wish we hadn't done. It can even separate friends, spouses, and entire families. Regrettably, many times what causes us to become angry is actually insignificant.

When we are unable to do anything else but think about how someone has offended us, we are allowing anger to fester and grow deep within us. If left unchecked, this anger will cause damage to our minds, emotions, spirits, and even our bodies. Anger also can cause us to be unproductive in the classroom, which causes our students, who need us so much, to suffer as well.

We teach our students to ignore other children when they are bothering them and to try to get along. As adults, we need to take the same advice we give our students. When someone makes us angry, we must let it roll off of our shoulders, taking our concerns to God. If we will prevent anger from "taking us over," then we will have the peace to make it through the situation.

In the song "Stand by Me," Charles A. Tindley writes, "When I do the best I can and my friends misunderstand, thou who knowest all about me, stand by me." Whatever anger we feel, we must allow God to stand by us and lead us through.

Lord, help me to be slow in becoming angry and, when I do, to turn my anger over to you. Amen.

September 28

Songs of Praise—Read Psalm 104:33.

Many of the songs I sang in my father's church as a little girl have helped me tremendously in my years as an educator. Songs such as "We'll Understand It Better By and By," "Have Thine Own Way," "Trust in the Lord," "Stand By Me," and

"Amazing Grace" have carried me through some very challenging times.

The one song that stands out most of all is "We'll Understand It Better By and By," written by Charles A. Tindley. One stanza in the song says, "We wonder why the test, when we try to do our best, we'll understand it better by and by." Those words have helped me make it through many storms.

Knowing that we are going to be tested in this lifetime, we have to remember that God will take care of us. There are times when we do everything right and we still go through trials, and we wonder why this is happening to us. We were not promised a life of pure joy. But when those trials come, we need to continue to remind ourselves that we can go to Someone who will carry us through like no other.

Start your day with a song of praise and see how peaceful you will remain.

Lord, I will praise you with everything I have. Amen.

SEPTEMBER 29
MUTUAL LOVE—READ HEBREWS 13:1.

One year I had a student who always defied me no matter what I directed her to do. If I asked her to sit, she would stand; if I asked her to stop talking, she would talk. Because I was a young teacher and had never encountered this kind of behavior before, this was confusing to me. I decided that I would meet with her parents to discuss her behavior.

After talking with the parents, they agreed to speak with their daughter when they got home. The next day I met with her and lovingly explained my expectations and consequences. I communicated my care for her and my desire to help her learn.

Over the next several days, I noticed a change in her behavior. She began to listen more intently. We both started on a "new page," and the year ended with the two of us having a successful relationship.

Lord, help me work toward a relationship of "mutual love" with all of my students. Amen.

SEPTEMBER 30

CLOTHED IN LOVE—READ COLOSSIANS 3:14.

Through the years I have discovered that all children are different and yet basically the same: They all need and want to be loved. No matter how bad, smart, slow, good, sassy, or obedient they have been, they have all wanted one thing: love. Even in my relationships with parents through the years, love has been the cornerstone. Of course there have been conflicts, but all of the battles have been won with love. When we show love, any negative or evil thoughts that the other person may have been thinking are more quickly dissolved.

The Bible says there is nothing above love. Joseph showed love to his brothers when they treated him unfairly. Job showed loved to God even though he was going through so many trials. Again and again, we see love in action, redeeming individuals and situations.

A parent was very upset because she thought I was not treating her child appropriately. Then, after I was sympathetic of her feelings and opinion, she began to realize all the plans I had made for her daughter. What easily could have turned into a negative conference became a positive experience because I decided to listen and show love.

Parents send us their children, and it's up to us to love them while they are with us.

Lord, help me clothe myself in love today and every day. Amen.

OCTOBER
Your Spiritual Wardrobe

Danny Hill

OCTOBER 1
CLOTHING YOURSELF SPIRITUALLY—
READ COLOSSIANS 3:12.

AS PRINCIPAL OF A K-8 SCHOOL, ONE OF THE EASIEST WAYS FOR ME to ensure a great day at school is to allow the staff to wear blue jeans. It seems fewer students are sent to the office on "blue jean" days—perhaps because teachers are in a better mood.

Although we tend to focus on our physical clothing, God's priority is our spiritual clothing. God sent his son Jesus to show us how to dress spiritually.

The woman who had a bleeding condition was an outcast who touched Jesus' garment as a last resort. As he turned and looked at her, he said, "Daughter, your faith has made you well" (Luke 8:48 NRSV). This is the only time in the Bible when Jesus called anyone "daughter." He knew she was starved for kindness, so he used a word of special affection. Max Lucado says it best in his book *He Still Moves Stones*: "To the loved a word of affection is a morsel, but to the love starved a word of affection can be a feast." When we clothe ourselves with things such as compassion and kindness, we are the presence of Christ to a starving world.

How is your spiritual wardrobe? Do you take as much time and effort to clothe yourself spiritually as you do physically? This month we will take a look at the kind of "clothing" we need in our spiritual wardrobe.

Lord, clothe me in your spiritual wardrobe today so I can respond with real love and kindness to everyone. Amen.

October 2
Serving Others—Read John 13:1-5.

After teaching middle-school science for ten years, I became assistant principal at a nearby high school. I was in charge of student management (discipline), with more than 1,200 students to manage. Every day that first year I listened to Christian tapes while driving to school, praying, "What am I to do today, Lord?" and "Help me, Lord." The Lord kept bringing me back to Jesus washing his disciples' feet. The message was loud and clear: Serve the teachers.

Four years later, I became principal of a K-8 school, which has been my passion for the past twelve years. Once again, the biblical truth of servant-leadership prepared me for my role. Within a week there was a relationship problem between two teachers who were arguing over a broom. After buying and delivering new brooms to both teachers, I spread the word that I had brooms in my office for anyone who wanted one.

When I hired my assistant Clint, he asked, "What do I do?" I talked about serving the teachers, staff, parents, and children. On any given day, he moves desks, delivers books, sets up for programs, and does any task necessary to take care of our school. Clint, a Christian educator, never resents it because he daily visualizes the King of Kings, Jesus, washing the disciples' feet.

Are you willing to serve others?

Lord, show me how I can serve my students, parents, and colleagues today. Amen.

October 3
A Daily "Quiz" in Kindness—
Read 1 Corinthians 13:4-6.

I once heard a speaker replace the word *love* with *God*. He said, "God is patient with me, God is kind to me," and so forth. When I think about kindness, it helps me to remember that because God is kind to me, I must be kind to others.

One of my favorite stories about kindness involves two teenage boys. One of the boys, who had no friends, was carrying all his books home from school one day and dropped them. Another boy, who was popular, noticed and offered his help. They began to talk and walk together, and over the course of their high school years became great friends. The boy who had dropped his books became valedictorian. In his graduation speech, he explained for the first time why he had been carrying his books home that day: He had cleaned out his locker and had been on his way home to commit suicide. The simple act of kindness by his friend had made all the difference in the world.

When we love others unconditionally as Jesus loves us, kindness comes naturally. Jesus' kindness doesn't fluctuate with our performance. Therefore, we can treat others with kindness even when they don't deserve it. As you encounter unkind coworkers, parents, and students, think of it as your daily quiz in kindness.

Father, help me realize how important kindness is to people who are hurting. Help me look for opportunities today to be kind. Amen.

OCTOBER 4

EMBRACING STRANGERS—READ MATTHEW 25:35.

I was asked to be on a regional planning board a few years ago. I drove to my first meeting in my 1988 Dodge Dakota truck, affectionately called Leonard by our family. When you'd put Leonard in reverse, he would react violently. After bouncing up and down, he would move backward. If you turned Leonard's steering wheel too far to the right, he would make a loud screaming noise.

When I arrived, the chairman had us introduce ourselves. It went something like this: "My name is John D. Rockefeller IV and I am the CEO of such-and-such company; my name is Bill Sanders III and I am the Chairman of the Board of so-and-so bank." When it was my turn, I sheepishly said, "I am Danny Hill, principal of Southside Elementary." I felt so out of place.

As we were leaving, suddenly I remembered that I had driven Leonard, so I tried to beat them out of the parking garage. All of the Jaguars and BMWs had to wait for Leonard to bounce and scream out of the lot.

I don't want any student to feel like a stranger, do you? Do you embrace the new students and handle them with love? Remember, we were all strangers, and Jesus invited us in. Never forget how uncomfortable and scary it is to be a stranger.

Lord, I was a stranger and you invited me in; help me embrace my new students with your love. Amen.

OCTOBER 5

PROTECT YOUR TEACHER HEART—READ 1 SAMUEL 16:7.

While interviewing teacher applicants, the most important question I ask is, "Why did you choose teaching as a career?" I hope for a sincere answer such as, "I love to help and work with young people."

Recently a highly qualified applicant was seeking a transfer to our school. When I asked the key question, the answer was, "Well, I kind of bounced around from job to job after college, and then I just sort of landed in teaching and have been there ever since." I then asked, "Tell me about your relationship with your students." The applicant replied, "Oh, I guess you could say that we get along to some degree, but you know how difficult kids are today." I wanted to say sarcastically, "Your enthusiasm and love for children really impresses me, and I would love to have you here every day!"

When the Lord spoke to Samuel about "interviewing" individuals for Saul's replacement as king, he emphasized the heart. While interviewing and evaluating teachers, secretaries, cafeteria staff, and educational assistants, I simply follow his directions: "Look on the heart."

Most of us go into teaching because of our "teacher heart," and then circumstances try to harden our heart. How soft is your heart today? Pray for the Lord to protect your heart so your children will know your love.

Lord, I need a soft heart every day. Protect my heart from being hardened by circumstances. Amen.

OCTOBER 6
LOVE FOR ALL—READ JOHN 13:1, 5.

Several years ago a man shouted obscenities at me in my office in front of his wife and children. He didn't want me to discipline his son because the teachers, of course, were at fault. Mom cheered him on while the student stood there with a big grin on his face.

The next day we explained to the young man that he would be disciplined despite his father's cussing abilities. I was tempted to rationalize that it was OK not to love this man and his family. My flesh said, "He can't talk to me that way in front of the children—especially in my own office."

Is it OK to love only those who are easy to love? Is it OK to pick and choose favorites? Jesus gives us guidelines in his treatment of the disciples at the Last Supper. Jesus knew they would desert him, yet he served them with a heart bursting with love.

Because I asked God to get me out of the flesh in dealing with these people, our relationship healed within a few months. Evidently the son started showing his disrespectful attitude at home, and the dad came in to apologize. Three years later, when his son moved on to high school, the dad came up to me and gave me a big hug and thank you.

Lord, help me not to have favorites. I want to burst with love for all my students. Amen.

OCTOBER 7
KNOW YOUR STUDENTS—READ PSALM 10:12-15.

It took several years for me to realize the importance of digging a little deeper to get to know our students. About six years ago, a detective from the sheriff's department came to my office about a half hour before dismissal. He took me to the gym and pointed outside, explaining that there were patrol cars hidden in five areas. In a few minutes, two of our students would be picked up by their father, who then would be arrested by the officers. The father had been prostituting both children as he moved one step ahead of the police across three states.

As the deputies arrived, I was thankful we could help put this monster behind bars. However, within minutes our staff was in tears as we watched the two innocent children get into a lonely squad car.

I learned a lot that day about looking beyond the surface with my students. I wondered, *Had either one of those children ever tried to talk to me—maybe just to say hi—and I was too busy to stop and listen?* How many others have come and gone in similar situations?

Jesus changed people's lives, and he can help us do the same. He will use willing teachers to heal hurting children. We can make a difference when we surrender to him daily.

Lord, I surrender myself to you. Please make me sensitive to my children's needs and give me wisdom to know how to help. Amen.

OCTOBER 8

RELYING ON OUR COUNSELOR—READ JOHN 14:16.

A good guidance counselor is invaluable to a school. Our two counselors, Linda and Emily, are fantastic. Their main role is to be advocates for the children. Almost daily I attend meetings with parents and teachers, called by our counselors, to discuss children's needs. Over the past few years, our parents and teachers have grown to trust our counselors. I have discovered that even our adult staff members go to the counselors for advice and comfort.

As Jesus was preparing to go to his heavenly Father, he said, "And I will ask the Father, and he will give you another Counselor to be with you forever." We have a Counselor with a capital C who has a direct line to God, and this Counselor is always there for us. Just as our school counselors make sure the students have all they need, so our Counselor, the Holy Spirit, will make sure our needs are met. Just as a school community grows to trust and rely on its school counselors, so we should rely on our Counselor all day long. Remember, we are working with precious lives, and we need all the help we can get.

Lord, thank you for giving me your Counselor, the Holy Spirit, to guide me each day. Teach me to seek your counsel in all situations. Amen.

OCTOBER 9

GOD'S COMFORT—READ 2 CORINTHIANS 1:4.

A year and a half ago, my wife, Debbie, was diagnosed with stage two breast cancer. When the doctor gave us the news, I almost collapsed. Fear gripped me as nothing I've ever felt before. For several days I could hardly eat or sleep.

Before going to the oncologist for the first time to get some important test results, I called my guidance counselor and spiritual mentor, Linda, to pray with me. Her prayer and words of comfort reminded me that God is in control. She also reminded me that to rest in God's comforting hands would free me of my fears.

Comfort poured in over the next few months in the form of food, cards, visits, money, and most of all, prayer. Breast cancer survivors called and sent cards—most of whom we did not know personally. My school staff was like an army of angels carrying me through the school year. God turned a trial into a blessing, comforting us in our time of trouble.

Just a few months ago a teacher at our school received almost the exact same news we had received. She and her husband have three children almost the same ages as ours. Now we will be able to pass on the comfort God gave to us, just as God's Word says. Isn't God wonderful?

Lord, may I allow you to comfort me so that I can pass it on to my coworkers and students. Amen.

OCTOBER 10

KEEPING SCORE—READ EPHESIANS 2:14-16.

A parent donated a slab of concrete to help our traffic flow. Then, one day I was called to the office to meet with her about a concern. After she ripped one of my teachers over something minor, I calmly let her know the teacher's decision would stand. She blew up. I had forgotten about the concrete slab, but she reminded me. "I'll come down here with a sledge hammer and take that concrete back if you don't give me what I want," she threatened. *Oh, no,* I thought, *not that tiny little slab that we could replace for fifty dollars.*

Keeping score is common in today's performance-based society. Marriage counselors say that keeping score leads to disaster. Couples expecting an even fifty-fifty split in job responsibilities are quickly disillusioned.

Isn't a school faculty a lot like a marriage? We work in close contact with one another. Those who keep score are generally grouchy and irritable. Comments like, "She never picks up her kids on time," and "I wish he'd make them behave" keep things stirred up.

Aren't you glad Jesus doesn't keep score? His grace should lead to our peace. We can only have God's peace after we accept and experience his grace.

If you're in the habit of keeping score, understanding and accepting God's grace for your own weaknesses will set you free.

Lord, I don't want to keep score in my relationships. Mature me in your truth, and show me how to experience your peace daily. Amen.

OCTOBER 11

EXCESSIVE LOVE—READ EPHESIANS 3:18.

A boy was born without ears. As he grew and became more sensitive about his looks, he really wanted ears. The plastic surgeon tried several things that his body rejected. Then, one school year, he showed up with a good-looking set of ears that had been accepted by his body.

For years no one knew where he had gotten the ears. Then his mom died. While getting her body ready for burial, the funeral director pulled her long hair back and discovered her ears were gone.

Wow, what love! We would do that for our own children, wouldn't we? We would even die for them. Keep that thought for a moment while you think about how much you love your *students*. Have you placed limitations in this area of your job? When you entered the teaching profession to help children, no one expected you to donate your ears. Aren't you glad, however, that your heavenly Father hasn't placed a limit on how much he loves us? Ephesians 3:18 tells us, "How wide and long and high and deep is the love of Christ."

Don't let your love for your students shrink from year to year. Just imagine Jesus' arms stretched out on the cross, saying to you, "I love you this much."

Lord, the paperwork, parents, and children wear me out sometimes. Please stretch my love for the children and keep my teacher heart fresh. Amen.

OCTOBER 12

NOT AFRAID TO TOUCH—READ EPHESIANS 6:10-20.

How can we touch lives without touching children? The question may seem odd, but it has become a real issue today. Last night at a restaurant, one of our second graders came out of nowhere to give me a big hug. I could tell the hug meant a lot to her, and it was a comfortable way for me to show that I love her.

My wife was told by an attorney for the State Department of Education to "keep your hands off students." It was a sexual harassment workshop, and the attorney demonstrated a hug like the one I gave my student last night. "All touching, including this friendly hug, is off-limits to teachers," she said. Wow, what a dilemma. Parents want us to love their kids, but we can't touch them.

Everyone needs to do what is comfortable for him or her, but I refuse to live in fear of a lawsuit. I pray for spiritual protection consistently. More and more children are coming to school without having received any positive verbal or physical affection at home. If a child wants to hug me, I will not refuse.

God says we're not fighting against flesh and blood but against "powers of the dark world." As Christian educators, let us pray for the wisdom, discernment, and courage we need to share God's love.

Lord, give me wisdom to know what is right and to have the courage to act on it without fear. Amen.

OCTOBER 13

PRACTICING SELF-CONTROL—READ GALATIANS 5:22-23.

Not long after school started, I listened as a kindergarten girl tattled on a second-grade boy. "Mr. Hill, Adam can't keep his hands or other objects to himself," she said. "I will talk to Adam about keeping his hands and other objects to himself," I said to her satisfaction. She obviously was restating a classroom rule she had learned, while getting to fulfill her tattling needs for the day.

Self-control is still a behavior assessment on many report cards. Isn't it ironic that we rate our students in areas in which we also could be given an unsatisfactory mark? Students usually need to practice self-control with physical things, whereas we adults struggle with what we say. Have you said anything lately you wish you could take back? I often make inappropriate remarks that I wish could be erased. The Bible says "no man can tame the tongue" (James 3:8). That doesn't make sense. If we try hard enough, we can control everything, right?

Actually, self-control is a result of our giving *God* control. Paul lists self-control as a fruit of the spirit. He says in Galatians 5:24-25 that those who belong to Christ Jesus have crucified the sinful nature and must keep in step with the

Spirit. Jesus always practiced self-control, and he offers us this fruit every day.

Lord, help me enjoy the self-control you have made available to me by keeping in step daily with your Spirit. Amen.

OCTOBER 14

LOVE ALWAYS PROTECTS—READ 1 CORINTHIANS 13:6-7.

Several years ago, numerous tornadoes were touching down within a mile of our school. On this day, we didn't have to tell the students to be quiet while they sat in the hallway for more than two hours. As I walked our halls making sure everyone was accounted for, I tried to be calm and confident. I stopped in several closets without being noticed to pray for God's help. Approximately sixteen tornadoes were counted within a fifty-mile radius of our school, but none came our way.

Protection is one of my biggest responsibilities. Along with physical protection, spiritual and emotional protection are high priorities. I regularly pray for wisdom to discern what to share with my staff. Often I keep poor state or local decisions and rumors of what "might happen" quiet until time to discuss them with staff members as necessary truths. Just today a staff member thanked me for protecting her so that she could keep her mind on our precious children.

Protection is a result of love. First Corinthians 13:6-7 says, "Love does not delight in evil but rejoices with the truth. It always protects." We teachers can protect one another from gossip and lies, and we can protect our students from hopelessness, self-doubt, and worry.

Jesus loves and protects you; he expects you to pass it on.

Father, I pray for protection around each child in my classroom. Teach me to protect others as you protect me. Amen.

October 15

Love Perseveres—Read 1 Corinthians 13:7.

Our professional development presenter today quoted recent research about special problems facing our young boys. An increasing number of boys are being raised with no positive male role model, and the research shows they learn how to be men from television characters. The lack of male teachers doesn't help the problem. The research also revealed a much higher rate of discipline and apathy problems among boys in school.

Our presenter made several statements that sounded so typical of many teachers. The one that jumped out at me and made my skin crawl was, "I've tried everything with Billy and nothing works." Sometimes we forget that we are the adults, and we are dealing with children—which includes high-school students. One of the most important truths we can remember is that all children are made special, have potential, and need hope. Some teachers, however, choose to teach a particular subject rather than teaching children.

As Christian teachers, we have been placed by our heavenly Father to mirror him and spread his truth each day. First Corinthians 13:7 says love "always protects, always trusts, always hopes, always perseveres." When God has tried everything with us, thank goodness he perseveres until he finds what works. Give your students hope by never giving up on them.

Lord, I want to give my students hope, but I need your help. Show me how to persevere beyond my own capability. Amen.

October 16

Your Spiritual Achievement Test—Read James 1:12.

Many politicians seem to be jumping on the achievement test bandwagon. Supposedly, if we have high achievement tests, then we're doing a great job. Of course, the implication follows that if our scores are not good, we're doing a poor job. This is so unfair, but it's a game we must play. What is the purpose of the achievement test anyway? I thought it was to give teachers an instrument for measuring a child's strengths and weaknesses.

Take this emphasis on testing and add in that almost unbearable child or parent you have to deal with, and you're ready to start thinking about another profession! Unless . . .

Could there be a connection? Did God give me that difficult parent or child as my "spiritual achievement test" for this year? Does God want to measure my strengths and weaknesses in spiritual growth? Maybe if I ask for the Master Teacher's help every day, I will learn something.

God teaches us to love by putting some unlovely people around us. It takes no depth of character to love people who are lovely and loving to us. James 1:12 says, "Blessed is the man who perseveres under trial." Are you showing improvement in character development? The real improvement comes in dependency on God.

Lord, please help me help this parent or student who is driving me crazy. Give me wisdom. HELP! Amen.

OCTOBER 17

SOWING SEEDS OF PEACE—READ JAMES 3:18.

Never underestimate the power of a seed. When I taught eighth-grade earth science, one of the units we covered was "weathering and erosion." The students' favorite part was walking around the school and finding grass and weeds growing through rock or cement. They were amazed at how a tiny blade of grass could break through the tough surface above. A small grass seed planted in rich soil grows into a powerful weathering tool that changes the earth's topography.

James 3:18 says, "Peacemakers who sow in peace raise a harvest of righteousness." Teaching is one of the best professions for being a sower of seeds. We have opportunities to sow seeds of God's peace with parents, coworkers, and students every day. Jesus placed a high priority on relationships and set the perfect example for us as the "Prince of Peace." He built relationship bridges everywhere he went.

As the school year begins to wear you down, plant seeds of peace: compliment and don't gripe, give and don't take, hug and don't push away, praise and don't criticize. Sowing seeds of peace is like sowing grass seeds—you don't know why it works, you just know it does!

Lord, make me a peacemaker at school. Help me sow seeds of peace all day long. Amen.

OCTOBER 18

FILLED WITH JOY—READ ACTS 13:51-52.

Our high percentage of transient students can be stressful on the teachers, guidance counselors, educational assistants, and administrators. Tomorrow we're meeting with the mother of a new student who is constantly faking being sick. We already know that Mom lives with her boyfriend, who drinks a lot. Tomorrow we will find out the rest of this student's story. Each new student has a story. A change of custody, a recent divorce, a lost job, or an eviction brings many new students to our school. The only thing they have in common is their need for a fresh start.

Linda and Emily, our guidance counselors, do an awesome job learning about the new children while providing support for the students and teachers. Their attitudes are always positive, enthusiastic, and encouraging. What keeps them so positive? They are Christians who find joy in working for the Lord.

Paul and Barnabus "shook the dust from their feet. . . . And [they] were filled with joy and with the Holy Spirit." They were rejected and run out of town, but they were filled with joy anyway because they had completed God's assignment.

The Lord will shower us with joy when we work for him. We can start by making sure each child has a fresh start no matter how short his or her stay with us.

Lord, help me give each of my children a fresh start today, and shower me with joy as I work for you. Amen.

OCTOBER 19

MAKING A DIFFERENCE—READ JOHN 4:7-42.

Mary Jean, our librarian, is an excellent example of a teacher who makes a difference in children's lives. She loves books. She even holds them with a certain unique reverence. Mary Jean often says, "If you have read two chapters and aren't hooked on the book, bring it back and we'll find you one you'll love."

One of Mary Jean's biggest accomplishments is how she changed *me*. I hated to read in high school and college. Then Mary Jean started giving me Max Lucado's books as birthday and Christmas presents. After putting them in a drawer, I finally opened one and began to read. I was amazed by how clear his writing was—and how short the chapters were! Over the past several years, I have enjoyed reading dozens of books by different authors. God needed me to be turned on to reading so that he could use me to teach adult Sunday school. Mary Jean made a difference in my life.

Jesus made a difference in the lives of everyone he touched. Remember the Samaritan woman at the well? All he did was ask her for a drink of water, and her life was changed forever—along with those of many in her town. Never underestimate the impact you have in people's lives. Trust God to use you each day to make a difference.

Lord, help me sow seeds today that will make a difference in someone's life. Amen.

OCTOBER 20

HANDLING CONFLICT—READ JOHN 8:6-8.

Before our county adopted a dress code, I made a boy turn his shirt inside out because it had profanity on it. I told him not to wear the shirt again because it was inappropriate for school. That night the boy's mother called me at home. Believe it or not, she was angry with me for prohibiting her son from wearing the shirt to school. After all, he had purchased it with his own money. My sarcasm almost broke loose. Instead, I was able to stay calm and ask, "Do you think a shirt with that word on it is appropriate for school?" Every time she wailed at me, I calmly asked a question.

One of the most applicable lessons Jesus taught us was how to handle conflict without being abrasive or argumentative. He was verbally attacked again and again, yet he always remained calm. When the adulterous woman was going to be stoned, the Pharisees tried to trap Jesus by quoting the law of Moses. Jesus replied: "If any of you is without sin, let him be the first to throw a stone at her." This is just one example of Jesus' perfect way of handing conflict.

When dealing with angry parents, we can follow Jesus' example. Remaining calm rather than arguing has a much better ending. An argumentative Christian does not represent Jesus.

Lord, help me to be Christlike in handling tough situations. Teach me to be more like you. Amen.

OCTOBER 21

WE ARE GOD'S HANDS—READ MARK 1:40-45.

"Keep your hands to yourself" is one of the few school-wide rules we have at our school. Hands give gifts, prepare meals, show affection, and put on bandages. However, because children often slap, hit, grab, push, pinch, and choke, we have a cut-and-dried rule not to touch others.

Have you ever thought of your hands as an extension of God's hands? Jesus did. Jesus always touched with compassion. He was a master at communicating love and acceptance. The leper's disease caused others to step back, yet Jesus stepped *toward* him. His leprosy meant "hands off," yet Jesus reached out and *touched* him. If you think Jesus' touch healed the man's leprosy, read the verses again.

Verse 41 (KJV) says, "Jesus, moved with compassion, put forth his hand, and touched him." The next verse says, "As soon as he had spoken, immediately the leprosy departed from him." Jesus touched him because he needed to be touched, and he needed for those who had shunned him to see Jesus touch him.

Each day we are surrounded by children who have emotional leprosy—the physically challenged, the impoverished, and the love starved. We can handle these children just like Jesus, allowing our hands to become extensions of our heavenly Father's hands. Through our compassion, love, and acceptance, we can make a difference in their lives.

Lord, don't allow the sorrow and pain I see make me step away. I want to serve you by touching as you did. Amen.

OCTOBER 22
THE BLESSING OF ENCOURAGEMENT—
READ MARK 10:13-16.

Two psychiatrists were at a convention. One asked the other what his most difficult case was. He answered, "I had a patient who believed that a wildly rich uncle in South Africa was going to leave him a fortune. All day he would wait for a make-believe letter to arrive from a fictitious attorney. He never went out or did anything. He just sat around waiting."

"What was the result?" asked the first psychiatrist.

"It was an eight-year struggle, but I finally cured him," he said. "And then that stupid letter arrived."

We should never discourage children from their dreams, hopes, and aspirations. God has something special planned for each child's future. When the disciples seemed irritated by the little children, Jesus "took the children in his arms . . . and blessed them." He didn't take only those who were good-looking, smart, or well behaved. One of the biggest mistakes we make is labeling children based on their cleanliness, neatness, intelligence, and behavior.

Last year we retested every student to get an accurate, up-to-date reading level. We discovered that several good readers who belonged in the high reading group had been placed in the lower group. Further review showed that this had happened because of behavior issues. When we moved them to the higher group, each child responded positively to the higher expectations.

Bless your students with encouragement!

Lord, help me be optimistic with all my children. Give me the right words of encouragement to pass on to them. Amen.

OCTOBER 23

GUARD AGAINST PREJUDICE—READ MARK 6:2-3.

When Jesus performed miracles in his hometown, the people were amazed—at first. Then they began to rationalize that he couldn't be anyone special. After all, they said, "Isn't this the carpenter?" They knew his mother, brothers, and sisters. The people decided he was no better than they were, and they were offended. Their preconceived notions about who he was made it impossible for them to see who Jesus really was.

As teachers, we must guard against prejudice, which blinds us from the truth. Students come in all shapes and sizes. Some are clean, whereas dirt and sloppiness hide the beauty of others.

When I was a teenager, I grew my hair really long and experienced prejudice daily. One time when my car broke down on a dark road, I received threats instead of help. In this day of tattoos and pierced body parts, my teenage experience has helped me look past outward appearance.

One of the best ways to look past tattoos, pierced tongues, sloppy dress, and dirty faces is to look at children's eyes. Their eyes are beautiful. They remind me that God is the sculptor who put each of us together with special qualities. When children know that their teacher thinks they are special, it plants seeds of hope for God to grow.

Lord, teach me to look beyond outward appearances so I can love all of my students without prejudice. Amen.

October 24

Serving Others Pleases God—Read Matthew 20:28.

The movie *Chariots of Fire* tells the story of Eric Liddell, a gold medalist in the 1924 Olympics. Eric was a sprinter but won his medal in the long-distance race because he refused to run on Sunday when the sprints took place. When he interrupted his work as a missionary to train for the Olympics, his sister challenged his commitment to mission work and disagreed with his decision. Eric replied, "God made me fast. When I run, I feel his pleasure."

Does God get pleasure watching you teach? Of course! After all, he knit you together and enabled you to teach. Does God get as much pleasure watching you teach as he does watching fast runners run? Of course! If you think, however, that running fast is *more* exciting than teaching and, therefore, that it brings more pleasure to God, you have been deceived.

Jesus told the disciples that whoever wanted to be great must become a servant. We serve children on a daily basis. So, though we may not bring pleasure to society in the same way that a great athlete does, we can know for sure that we bring great pleasure to God, our Father.

Yesterday I helped a frustrated eighth-grader open her locker. It was my pleasure to do it even though no one was watching or applauding. On second thought, God was watching, and Jesus' nail-scarred hands were applauding.

Lord, to be great in your eyes, I must be a servant. Help me serve the children in my class today. Amen.

October 25

Let Us Pray—Read Philippians 4:6.

On the evening before the new school year, my assistant principal, Clint, and I were making final preparations. Tables and chairs were blocking the hallways. Trash, old books, and discarded boxes had to be thrown away.

Suddenly, visitors began to arrive. As we walked the halls to see what was going on, we passed classroom after classroom with small groups of adults and children holding hands. *I hope they stay out of our way or we will be here all night,* I thought. I was getting anxious.

When I slowed down to see what they were doing, I had a change of heart. They were praying. Several small groups from area churches had come into our school to pray. They spent time in the library, the office, the restrooms, the gym, the computer lab, the guidance office, and every classroom. Children had come with their parents to pray in their teachers' classrooms. I had prepared for the new school year mentally and physically, but I had neglected to prepare in the most important way—spiritually.

As they began to leave, they circled Clint and me to pray for us. The children bowed their heads while the adults prayed. When we were ready to break up, one of the children asked if he could pray. *Now* it was time to start the new school year!

Lord, help me remember to bathe every day in prayer. Amen.

OCTOBER 26

BECOMING A GOOD LISTENER—READ PROVERBS 18:13.

Teaching and being a principal are demanding. We have so many different things pulling us in so many directions. Also, the range of things we have to do is so wide that it's almost funny. I was preparing my notes for our in-service when one of our custodial staff told me that a commode in the girls' restroom was heating up. That was a new one on me! The range of issues is almost overwhelming, and we want to do a great job at everything.

I especially want to be a better listener. No matter how busy I get, I want to look people in the eye and really listen. Angry parents, nice parents, well-behaved children, troubled children, teachers, aides, secretaries, bookkeepers, lunch staff, custodians, supervisors, board members—all are significant people who deserve my attention.

Jesus was busier and had more important things to do than we, yet he listened to everybody's problems and, even when exhausted, continued to meet people's needs. I bet he never interrupted people or let his mind wander when listening, either. If we ask him, he will teach us to be good listeners, too.

Lord, I need your help every day to be a good listener. My day is so busy, I can't do it without you. Amen.

OCTOBER 27
SPIRITUAL "QUIZZES"—READ PSALM 26:2.

This year our cafeteria staff is new, our computer keypads are new, and the store for à la carte items is new. Normally our lunchtimes are in perfect rhythm by the third day of school, but not this year. They're still backed up ten to fifteen minutes. Teachers and students are getting impatient.

Isn't it amazing how this sort of thing can become a bigger and bigger irritation each day? Morale problems can grow like spiritual cancers throughout the school.

We need to remember that God gives us daily, weekly, and monthly "quizzes" to see how we are doing spiritually. Without quizzes, we might think we have arrived spiritually and lose our hunger for God's "food." Many Christians suffer from spiritual bulimia, a condition in which they chew on the food and swallow it, but they spit it out before digesting it. They don't realize their need for God's "vitamins and minerals." Daily quizzes—such as cafeteria times getting backed up ten to fifteen minutes—are spiritual tests from the Lord.

Are you communicating with the Lord daily so you will recognize what he is quizzing you on?

Show me how you are testing me, Lord, and lead me to the wisdom and truth in your Word that will help me "pass" the test. Amen.

OCTOBER 28

A "JESUS CONTACT"—READ PROVERBS 3:5.

I receive many phone calls related to a parent questioning something a teacher said or did. Thankfully, allegations are almost always the result of a misunderstanding. Misunderstandings occur when communication is weak, resulting in a lack of trust. By listening and understanding each other's point of view, teachers and parents can build healthy relationships for the benefit of the children.

This year I have asked our sixth-, seventh-, and eighth-grade teachers to contact one parent each day. The parent contact can be by e-mail, in person, or by phone. Our goal is to have a balance of positive and negative contacts.

One teacher saw a new student and his parent in a restaurant and made her parent contact for the day by introducing herself. Another has developed a spreadsheet of parents' e-mail addresses to make easy and quick contact. Teachers are also speaking to parents in the hallway before or after school. I am excited about our new routine because it is building a strong bridge of trust.

Proverbs 3:5 says we're to trust in the Lord with all our heart and lean not on our own understanding. This means we must make contact with Jesus every day. If we do, we'll learn to trust him with all our heart, all the time.

Lord, thank you for wanting to listen and talk to me daily. Help me trust you more. Amen.

OCTOBER 29

A PERMANENT BRIDGE OF TRUST—READ MARK 8:14-21.

Many educators feel parents just want us to baby-sit their children. We often joke that if we just gave every child an A, the parents would "leave us alone."

After twelve weeks of intentional contact with parents, our middle-school teachers are reporting that most parents really do want to help. By calling and e-mailing more frequent information, parents are responding and students are being more successful.

One sixth-grader last year had his mom wrapped around his finger. He convinced her that the teachers were unfair, that children were picking on him, and that I didn't like him. Every time I called this mom, I had to defend the teacher's position, and she always hung up angry. Our frequent contact system this year, however, has developed a solid bridge of trust between us. Her son is rarely in trouble because when I call her now, it is a simple one-minute conversation. She tells me, "Do what you need to do; I trust you."

The disciples had already witnessed Jesus feed more than five thousand people with five loaves and two fish, yet they doubted whether he could feed another large group. They shortchanged Jesus.

Let's not shortchange Jesus. When we ask for his help, let's believe that he will always respond; and a permanent bridge of trust will remain.

Lord, open my eyes so I can see you and my ears so I can hear you throughout the day. Help me trust you. Amen.

OCTOBER 30
SEEKING THE TRUTH—READ JOHN 8:32.

The truth will set you free. These are powerful words from John's Gospel that have a variety of applications in school. As teachers, we must seek the truth in every situation, especially discipline issues. By spending a little extra time to find out what really happened, we teach the importance of telling the truth.

One day an eighth-grade girl came to my office very upset. She said that a boy had been sexually harassing her on the bus. *Uh-oh, this is going to be a mess,* I thought. From years of dealing with student discipline, I knew to get both sides of the story and seek the truth. After talking with the young man, I got a totally different story. Fortunately, the whole thing was caught on the bus video camera. The tape clearly showed the girl flirting, harassing, and aggressively enticing the young man. When confronted with the tape, she confessed; and the truth set us all free.

Make this scriptural truth a daily foundation for your classroom by modeling and emphasizing its importance.

Lord, help me model truth in the big and small things so that my children will learn from me. Amen.

OCTOBER 31

BEING A GREAT TEACHER—READ JAMES 3:1.

I attended a workshop called "Great Teachers Make Great Schools," and it's the truth. A school with great teachers and a weak principal will be fine because the teachers will take care of the students. One characteristic of a great teacher is seeing the potential in every student. One of my teachers, Erica, sent me the following e-mail and gave me permission to share it:

> When my husband and I moved into our house, I noticed an ugly bush beside our porch. It was brown and droopy, and I was sure it was dead. I asked Tommy to uproot it and throw it away ASAP! I was proud of the decision because things looked much better without the ugly bush. Soon afterward, I noticed another ugly bush but decided to leave it alone since it was out of sight. Six months went by, and I didn't give any more thought to the bush. Then one day I was lying in my hammock when I saw an incredible sight! The bush on the side of our house, the one I had thought was dead, had changed. It was a beautiful green color with gorgeous flowers. God brought to my attention the hasty decision I had made to uproot that other bush without investigating its potential. He then asked me, "How many children have you uprooted from your mind or classroom because you assumed they were too far gone?" I learned that day that God truly does have a plan for every student. However, if I hastily uproot them the same way I did that bush, they will never have the opportunity to develop roots, blossom, and grow into what God has planned for them.

Great teachers make great schools!

Lord, help me be the best teacher I can be by seeing the potential in every student. Amen.

NOVEMBER
Nourished by God's Word

Danny Hill

NOVEMBER 1
LISTENING TO GOD'S "MUSIC"—READ PSALM 1:2.

I STRUGGLED THROUGH MY WORKOUT THIS MORNING. IT WAS DIFFI-cult to run two miles even though three miles seemed easy yesterday. There was one small thing missing today that made a huge difference: no music. Whenever I put on my head-phones, close my eyes, and focus on the beat of the music, I don't notice the pain. But without the music, I couldn't get my mind off the burning pain in my leg and lungs. I kept looking at the time and became so discouraged that I stopped short of my goal.

It's much the same when we don't "listen to God's music" as we work. When we go through the day without focusing on God's Word, we can get so discouraged. The children are act-ing up, a parent is angry, there are tests to give, and the next day off is nowhere in sight. However, when we "listen to God's music" during the day by meditating on God's word, the truth sets us free from the bondage of our circumstances.

A great habit to keep us refreshed is to meditate on God's Word throughout the day. This month we will focus on tast-ing (reading), chewing (reflecting on), and then swallowing (applying) each day's scripture reading so that God may nour-ish us for his purposes.

Lord, starting today, help me meditate on your words of truth throughout the day. Amen.

November 2
Spiritual Anorexia—Read Psalm 119:131.

In his book *Point Man,* Steve Farrar speaks of a spiritual condition he calls "spiritual anorexia." He says that many of us know just a little truth from God's Word but see ourselves as healthy spiritually. Often we're deceived into thinking we're spiritually fat when in reality we're spiritually anorexic. We think we don't need spiritual food, and we become apathetic toward chewing on God's Word.

Apathy toward schoolwork is one of the biggest problems we face in education. Some children seem to lap up our lessons like starving animals, while others could care less. Though we get many of them to do the work, it's frustrating when they just don't seem to care.

Can we become better teachers by relating spiritual apathy to student apathy? When are we hungry for God's Word?

In my own life, when my wife was diagnosed with breast cancer, I was starving for God's Word to comfort me. When I read in Psalm 34 that "the angel of the LORD encamps around those who fear him," I knew I was not alone.

Though there's no single solution to student apathy, helping students apply each lesson to their daily lives is an important strategy. Likewise, we will learn and retain God's spiritual truths if we hunger for his words and apply them to our daily lives.

Help me, Lord, to learn from you each day by applying your word to my life. Amen.

November 3
What's Your Motivation?—Read 2 Peter 3:17.

When a kindergartener comes home from school, we ask, "What did you learn today?" Around third or fourth grade, the question becomes, "What did you make on that test today?" This is one reason many children stop liking school.

When we stop asking, "What did you learn?" we stop emphasizing the most important thing: learning. This contributes to an unhealthy mindset in our students and can lead to apathy or cheating, because grades don't motivate all students. Learning is fun, and this should be the motivator.

What about your mind-set toward God's Word? Have you been told, "You need to read your Bible"? I get a knot in my stomach every time I hear the "phantom Christian" talk about getting up at 4:00 A.M. to read and pray for hours. When I finally discovered God didn't make me that way, it freed me to develop my own habits and routines.

Do you read God's Word because you're supposed to, or do you want to read the most awesome book ever written? Maybe you've learned a few of God's truths and have become like the student who sees no need to learn. Peter's instruction to believers in 2 Peter 3:18 is to "grow in the grace and knowledge of our Lord and Savior Jesus Christ." Growth comes from learning, and learning is the long-term motivator.

Lord, help me develop my own routine for spending time with you and your word. Amen.

NOVEMBER 4
FROM BELIEF TO CONVICTION—READ JOHN 14:6.

I taught a study at church on moving from belief to conviction based on several of Josh McDowell's books. He cites a survey of Christian youth that indicates 81 percent believe truth is relative to the individual. Yet Jesus said, "I am the way and the truth and the life. No one comes to the Father except through me." Jesus, Son of the one and only God, is the one and only Truth. How can we be sure?

God placed scribes as the custodians of the Old Testament to preserve the accuracy of his word. God's Word predicted in detail Jesus' birth, life, and death hundreds of years before the actual events. His crucifixion was predicted eight hundred years before the Romans had even heard of crucifixion. The New Testament was written by eyewitnesses and those who interviewed eyewitnesses. Jesus performed miracle after miracle to help us believe. Opposing theories of the empty tomb are easily shot down by common sense and eyewitness accounts of the risen Lord. Jesus' disciples must have been totally convinced of his resurrection because they went from being frightened deserters to bold preachers who died because they couldn't keep from sharing what they had seen.

We want our students to be certain and confident—convicted—of what we teach them. Only then can they apply their knowledge in a meaningful way. Likewise, God wants us to be certain and confident of the truth of his word—both the written word and the Living Word, Jesus.

God, help me move from belief to conviction. Amen.

NOVEMBER 5

DOING GOD'S WILL—READ PSALM 143:10-12.

When I was five, I had a bad bicycle wreck and was rushed to the hospital. After several X rays, it was determined that I had a slightly fractured skull that would heal in time.

At age ten, I had my first hearing test at school. The lady testing me became concerned when I didn't indicate I was able to hear in my left ear. My parents took me to an ear specialist who discovered I was deaf in my left ear. My middle ear had been destroyed in the bike wreck five years earlier.

No wonder I had never been a good listener in class. It took so much effort to hear that I usually tuned the teacher out. As a result, I had difficulty understanding the assignments.

Often people say they're seeking God's will but don't know what God wants them to do. Maybe you're unsure how God wants you to handle a certain parent, child, coworker, or problem. My teachers gave clear instructions, but I had difficulty understanding them because of my poor hearing. Similarly, God's will can be elusive if we're not "listening" carefully.

Meditating on God's Word and walking with Jesus every day is the key. The disciples never asked Jesus where they were going next. They just looked to see where he was going and stayed close to him so they could hear his instructions.

Lord, please help me stay close to you so I can follow you and do your will. Amen.

NOVEMBER 6
ARGUING—READ PROVERBS 8:13.

I had to apologize today for getting angry and raising my voice in a meeting with a coworker. I used to argue a lot because I believed it was important to "win" all arguments. Growing up with two very intelligent brothers taught me how to "out argue" most people. One of my brothers went on to be a very successful trial attorney.

Over the past few years, God has been teaching me how to hand him this desire of the flesh so he can exchange it for his spirit of peace. Jesus was never abrasive in his dealings with people, and he is my perfect example.

I wish I could relive today. Pride and ego, along with a poison tongue, have no hold on me unless I think I can handle the day alone. The first mistake I made was not saying a quick, "Help me, Lord," before the meeting.

Do people know you are a Christian? Remember the lyrics "They will know we are Christians by our love." Proverbs 8:13 says, "[Wisdom] hate[s] pride and arrogance, evil behavior and perverse speech." Ask for God's wisdom every day—all day long.

Lord, I want to trade my flesh for your spirit each day, but I need your help. Amen.

NOVEMBER 7
BEAUTIFULLY KNIT—READ PSALM 139:13-14.

I have a comprehensive development class for middle-grade students. Some are high functioning and can be mainstreamed for part of the day, while others require an individual aide at all times. Everyone knows it takes the right people to work with autism, Down's syndrome, and mentally challenged children. The teacher and two aides at our school do a tremendous job.

Diane, the teacher, had several bruises on her left arm today after being bitten by a new student. Instead of complaining, she laughed it off and assured me the child will be fine in a few days. Parents tear up many times when they describe the miracles she performs with their children. When God was putting Diane together, he placed several special ingredients in her so she would enjoy and succeed in working with special needs children.

God put special ingredients in each of us. As you look at each child today, reflect on Psalm 139:13-14 and remember that helping children discover the "special ingredients" God has put in them is an important part of our job as educators. Even when the stresses of teaching try to bury our enthusiasm, we must treat each child as a beautifully knit product of God.

Lord, help me look for the special traits within my students so I may lead them to discover their gifts and talents. Amen.

NOVEMBER 8
NEVER GIVE UP—REREAD PSALM 139:13.

Bryan arrived at our school as a homeless eighth-grader. He arrived late every day, did nothing in class, and soon had an attendance problem. Our guidance counselor had an intervention meeting with several teachers and Bryan's mom. We gave Bryan an alarm clock, some clothes, and a new plan. Within a few days I met with him again about not doing his work. During this conversation, he shared with me about being sexually abused when he was younger. His most alarming statement that day was, "I don't think I should have been born. . . . What I'm trying to say, Mr. Hill, is it would have been better if I hadn't been born."

Thankfully, I have several staff members who believe Psalm 139:13. If God "knit" Bryan together, then he must be special. And if God placed Bryan with us, then God must have "knit" within us the ability to help him. Bryan's P.E. teacher believed this, and consequently he earned Bryan's trust as the weeks and months passed. Then, one night in the spring, Bryan asked him for a ride to a revival at a local church. That night Bryan went forward during the invitation and received Jesus Christ as his Savior and Lord.

The next day at school Bryan still looked sloppy with his shoelaces untied, his zipper down, and his shirttail out. But his eyes had new hope and his face was much brighter. At the end of the school year we did not have to "socially promote" Bryan to high school because he had earned passing grades.

Today Bryan has an eternal home and a sustaining hope. We must never give up on a child because God never gives up on us.

Lord, I believe you knit together every child. Help me teach all of them how special they are. Amen.

NOVEMBER 9

LEARN TO RESPOND—READ PSALM 46:10.

Several years ago I heard the story of a girl who was murdered and whose heart went to another young girl. Amazingly, the eight-year-old heart recipient, who never knew the victim, was later able to identify the murderer for the police. The man was tried and convicted. Incredible, isn't it? This story reminds me that it's all about the heart.

Jesus said to love the Lord your God with all your heart. Though we worry about the condition of our physical hearts, the Lord is more concerned with the health of our spiritual hearts. God knows that when our hearts are right, our actions will reflect and honor him.

In the school setting, conflicts and disagreements occur daily. If our spiritual hearts are not healthy, we can react without thinking. Zig Ziglar says when we *react* to something, it turns out bad. However, when we *respond* to something, it turns out good. When we get angry and upset with people, it is wise to be still and ask God to change our hearts so that we are able to respond properly.

Lord, when I become angry, help me be still and allow you to change my heart so I can respond rather than react. Amen.

NOVEMBER 10

DO IT FOR THE LORD—READ COLOSSIANS 3:23.

John had spina bifida, and it was serious enough to keep him permanently confined to a wheelchair. One day on the playground, he suddenly realized how permanent his situation was. He looked at one of our staff members and said, "I'm never going to be able to get out of this wheelchair and play, am I?"

After sharing this story with some children at a retreat, I asked them, "If Jesus were nearby, would you take John to him to be healed?" They all responded with an enthusiastic "Yes!" I said, "What if you got really hot and tired, or hungry? Would you set him down and go home?" They shouted, "No way!"

The scripture for the retreat was Colossians 3:23. I tried to "bring home" the scripture by relating the effort they were willing to give for John to other areas of their lives.

I would love to be a student in a teacher's class who meditated on and applied this scripture in the classroom. It tells us to do it "for the Lord," not for men. Teachers have all kinds of great excuses for being discouraged because society does not reward us for our hard work. After all, the lazy teacher gets paid the same. Yet God's reward awaits us when we "work at it with all our heart" for him.

Lord, help me become more motivated and enthusiastic in all things. Show me how to work for you and not for men. Amen.

NOVEMBER 11

FLEXIBILITY IN TOUGH TIMES—READ 1 PETER 1:3-7.

This year there were not enough students in fourth grade, and I had to choose one of four excellent teachers to move to first. Whatever decision I made would surely produce tears. I asked God for his wisdom and then made sure I got my own feelings out of the way. As always, he gave me a clear, decisive answer, and I had peace. However, I still don't like to make people I love unhappy.

Teaching calls for a lot of flexibility. Teaching assignments can change at any time. Leadership may change along with expectations every few years. Flexibility is also necessary on a daily basis. We get called to an unexpected meeting or program. The cafeteria has a problem, so lunch is delayed for thirty minutes. Sometimes there are not enough substitute teachers.

If God shelters us during life's storms, then surely he will shelter us during life's showers and drizzles. As you face each day with God's precious children, see the showers that come your way as opportunities to be flexible and show your faith, bringing glory and honor to God.

Lord, keep me flexible and help me see trials as opportunities to show my faith and bring you glory. Amen.

NOVEMBER 12

A LIVING SACRIFICE—READ ROMANS 12:1.

When I decided to accept the principal's job at a K-8 school after being assistant principal at a high school, a friend who had made the move from secondary to elementary said I would love it. Then she said, "The kids will love you." When I asked why, she answered, "Because you are the principal."

The change was unbelievable. Every day for the past thirteen years I have had as many hugs and high fives as I can handle in one day. Once as I walked past a kindergarten class, a little one looked up and proclaimed, "There goes the principal . . . of the United States of America." It was another moment of joy amid the chaos of the day.

I believe even the older students think highly of teachers, though some won't admit it. We teachers have more impact on young lives than we realize. We serve as role models for so many children each day. So, we had better "get our act together" by saying a simple prayer each morning, offering ourselves to the Lord and asking for his help. As Romans 12:1 says, let us "offer [our] bodies as living sacrifices, holy and pleasing to God—which is [our] spiritual act of worship."

Lord, today I offer myself to you as a living sacrifice. Help me be all you would have me be for my students. Amen.

NOVEMBER 13
WHEN YOU'RE CRITICIZED—READ JAMES 1:2-4.

Most of us start the year fired up and ready to go, but by Christmas our batteries are usually running low. Trials of all kinds drain us. One of the most draining is personal criticism. Two years ago we had a student whose mother attacked, accused, and manipulated the teacher, refusing to discuss anything without blowing up and stomping off. Although the child and teacher got along fine, there was nothing I could say to keep the teacher from taking the attacks personally. It was an energy drain, and it affected the teacher even though she handled the situation well.

Is it possible to keep our batteries charged throughout the year—even when we're criticized? What if everyone wore a sign that said "under construction"? Perhaps that would help us view one another differently. Then, when a parent "goes off," we'd read his or her "under construction" sign and be reminded that we're wearing the same sign; and we'd realize God is still working on us, too.

The "under construction" analogy can help us be more tolerant when we're being criticized. After all, God allows these people in our paths to see how we're doing spiritually. There will always be people to drain our batteries. If we will turn to Jesus, he will recharge us with his truth and give us patience.

Lord, help me remember that we're all "under construction," and give me patience and understanding when others are critical of me. Amen.

NOVEMBER 14
THE SAME MEASURE OF LOVE—
READ EPHESIANS 3:18-19 AND JOHN 13:34-35.

In his book *Classic Christianity*, Bob George gives an illustration about Christian imitators. A man is listening and dancing to some upbeat music. A deaf man enters the room and begins to imitate the first man. A third person then enters the room and sees both men dancing. He can't tell by the exterior gyrations that one of the men is deaf.

The deaf man represents a legalist who says to himself, "I've got to do better." He has knowledge of Jesus, but he doesn't have a personal relationship with the Lord. The imitator will become grouchy and eventually tire of trying to figure what move to make next. The man who really hears the music represents someone who has a personal relationship with Jesus. His dancing, which represents his actions throughout the day, is a natural response to the music he hears.

As a teacher, your greatest effort should be in growing your understanding of God's love and grace for you, because you will treat your students and coworkers with the same measure of love, acceptance, and forgiveness that you think God has for you. If you think God is constantly angry or upset with you, that's probably how you'll treat others. However, once you have a true awareness of God's love, it will produce a response that's as irresistible as upbeat music!

Lord, help me grow in my understanding of your love and grace so I may love others with the same measure of love. Amen.

November 15

Don't Worry—Read Matthew 6:34.

A boy called a girl a racist name in the hallway. Whenever this kind of language is used, I require an apology, punish the guilty party, and make the individual meet with Linda, my African American guidance counselor. Linda's understanding of racism makes the meeting a valuable learning experience. This time, however, the girl's family went to see a lawyer and wrote a very aggressive letter to my boss, criticizing the way I had handled the situation.

If this had happened a few years ago, I probably would have lost sleep. But I've learned to remember God's faithfulness and to rest in the knowledge that he will take care of me. My heavenly Father has "parted the Red Sea" many times in my past. He took care of my mom after my dad died. He took care of me after a failed marriage. He has sent his angels to carry my family during my wife's battle with breast cancer. Wouldn't it be a sin if I worried about unfair attacks?

Worry and fear will paralyze us. Don't let these favorite tools of the enemy rob you of your joy in teaching and keep you from receiving God's blessings for helping his children.

Lord, teach me how harmful worry and fear can be to my spiritual growth, and help me enjoy teaching your children each day. Amen.

November 16

Letting Go of Worry—Read Matthew 6:25-34.

Teachers often worry: *What if I get a bad group of students? What if I'm asked to move next year? What if I'm not able to cover everything before achievement tests?* The "what ifs" put lots of extra weight on our shoulders, and the extra weight takes more energy to carry. I wish all of my staff members could let go of worry so they would have more energy to love and care for the children. Letting go of worry is a step of faith.

A Sunday school teacher put a chair in the middle of the floor and said, "I believe this chair will hold me because it looks strong." This, he explained, represented our beliefs. After praising the color, shape, and size of the chair, he explained that this represented our worship. "Now I am going to demonstrate faith," he said, and he sat down. Faith, he explained, is an action verb. Belief and worship without action have no meaning. When he sat in the chair, he demonstrated faith that the chair would hold him. The burden and weight rested on the chair, not on his feet.

What if you placed *all* your "what ifs" in the strong hands of Jesus? I believe your shoulders would be available for your students, who need all your energy.

Lord, help me give you all of my "what ifs" and worries, trusting you to take care of everything. Amen.

NOVEMBER 17
BEING A LIGHT—READ PSALM 119:103-105.

The staff at our school is incredible. In thirteen years I have never had a staff member refuse to help load buses, coordinate homecoming, or go the extra mile. Love is a much higher standard than rules and contracts.

During the school year, certain staff members need to be lifted up by the others. Miscarriages, sickness, and problems at home are personal issues that can drain teachers' energy from their students. Instead of allowing these things to become draining, our staff has learned to turn them into opportunities. Phone calls, letters, cards, prayer, food, and more prayer consistently shower blessings throughout the school. When my own wife, Debbie, went through chemo for breast cancer, we were flooded with cards and food.

During tough times, the enemy wants us to worry and be paralyzed in fear. Jesus wants us to rest in him and be free from the bondage problems can bring. How do your coworkers view you? Are you a light during dark times? If we allow his word to be a lamp to guide our actions, we will become a light to others.

Lord, please help me be a light to my coworkers during their dark times. Amen.

November 18

Do Not Fear—Read Isaiah 41:10.

Several years ago, the mom of two of our students was a self-proclaimed witch. One day one of the girls was upset because she said her mom had cast a spell on the school and she was worried about what might happen. Linda, our guidance counselor, said that she wasn't worried because she and the school had the protection of Jesus Christ. The little girl said she'd never heard of the guy and wanted to know where he was from.

Jesus commanded us to teach others about him. Even though many believe this cannot be done in a public school, the truth is that the Lord's work cannot be stopped. Prayer by staff members and the community is powerful.

Linda and other staff members prayed for an answer. One of our teachers had a relative who was looking to adopt. He and his wife were not afraid. The judge removed the children from the physically and emotionally abusive home and placed them in foster care with the young couple. After several years of fighting, the witch gave up her children, and the young couple has legally adopted them.

Isaiah 41:10 says, "So do not fear, for I am with you; do not be dismayed. . . . I will strengthen you." I'm thankful our staff and the young couple rested in this truth.

I invite you, Lord, into my classroom every day. Protect my children and intervene when they're being harmed. Teach me to rest in your truth. Amen.

November 19

Goodness and Mercy—Read Psalm 23:6.

Taylor, a sixth grade boy, has big, brown eyes that can only be seen when you push away his long, mopped hair. His apparent laziness and constant misbehavior led to many meetings between the two of us.

A few months ago we called a meeting with his teachers, mother, and grandmother. During the meeting, Taylor broke down while sharing how his mother's boyfriend had been bullying him when Mom was not around. Since we knew Mom would choose the boyfriend over her son, we suggested Taylor move in with his grandmother, and everyone agreed. Taylor loves his granny and grandpa.

As we walked back to his classroom, I told him how proud I was of him and reached out my arms to give him a hug. He buried his head in my chest and cried for several minutes. We both sensed God's goodness.

Taylor's grades and behavior improved dramatically. However, one day he lost his temper with another student and had to be disciplined. I was very careful to show mercy and let him know he was still very special to me. As I spoke to him about learning from his mistake, I sensed his heart's desire to not disappoint me again.

Psalm 23:6 says God's goodness and mercy follow us every day of our lives to bring us back into his will. As you accept God's goodness and mercy in your own life, be sure to extend the same with your students and coworkers each day.

Lord, thank you for always giving me what I need to draw me back to you. Help me to do the same with my coworkers and students each day. Amen.

NOVEMBER 20
LOVING STUDENTS FIRST—READ 1 JOHN 4:19.

When I was seven, we moved from Michigan to Tennessee, and I entered second grade having no idea of the cultural differences I would face. Although "yes" and "no" had been acceptable responses in Michigan, it was "yes, ma'am" and "no, ma'am" in Tennessee. My teacher spanked my hand every time I forgot to say *ma'am*. I soon hated school. I never told Mom and Dad because they'd taught me to obey my teachers. Then one morning I was waiting at the bus stop, and when the bus came into view, I took off in a sprint. My mom had to chase me down and wait with me to make sure I would get on the bus.

I don't think my second-grade teacher liked me. More important, I didn't learn anything that year. Experts say children cannot learn if they believe their teachers don't like them. I believe it's the teacher's job to convince every child that she or he loves that child.

Some students get under your skin and test you daily. However, the minute they think you don't like them, they won't like you either and will turn you off.

We're no different. We're able to love only because Jesus loved us first. And just as Jesus loved us first, so we must love our students first.

Lord, help me love all of my students and convince them of my love. Amen.

NOVEMBER 21

GROWING OUR LOVE—READ 1 JOHN 4:10, 18-19.

One difference in being an administrator of a high school and being principal of an elementary school is the way the students view you. High-school students don't like you at first. If you are fair and honest with them, they eventually warm up. Elementary students, however, love you from the start. It's easier to love the elementary students because they love you first. The students at my school want to hug me, get high fives, and tell me every little thing. The warmth and excitement in their eyes make it easy to reciprocate their love.

As we saw yesterday, God loves us first—just like the elementary students. First John 4:10 says, " . . . not that we loved God, but that he loved us and sent his Son as a sacrifice to take away our sins" (NLT). Many people wonder why they find it difficult to love God, even though they know they should. The truth is, our love for God can grow only when we understand how much he loves us. We love because he first loved us.

Have you ever wondered if you are an easy person to love? God has shown us the perfect way to start and retain relationships. If we love others first, they will be drawn to us and give us the opportunity to share God's love.

Thank you for loving us first, Lord. Please grow my love so that my heart is filled with love for others. Amen.

NOVEMBER 22

A DISCERNING HEART—READ 1 KINGS 3:7-12.

I'm sure you've read examples of people who failed many times before they became famous. Michael Jordan, for example, was cut from his high-school basketball team. Beethoven's music teacher once said of him, "As a composer, he is hopeless." However, the best one might be Walt Disney, who was fired from a newspaper because he "lacked imagination and had no good ideas."

It's good to hear these stories because sometimes we categorize students and see only their poor behavior or lack of responsibility. This is why smart students with behavior issues are sometimes placed with students with less ability.

We must look for the potential in *all* our students. Instead of dwelling on the day-to-day grades and behavior, we should never lose sight of the big picture. Godly wisdom and discernment can help us achieve this very important aspect of our job.

King Solomon told God, "But I am only a little child and do not know how to carry out my duties." Maybe we need to make a similar confession to God, because teaching children is such a huge responsibility. Then, like Solomon, we could ask for a "discerning heart." When we truly seek God, he will grant our request for wisdom and discernment in helping to encourage and grow our students.

Lord, grant me wisdom and discernment in every area. I want to look deeper to see children's potential and help them reach it. Amen.

NOVEMBER 23

FILLED WITH LAUGHTER—READ PSALM 126.

Family means getting together for food, fellowship, and laughter. I was born into a fantastic family who has always enjoyed getting together. My in-laws are also a great bunch to fellowship with. And what a special blessing it is to enjoy being with my school family.

Today we went off campus to my brother's lake house. My large teaching staff enjoyed food, fellowship, and a lot of laughter while soaking in a short but effective workshop. While sitting on the back porch overlooking the lake, I loved hearing the sound of conversation and laughter as everyone enjoyed being together away from school.

Psalm 126 says, "Our mouths were filled with laughter, our tongues with songs of joy." In between the laughter today, I could sense the joy it brought all of us to be together.

At this time of year, we are usually frustrated by the lazy students, tired of the discipline problems, irritated with one another, and starting to feel stressed by the upcoming holidays. Instead, we left our meeting revived with a fresh spirit for the next few weeks.

God's ability to restore life is beyond our understanding. Forests burn down and grow back. Broken bones heal. God uses our "family time" to restore our energy and enthusiasm, because he expects our best every day.

Lord, help shape our faculty into a family atmosphere. Restore my spirit today as I read your truth in Psalm 126. Amen.

NOVEMBER 24

SHOWERS OF BLESSINGS—READ EZEKIEL 34:25-31.

James was president of our junior class in high school and one of the smartest students in our class. His parents were smart and successful; his two older brothers had been graduated from high school with honors and were doing very well in college. James had unlimited potential.

I visited the funeral home a few weeks ago after hearing about the passing of James's father. My friend's physical and mental health resembled a feeble old man. At age fifty, I expected some aging, but his appearance was startling.

While offering my sympathy to one of his brothers, I asked about James's health. His brother said he didn't believe James would be alive in two years if he didn't stop drinking. He had lost his driver's license, his family, and was working the third shift at a local gas station for minimum wage. What a wasted life.

Many Christians never reach their potential, choosing to live in spiritual poverty. Ezekiel 34:26 talks about God showering us with his blessings. However, many of us settle for short periods of drizzle. Just like alcohol kept my friend James from reaching his potential, fear and worry can grip us spiritually. How sad it must be for Jesus to watch his children wasting their spiritual potential and settling for a small portion of the blessings he has waiting for us.

Lord, deliver me from any spiritual poverty in my life. Shower me with your blessings, and I promise to enjoy your rain. Amen.

November 25
Live by the Spirit—Read Galatians 5:11-18.

I read an article recently that said that selfishness—which speaks of *my* identity, *my* rights, *my* fulfillment, and *my* happiness—probably kills more marriages than anything else. Working together in a school setting is sort of like a marriage. We share space and furniture and see a lot of each other!

Do you work with people who are selfish? You can almost guarantee they're going to start talking about themselves if you give them a few minutes of your time. They'll tell you about their bad students or problems, or brag about their recent accomplishment.

Paul says in Galatians to "live by the Spirit, and you will not gratify the desires of the sinful nature." Jesus has given us the free will to choose each and every day to live by the Spirit of truth he left us. That means that each day we can enjoy the fruit of Spirit.

During my wife's illness, I've learned that it is not selfish to allow others to minister to our family. On the contrary, it has been a spiritual lesson for us to watch and learn from the unselfish acts of friends and family.

Because of Jesus' perfect example, we are empowered to build healthy relationships at work and set a good example for our students.

Lord, help me know if my relationships at school are what you want them to be, and help me reflect your Spirit today. Amen.

NOVEMBER 26

TRUE SUCCESS—READ JEREMIAH 9:23-24.

Teachers are leaving our county in large numbers for higher-paying positions in a nearby county. It's difficult to blame them when the average pay is six thousand dollars more there. Although most of us enter the profession because of our desire to help children, the cost of living begins to weigh on us; and our income becomes increasingly important.

But what if the Lord's plan for us means staying where we are? Are we following our own agenda or surrendering everything to God? God's plan should be the only issue we consider. Trusting him in decisions about staying where we are or leaving for more money is simply an opportunity to let God reveal his plan for us.

Jeremiah 9:23-24 tells us the truth about success, which contradicts the world's definition. "This is what the LORD says: 'Let not the wise man boast of his wisdom or the strong man boast of his strength or the rich man boast of his riches, but let him who boasts boast about this: that he understands and knows me, that I am the LORD.'"

True success can occur only when we enter into a personal relationship with Jesus. When we know, meditate on, and obey his word, we are considered successful in his eyes. The real question is whose agenda takes priority.

Lord, I'm not always sure this is where you want me to teach. Help me see clearly what your agenda is for me. Amen.

NOVEMBER 27

FAILURE IS NOT AN OPTION—READ JOHN 21:15-19.

In school, F stands for failure. Many students coming into our schools already feel like an F. They've been verbally abused or neglected. When school is their only hope, receiving F's only reinforces their poor self-image.

In our middle grades, we have adopted a new guideline: Failure is not an option. F's have been replaced with I's, for Incomplete. Parents no longer get angry with the teacher for giving their child an F. Instead, teachers accept only quality work and question students about what assignments were not turned in, giving them the opportunity to complete or redo the work.

At first, apathetic students begged us to give them an F and leave them alone. Over time, however, student apathy has been greatly reduced, and many students are experiencing success at school for the first time.

Isn't this system more in line with the way God treats us? Think about all the figures in the Bible who appeared to fail— King David, Peter, and other disciples. Thankfully, in God's system, there is no such thing as being a failure. Though we fail temporarily, God continues to allow us to revise, correct, and learn from our mistakes.

Modifying our grading system so that it's more in line with the way God treats us just makes sense.

Lord, thanks for never giving up on me and for allowing me to learn from past mistakes. Teach me to reflect this with my students. Amen.

NOVEMBER 28

INTERCEDING—READ ROMANS 8:26-27, 34.

Emphasis on intervention for struggling students has increased dramatically in the past few years. With the No Child Left Behind legislation, intervention is required. Teachers must be able to show specific attempts to turn a child around.

At our school, we have intercession at the end of every nine-week grading period. Each month we have Intensive Care—ICU—for students whose work is slowly dying. Parent phone calls, after-school tutoring, and extra help during the school day are proving successful in preventing students from being left behind.

One of the most promising changes we have made is giving each child an advisor adult. Sixth-grade students will have the same advisor all through middle grades. The adult advisor is supposed to intercede for his or her students. The other day one of the boys who had lost some of his work complained that his teacher would not let him make it up. He said, "My teacher won't give me another worksheet because I lost the other one." The boy's advisor teacher interceded for him by simply discussing the situation with the classroom teacher, and it was easily resolved.

Jesus intercedes for us. Paul repeats this truth three times in Romans 8. Just like the boy whose advisor took up for him, Jesus sits at the right hand of God and stands up for us.

Lord, help me look for opportunities to intercede for my students. Thank you for being my advocate in heaven. Amen.

NOVEMBER 29

SPIRITUAL ARMOR—READ EPHESIANS 6:11-14.

We have several new teachers this year. Although each of them has the raw talent to be exceptional some day, they will need more information and experience to reach their potential. One of my roles as principal is to arm teachers with the best practices in planning, teaching strategies, communication, and classroom management. Without proper training, these new teachers will not be equipped to become master teachers.

The same is true of us as Christians. To be spiritually prepared, we must learn to put on our spiritual armor. Ephesians 6:11-14 says to "put on the full armor of God so that you can take your stand against the devil's schemes."

The Bible clearly says the war is in the spiritual realm rather than the physical. We must get in the habit of putting on the armor of God, including the "belt of truth" and the "shield of faith," each and every day.

Jesus gave us spiritual "best practices" to use each day. Without following his example, we will never reach the potential he created us for.

Lord, remind me each day to prepare myself spiritually by putting on your spiritual armor to protect and guide me. Amen.

NOVEMBER 30
THE LORD IS MY SHEPHERD—READ PSALM 23.

I went with Debbie to see her oncologist yesterday. Our nurse and doctor visited with us for almost an hour. With regular weekly or monthly treatments over the past year, we have become good friends. I told them both how strongly we believe they were clear and undeniable answers to many prayers. They told us we did not have to come back for three months this time!

As Debbie and I got in the elevator to leave, we just had to hug. As we walked to the car, we just had to hold hands. We were not sad, happy, or scared—just totally at peace. The deepened love and respect we developed for each other over the past sixteen months is priceless. Our bond in trusting Jesus for the future is permanent. Only the creator of the universe could turn breast cancer into a blessing.

The Twenty-third Psalm puts it all in perspective. The Lord is my shepherd, and I am one of his sheep. During the breast cancer, it was really comforting to know I wasn't the shepherd. When I couldn't breathe because fear had a grip on me, God made me lie down in his green pasture so I could rest and breathe. When the waves of worry tried to drown me, he quieted the waters; and I have slept like a baby every night. Of course, verse four will always be my favorite because God has taught me that for the rest of my life here on earth, he is always with me—even in the face of death.

Through the rest of this school year, may you remember that God is always with you, too.

Lord, thank you for being my shepherd and meeting all my needs. Amen.

DECEMBER
Glad Tidings

Amy Maze

DECEMBER 1
ENCOURAGING WORDS—READ LUKE 2:10.

I BELIEVE THAT TEACHERS ARE THE EASIEST PEOPLE TO SURPRISE. We get excited over the smallest things. Have you ever felt overjoyed with the announcement, "There will be no faculty meeting today," or "We have purchased every teacher dry erase markers for your classroom," or "Little Timmy (the student who has become a thorn in your side this year) is absent today," or simply "Thank you"? Those words mean so much to us because in the hectic busyness of our demanding days, we rarely hear encouraging words.

I once had a principal who would occasionally put a note in my mailbox praising me for specific things he saw me doing with my students. The night before the first day of school, he would "tour" the classrooms and make sure we were prepared. While he was there, he would leave a little note and a small gift to greet us on the first morning of school. It was so great to feel appreciated. It's the small things in life that really make a difference.

More than two thousand years ago, the world was changed by an angel giving encouraging words to an unsuspecting group of shepherds. The angel told them of the new Savior's birth. During the month of December, we will focus on the glad tidings surrounding Jesus' birth and life on Earth.

Dear Lord, help me give encouragement often because I never know when it may make a difference in someone's life. Amen.

DECEMBER 2

JESUS' FAMILY TREE—READ MATTHEW 1.

When I meet the parents of my students each year, it never ceases to amaze me that many questions are answered for me. Does the phrase "the apple doesn't fall far from the tree" mean anything to you? In my own family, I have noticed how I have many of the characteristics of my parents.

Many people research the generational histories of their families. It is a difficult task to trace your roots back through many decades; you may find things that you are exceptionally proud of, or not proud of at all. The same is true of Jesus' family.

I love the fact that Jesus' lineage can be traced back to Genesis. It makes the whole picture complete knowing that every part of the Bible is connected. In Jesus' family there were people with great reputations such as Abraham, Isaac, Ruth, and David. There also were some ordinary and even some evil people in his lineage. God used all kinds of people to bring his Son into the world.

If you are a Christian, you can add yourself to Jesus' family tree. We are all a part of Christ's family. You can make a difference in your family for generations to come if you will live a life representative of a child of God.

Dear Lord, thank you for preparing the way for your Son through many generations. Help me share his message with my family, friends, and students. Amen.

DECEMBER 3

PREPARE THE WAY—READ ISAIAH 40:3.

Have you ever felt defeated in your job? Have you ever questioned God about your purpose as an educator? All of us have felt similar frustrations at one time or another. Even when we have our students' best interests at heart, many times we are accused by overprotective parents of doing the wrong thing or making the wrong choice in a given situation.

One day in a faculty meeting, my principal was experiencing this particular frustration. She felt that all the complaining parents had conspired together to bombard the school with complaints on the same day. Taking it all in stride as she usually does, she calmly listened to each parent and explained to them that parents so desperately want to prepare the path their child will encounter each day. They want it to be perfect without challenge or complication. However, that is not the way life is.

As teachers, we must prepare our students for *whatever* path lies ahead. When we prepare them appropriately, they can handle any situation regardless of how fair or unfair it seems.

John the Baptist was sent to Earth to prepare the people for the coming Messiah. In a lost and broken world, he spoke the truth to prepare the hearts of the people. May we, like John, help prepare our students for what is to come.

Dear Lord, help me prepare my students for the road ahead. May they develop strong and sincere characters through my influence. Amen.

DECEMBER 4
THE POWER OF A NAME—READ ISAIAH 7:14.

Are there names floating around your school building of children known by all the teachers because they have a good or a bad reputation? When you get your class list each year, are there names you definitely do not want to see? Names are very powerful. We want people to call us by our names. Parents struggle for months and months during pregnancy to find the perfect name for their child.

My mom told me that when she was in fifth grade she was so excited because she was starting over at a new school and could be anyone she wanted to be. On the first day of school the teacher asked her what her name was, and she eagerly told her, "Gloria." Now, this was indeed her first name, but she always had gone by her middle name. She says she felt so bad the minute her teacher and new friends began calling her by that new name. She learned the importance of her real name.

For Mary and Joseph, naming their new baby was easy. His name had been prophesied many years before his birth. The baby was to be called Immanuel, which means "God with us."

Dear Lord, thank you for always being with us and for knowing us by name. Amen.

DECEMBER 5

"I DON'T GET IT"—READ LUKE 2:48-50.

Have you ever planned and prepared for a lesson that you were so excited to teach to your class, and it didn't turn out so great? You used visuals, manipulatives, technology, or other interesting things to capture their attention, and it didn't work. In the background of the classroom you could hear your students whining, "I don't get it." By the end of the lesson you were so frustrated and upset that you could scream!

I remember feeling this way when I taught first-graders. During my first year of teaching, I felt especially ill prepared to accomplish the many tasks expected of me. My mind was mush at the end of each day. I later realized that I had brought many of these feelings on myself by trying to do things that were not developmentally appropriate for first-graders. I would attempt art projects or multistepped home-made crafts, telling my first-graders exactly how to do it, and they would look so puzzled. They simply were incapable of processing so much information.

I imagine that Mary and Joseph had the same puzzled look when Jesus was speaking to the religious leaders in the Temple as a young boy. They knew he was unique, but they could not understand his thoughts.

Dear Lord, help me share your word more often with people who "don't get it." Amen.

DECEMBER 6

MARY'S MOTHER—READ LUKE 1:38.

I am not a mother, but being a teacher is similar in many ways. After a few weeks of school, I become connected with my students in a personal way. I want to know about their lives so I can better understand how to meet their needs in all areas. In addition to developing a connection with them, I begin to feel protective of them.

Have you ever thought of Mary's mother? We know that Mary was an exceptionally amazing person to be chosen by God and to be obedient to her call. But, I wonder about her parents and, in particular, her mother. What must this amazing woman have been like to raise such a special daughter? I mean, to think that as a young teenager her mother let Mary go off with Joseph on a donkey to a city far away.

I have a great Christian mother, but she says the fate of the world would have changed forever if she had been the mother of Mary. She would have asked, "How is he going to feed you?" "Where are you going to stay?" "Who will be there to help you if you go into labor?" Wouldn't most mothers agree? Although there is no specific mention of her in Scripture, I can imagine that the mother of Mary was a chosen one as well.

Dear Lord, thank you for the example of obedience you have given through Mary and her mother. Help me be more willing to trust you. Amen.

DECEMBER 7

BE STILL—READ PSALM 46:10.

I love the quiet stillness of my classroom before the school bell rings. I try to arrive at school early so that I can prepare myself for the day ahead. I know that when the doors open, the halls will roar with rolling backpacks and children's voices. The stillness of dawn will be exchanged for the noise of the day. The calm solitude of the early morning will be invaded by decisions to be made and deadlines to be met. My organized desk will be covered with notes from parents and field trip money to count. And, my classroom will come alive with the imaginations and creativity of children.

We are extremely busy during the school day, and we know our human limitations. This is why it is vital to our Christian growth to separate ourselves from the day-to-day demands and acknowledge where our strength comes from. God expects us to honor his power and majesty daily. It is not a selfish act to withdraw and replenish our minds and spirits; it is necessary. Learning to take care of ourselves is worthwhile and nurturing. We should take time each day to be still and to exalt God.

Dear Lord, thank you for honoring my time spent with you and for refreshing my spirit each day when I come before you. Amen.

DECEMBER 8

PUTTING PRAYER FIRST—READ MARK 1:35.

Oftentimes I mark "use time wisely" on the back of my students' report cards after each grading period. Time is a commodity in school these days because we are so pressured to teach the many standards and accomplishments in order to prepare for the yearly achievement test. When I see my students wasting time, it always frustrates me because there is always something to do. I explain to them each year the many things that can occupy their time if they are finished with their work. But it never fails; almost daily I am reminding someone to stay on task.

I must admit that I do the same thing in my daily life. I'm sure if Jesus could give me a report card, he would mark "use time wisely." I can usually think of a million things I "need" to do instead of being still with the Lord in prayer and devotion time. When I have time, I love to check my e-mail and correspond with my friends. I eagerly anticipate their e-mails or instant messages. Why am I not equally excited to hear what the Lord has to tell me for that day or that moment?

We learn from Jesus' own life to put prayer before anything else. The best time to speak with Christ is in the early morning, before our day begins.

Dear Lord, thank you for your great example of personal worship. Help us use our time wisely each day. Amen.

DECEMBER 9

HOPEFUL ENDURING—READ COLOSSIANS 1:11-12.

Every few years, it never fails; there is "a group." Somehow they all manage to get onto the same class roster, only to be your source of stress for the year to come. It can make for exhausting days!

Two years ago was my year to have "the group." They were a class of third-graders who had majored in trouble and minored in cheating. It actually seemed as if the whole grade level misbehaved. Each morning my neighboring teachers and I gathered in the hallway between our classrooms and tried to gear up for the day. We bemoaned the fact that we had never seen a group of children like these before.

We depend on well-behaved kids to be role models for the others, but in my class that year, there were none! I planned every moment, and still there were times when I felt I was making no progress. At the same time, I knew I had to continue trying because I wanted so desperately to succeed with every student. Even though I could not see the fruit of my labor, the following year some of the parents of those students came to me and thanked me for preparing their children for the next grade. My endurance had not been in vain.

Dear Lord, please help us not only to endure but also to continue trying even when we don't feel like we're making a difference. Amen.

DECEMBER 10

No Child Left Behind—Read Mark 9:36-37.

Recent politicians have made "No Child Left Behind" a catch phrase among educators. We are working harder than ever before in public schools to make sure our children are making gains, to be certain our schools are improving, and to be confident our teachers are highly qualified. Regardless of your political opinion, you want the best for all children or you wouldn't be an educator.

I love this quotation from the famous basketball star Magic Johnson: "All kids need is a little help, a little hope, and somebody who believes in them." We should believe in our students regardless of their backgrounds. Many times that is very difficult to do because the students who need the most help are the ones who drain us the most emotionally each day.

Jesus originated the concept of "No Child Left Behind." Children were treated as second-class citizens in the days of the New Testament, yet Jesus made a point to welcome them and teach them about his love. He has commanded us to do that as well. As teachers, we have the opportunity daily to touch children's lives and make an impact on them that will last forever. Let's not waste that opportunity!

Dear Lord, help me have the patience and compassion I need to share your love with my students each day. Amen.

DECEMBER 11

Mind Your Own Beeswax—Read Proverbs 21:23.

M.Y.O.B. stands for "Mind Your Own Beeswax." It seems I am sharing that phrase on a daily basis! My third-graders are constantly tattling on one another. They're constantly running back and forth between their peers and me, telling me tales of what they find difficult to believe. "Ms. Maze, Brian said that if I don't play with him . . . " or "Sally said she has a boyfriend . . . " or "Mary said her mom. . . . " It is always something. Of course, you can't trust any of them to keep a secret!

As I think of school faculties, I think we often resemble our students. Do you eat lunch in the teachers' lounge? Gossip, gossip, gossip! It is usually terrible! I stopped eating lunch in the lounge because it became too stressful. I don't want to know what Mrs. Smith did in her classroom or what Mr. Jones told the principal today. I really don't have time to deal with gossip or gossipmongers.

We can help our students learn God's standard for community and caring by setting the example. Perhaps our classroom rules can include standards of accountability and showing kindness to one another.

Dear Lord, help me guard my tongue so that my words will be pleasing to you. Amen.

DECEMBER 12
BEING REAL—READ HEBREWS 4:14-16.

My students are amazed to learn that I have a life away from school. I think they believe that I live at school and never leave. When they see me at a restaurant or store, they gasp in amazement. They can't wait to introduce me to their family. "Look, Mom, it's Ms. Maze!" They get the biggest grin on their faces and keep staring as I walk away.

I try to bring in pictures of my family, my house, and my hobbies so my students can understand that I am a real person, too. I share with them what I do in my spare time and tell them when I am worried about something or when I am not feeling well. When students know I am "real," they seem to be more prone to come and share their concerns with me.

Today many people are trying to find a hero, someone to look up to. People want to admire someone who is real, not someone who is fake. No one in the world will ever be as real as Jesus. Jesus came to Earth as a real man. He was a living, breathing, walking, and talking man with feelings and emotions. Jesus was real with people, which is why they flocked to him everywhere he went, and he's still real today.

Dear Lord, thank you for being real and for understanding my feelings and concerns. Help me follow your example by being real with my students each day. Amen.

DECEMBER 13
RELIABLE PROMISES—READ MICAH 5:2.

One of the things I love about teaching is that each day is full of new and different challenges. My students never fail to surprise me with the things they do and say, leading me to laughter or tears, depending on the circumstance! Children are unpredictable; they have no limitations in their thought process. They speak freely and openly about everything. I jokingly tell parents at open house each year that I will not believe what their children say about home life if they will not believe what they say about school life! As you know, the story can get very confused by the time the child embellishes it and adds on his or her interpretation. I just ask parents to always give me the benefit of the doubt, and I promise to do the same for them.

Unlike the stories of my students, the promises of the Bible are completely reliable. I am amazed by the fact that all of the messianic prophecies in the Old Testament are fulfilled in the New Testament, including today's verse, which was written several hundred years before Christ's birth. Isn't it amazing to realize that the entire Bible is built around the birth and death of our Messiah?

God's promises are reliable!

Dear Lord, thank you for the confirmation through your word that you set all things in motion from the beginning of time and will fulfill every one of your promises without fail. Amen.

DECEMBER 14

THE SALT OF OUR SCHOOLS—READ MATTHEW 5:13-16.

School cafeterias are interesting places. I often dread walking my students to lunch because of the boisterous sounds coming from behind those glass doors and the mingled aroma of children and fried food! Some days it is more than I can bear.

My students anxiously await lunchtime because they will be free at last to visit with their friends; eating is actually the last thing on their minds! As for myself, I bring my lunch to school each day because ketchup and salt can only do so much when it comes to school lunches. Never mind what all of the high-carb, high-calorie fried foods will do to my hips!

Jesus spoke of salt to illustrate a quality that should be found in his followers. If food has no seasoning, we usually do not want to eat it. Likewise, if we Christians are not dynamically different from the world, then we are of little value to God in building his kingdom. Rather than blend in with everyone else, we should make a positive impact on all of those who come into our world.

We have a wonderful opportunity each day to influence the lives of our students. Let's take on that challenge and be the salt of our schools, starting today!

Dear Lord, help me make a difference in the flavor of the world I live in, just as salt changes the flavor of my food. Amen.

DECEMBER 15

ORGANIZATION—READ MARK 6:30-44.

My strongest ability in the classroom is organization. I take time to teach organizational skills to my students each year; however, there are always a few students who never get into the routine of organization. Last year it was Joe. He came to school each morning with his backpack unzipped, papers crumpled in the bottom of his backpack, paperback books torn in half, graded papers from last year's teacher, and the permission slip for last month's field trip stuffed inside the wrong folder. Though I love them just the same, I have to pray especially hard for patience in dealing with students like Joe.

I tend to believe that Jesus was also very organized, structured, and systematic in his teaching and instructional practices. The story of the feeding of the five thousand is a good example of this. He began by asking the disciples to separate the people into small groups. After the disciples came back with the five loaves and two fish, he systematically divided the food into twelve baskets for the disciples to pass out to the crowd. Then he blessed the food and distributed it among the crowd.

I think Jesus was showing us that anything is possible when we first ask God's blessing and then divide it into small, practical steps.

Dear Lord, thank you for your wonderful example of organization and prayer. Help us remember your example when we are faced with an impossible task. Amen.

DECEMBER 16

TOO QUICK TO JUDGE—READ MATTHEW 7:1-5.

I have been called to report for jury duty on several occasions. It is such an interesting experience that I wouldn't mind doing it again. You really learn about the judicial system and all the intricacies that justice lawyers and judges deal with. Actually, in many ways it is very similar to teaching!

One thing the judge and lawyers always make clear to the jury is that the defendant is innocent until proved guilty. The burden is always on the prosecuting attorney to prove beyond a reasonable doubt that someone is guilty of a crime. We've all heard those words, but sometimes we have difficulty believing them. We, as a human race, are quick to judge others. We judge people by the way they look and talk, the decisions they make, the kind of car they drive, and so on.

Oftentimes, we are quick to judge in the classroom, too. We may feel that our past experiences allow us the evidence to pass judgment on a particular student or parent, even when we try not to. Sometimes our students surprise us, and we are actually proved wrong.

It is best not to make judgments about a student's academic ability or behavior based on prior experiences, because we never know which child will be used by God for a special task.

Dear Lord, help me not to pass judgment on my students, but to help them improve their weaknesses through hard work and effort. Amen.

DECEMBER 17
TAKING TIME—READ MARK 10:14.

I love adorning my desk with student-made cards and pictures—especially at this time of year. One of the greatest things about being an elementary school teacher is that regardless of how bad you may look or feel, your students always love you! I'm so thankful when they make me those special pieces of artwork. Many times I cannot tell what the pictures are of, but I know the students were thinking of me.

In one of my first years of teaching, I mistakenly threw away a picture that a student had drawn for me. When she saw it in the trash can, she was devastated that I had done such a thing. I felt horrible because I had crushed her spirit.

I tried to apologize, but she was still so hurt because, in the rush of the day, I hadn't taken time to show her how I appreciated her artwork. I decided that from that day forward, whenever I received a "gift," I would stop what I was doing, look into the child's eyes, and thank him or her for thinking of me. Then I would tape it onto my desk that very minute so that it wouldn't get lost in the shuffle!

It doesn't matter how many pieces of artwork we have on display; it is never acceptable to crush a child's spirit.

Dear Lord, remind me always to take time to show my love and thankfulness to my students. Amen.

119

DECEMBER 18
THE REASON WE CELEBRATE—READ MATTHEW 2:11.

In the month of December, I am often awakened from my sleep with startling questions running through my mind: Did I remember all of my family members and close friends? Did I mail my Christmas cards? Did I invite the family? Have I wrapped everything? When is that party? Did I get a hostess gift? The beauty of the season sometimes loses its appeal. In a matter of minutes, it is reduced to chores and endless "to do" lists. I find myself wishing the holiday was over, or that I could celebrate alone.

I have to get all of the shopping done before school is out for Christmas break. I have to find the right gifts for everyone. I have to research the best recipes for my parties. I have to go to Melissa's party since I missed it last year. I have to go to the school PTO program and show support for my students. I have to go to a student's church to see her as Mary in the Christmas play. I have to go to the faculty party. I have to go to my church's Christmas musical.

Are any of these activities wrong? As I think of the reason we celebrate, I realize that for all my good intentions, all I really *have* to do to celebrate Christmas is worship the Lord.

Dear Lord, may my worship be pleasing to you throughout this Christmas season. Amen.

DECEMBER 19
THE EXAMPLE OF THE WISE MEN—READ MATTHEW 2.

The wise men followed the star of the east, and it led them to the world's greatest treasure, Jesus, lying in a manger near Bethlehem. They traveled thousands of miles to see their Savior, and when they finally found him, they responded with joy, worship, and gifts—setting the precedent of how we should approach our Savior each day.

These wise men were very determined to find baby Jesus. In contrast, I often think of how undetermined I am to "find"

Jesus in the course of my day. I can delay my quiet time for so many reasons.

In their very deliberate efforts to follow the star, the wise men gave us a great example to follow. First, we must be deliberate in our efforts to seek Jesus, and second, we must be deliberate in guiding and encouraging our students. They need a "cheerleader" on their side to encourage them to dream or pursue a goal or simply work harder on a task. We can be our students' biggest fans, rooting them on toward their own particular "stars."

Dear Lord, give us exceptional vision to see what the "star" is in each student's life and to help point him or her in the right direction. Amen.

DECEMBER 20

SPECIAL MEMORIES—READ PHILIPPIANS 1:3-7.

Decorating the house for Christmas and trimming the Christmas tree have become a sentimental affair over the years. Thanks to years of teaching, my tree is adorned with special ornaments and my hearth is full of Santa Clauses and figurines from wonderful students I have taught in the past. As I unwrap each ornament or trinket, memories of how that particular student was extra special to me flood my mind. Some of the ornaments were handmade, some were store-bought, and some were taken from students' own Christmas trees in order to have a gift for the teacher. Each is equally special to me.

My students know that Christmas is my favorite time of the year. They are so eager to bring in their presents for me that they usually start coming in weeks before Christmas vacation. They will come to me and innocently ask, "Ms. Maze, I was just wondering . . . do you like perfume?" or "Do you like candles?" I can usually list my gifts before I open them.

When the frustrations of teaching have made me feel as if my efforts have been fruitless, these precious trinkets have validated my efforts. If I have reached one child during a single year, my efforts have not been in vain.

Dear Lord, thank you for the memories of each of my students. Bless them with peace and happiness during this holiday season and always. Amen.

DECEMBER 21

THE GREAT PHYSICIAN—READ MATTHEW 28:20.

I was trying to coordinate several doctor visits for the same day. You know how that is. You're off from school, and you try to make your appointments before all the students in your county make theirs!

The day I wanted to schedule the appointments for was a Friday. Well, imagine my extreme frustration when I discovered that the doctors I needed to see did not see patients on Fridays. *What? Are you kidding me?* I thought. *I have never heard of such a crazy idea!*

Then I thought, *Wouldn't it be great if we could have Fridays free from students? I mean, think of all the paperwork that we could accomplish without interruption!*

In the midst of my frustration, I realized how fortunate we are as Christians that God never takes a day off. I'm so glad that any time I need to speak to him, ask him questions, or make a request, he is always there to hear me. I am so thankful!

Dear Lord, thank you for always being with me; you are the one and only true great physician. Amen.

DECEMBER 22

OUR BREATH—READ GENESIS 2:7.

My dear friend's baby, Hadley, is a small miracle. She was born prematurely, weighing only fifteen ounces. When she was two months old, the physicians wanted to take out her breathing tube and allow her to breathe on her own. This was a terrifying day because we wanted her to be successful at breathing on her own, but we didn't want her to struggle. The doctors and nurses were close by all day, ready to reinsert the breathing tube if she needed it. At first she was irritated and restless as she developed her own breathing rhythm. But eventually she got the hang of it and rested peacefully.

It made me think of my first experience snorkeling in the ocean. I was frantic when I put on the mask and breathing tube. I went under the water and immediately came back up for air. Eventually, however, I adapted to breathing correctly.

I'm so glad God is our constant ventilator. There are times in our lives when he is doing all the "breathing" for us. As we get a little more experienced and brave, we begin backing away from him a little. Then we get agitated and irritated about something—whether at school or at home—and we go back to him for more oxygen. As a contemporary worship song puts it, he is the air that we breathe.

As Christmas quickly approaches, let us remember to give thanks for our Breath of Life!

Dear Lord, thank you for being our constant source of oxygen, breath, and life each day. Amen.

DECEMBER 23

COMPASSION—READ COLOSSIANS 3:12.

I love the frantic, festive days of the Christmas season! I love the tolerance we seem to develop for one another when Christmas is near. I love the Christmas spirit expressed in kindness and love toward others. I love the twinkling lights and the warm glow of the fireplace adorned with Christmas stockings. And I love to feel the excitement of the season as purely and honestly as children do.

I especially love to be around my students during the Christmas season. Since I am not a parent yet, I love to enjoy the excitement on their faces as they experience all of the wonders of the season. They have their Santa lists ready and can't wait for school to be out. I think of my students on Christmas morning as I wake up to a silent house. I can imagine the excitement they are feeling as they open their presents.

However, I also think of those students who I know will not be excited on Christmas morning. There are always those few in our classrooms who are going through many difficult home situations. I pray for protection on their young lives, knowing that their circumstances are building their character.

Dear Lord, may I always remember the students who will not experience life to the fullest. Help me have compassion on them. Amen.

DECEMBER 24

WAIT AND TRUST—READ PSALM 9:10 AND PSALM 130:5.

When I was a child, the anticipation of opening presents was too much for me to handle. I was a "snooper." I would search through closets, the attic, and car trunks to try to find my Christmas presents. I even unwrapped some that were under the tree and rewrapped them quickly before Mom saw me. I was rarely surprised on Christmas morning because I had already discovered many of my presents.

My brother, however, never wanted to find any of his presents. He calmly waited until Christmas morning and experienced the excitement of seeing his gifts for the first time. He could not understand why I spent time searching for something that I was going to receive anyway. I could not understand how he could be so calm and patient about waiting until Christmas morning.

Now, I experience the same struggle with waiting and trusting in God on a daily basis, and I don't like it! I want to know the what, when, and how—and sometimes the why not—of every detail of my future. Yet I know that it is a terrible way of robbing myself of the joy that comes when I am pleasantly surprised by what God does in my life.

Dear Lord, help me wait patiently on you and surrender to your perfect timing and plan, trusting that you want me to experience joy. Amen.

DECEMBER 25
SOLITARY LIFE—READ LUKE 2:8-20.

I love to attend local plays and musicals during the Advent season. During one especially memorable play, they read a poem during the manger scene. It was the first time I had ever heard it, and it brought a different perspective to the realization of how significant Jesus' life is to all people. Here is the original form of that poem, which actually was part of a sermon written by James Allan Francis in 1926:

One Solitary Life

Let us turn now to the story. A child is born in an obscure village. He is brought up in another obscure village. He works in a carpenter shop until he is thirty, and then for three brief years is an itinerant preacher, proclaiming a message and living a life. He never writes a book. He never holds an office. He never raises an army. He never has a family of his own. He never owns a home. He never goes to college. He never travels two hundred miles from the place where he was born. He gathers a little group of friends about him and teaches them his way of life. While still a young man the tide of popular feeling turns against him. The band of followers forsake him. One denies him; another betrays him. He is turned over to his enemies. He goes through the mockery of a trial; he is nailed on a cross between two thieves, and when dead is laid in a borrowed grave by the kindness of a friend. Those are the facts of his human life. He rises from the dead. Today we look back across nineteen hundred years and ask, What kind of a trail has he left across the centuries? When we try to sum up.his influence, all the armies that ever marched, all the parliaments that ever sat, all the kings that ever reigned are absolutely picayune in their influence on mankind compared with that of this one solitary life. . . .

(James Allan Francis, "Arise, Sir Knight!" in *The Real Jesus and Other Sermons* [Philadelphia: The Judson Press, 1926], pp. 123-24)

Dear Lord, thank you for that one solitary life that changed the course of eternity for all people. Amen.

December 26

Take Time to Rest—Read Mark 6:31.

The day after Christmas is usually a day of exhaustion for most people. Your days have been consumed with cooking, entertaining, shopping, calling old friends, and mailing holiday greetings to everyone you know. All of the excitement and anticipation of Christmas Day is over, and now you have decorations to take down, unwanted presents to return, and a house to clean! It can be overwhelming.

I think that is how the disciples felt after they returned from their missionary journey. They had done all that Jesus had commanded them to do, and they had had great success in their endeavors. Now, however, they were exhausted, and Jesus knew they needed physical and spiritual rest and relaxation. Jesus invited them to come with him to a quiet place to rest.

Jesus cares about every detail of our lives. He doesn't want us to be constantly on the go; he wants us to be well rested and ready for his next challenge. Our schedules are so demanding that they often drain us of our physical, spiritual, mental, and emotional strength.

I believe it is important to take time to rest and to enjoy being alone, even during holidays. If the disciples needed rest, so do we!

Dear Lord, thank you for the excitement of the season. Help me take time to rest, relax, and spend time with you. Amen.

December 27

Using Our Gifts—Read Romans 12:6-8.

Have you ever received gifts that you didn't use? Do you remember really longing for a particular item, receiving it, and then never putting it to good use? It is a great disappointment.

I love shopping! Unfortunately, I am an easy target. I see the demonstrator use an interesting gadget and describe how much easier that product will make my life, and I fall for it. I can't describe how disappointing it is to put those same wonderful items in a garage sale years later after they have practically never been used.

I wonder if Jesus feels the same way when we do not use our spiritual gifts. He has given each of us specific interests and talents to be used to build his kingdom. I'm sure he is disappointed when we put those gifts "on the shelf" and make excuses about why we don't use them. Many times we don't use our spiritual gifts because it would involve time.

The Magi brought gifts and worshiped Jesus for who he was. This is a great example of true worship: honoring Christ and being willing to give him what is valuable to us—our time.

Dear Lord, help us use our spiritual gifts and not withhold them because we are being selfish with our time. Amen.

DECEMBER 28

DIRECT REFLECTION—READ GENESIS 1:27.

Many of you have something in common with me: I have always wanted to be a teacher. I was the kind of child who wanted an overhead projector and teacher manuals for Christmas! I would spend many hours each day in our garage with a chalkboard, chalk, and stuffed animals, pretending to teach as I mimicked my own teachers. My mom would listen as I would repeat phrases they had said and act as they had acted in class. I wanted to be just like them.

Now, after many years of teaching, I watch my own students mimic me. Whenever they have free time, they want to write on the dry-erase board and hold my teacher manuals. They do and say exactly what I do and say when I am teaching. It can be a scary reality to think that my students are so in tune to what I do and say each day. They are a direct reflection of me, their teacher.

We have been created in the image of God with the purpose of reflecting God's glory. Each morning before school, let us pray that we will reflect God's character in all that we do and say.

Dear Lord, help me each day reflect more and more of your characteristics. Amen.

DECEMBER 29

FRUIT OF THE SPIRIT—READ GALATIANS 5:22-23.

At the start of each day, we must choose how we will respond to the day's demands. As we renew our souls and bodies during this holiday break, let's determine that when we return to school, we will make a conscious decision each day to choose love, joy, peace, patience, kindness, goodness, faithfulness, gentleness, and self-control.

Let us choose to love our students—and their parents. No occasion justifies hatred. Let us choose to be joyful in all circumstances, even when the week's math skill takes twice as long to teach. Let us refuse the temptation to be cynical—the tool of the lazy thinker. Let us have peace of mind, knowing that we live a forgiven life. Let us show patience when faced with frustrations, such as when all of the copy machines are jammed. Let us be kind to the unkind, and let us be good to others even when we'd rather be rude. Let us be faithful to our promises, especially when we'd rather use our time selfishly. Let us be gentle, remembering that nothing is won by force. Let us have self-control at all times, especially when we want to raise our voice at a student.

Which of these qualities do you most need to improve on? Ask the Holy Spirit to produce it in you.

Dear Lord, thank you for the fruit of the Spirit and for your example of how to incorporate the fruit into all areas of my life. Amen.

DECEMBER 30

GOD'S TIMETABLE—READ JEREMIAH 29:11.

Oftentimes I find myself in despair as a young, single woman because I want to be married—especially at this time of year with an abundance of family gatherings and parties. We all build up dreams for ourselves based on our plans, and then we hand over the timetable to God and say, "OK, God, this is how I want it to happen." God doesn't work that way. Maybe for you it is the struggle to conceive, or the battle of temptation, or any other need you think God hasn't met in your life.

Anytime I start to get exceptionally gloomy, I wonder why God hasn't blessed me in a particular way. After all, I've been faithful. Or I look at the lives of those who seem to have everything I want.

As Christians, we know the Lord does not give or take away based on merit. If he did, we would have nothing because we could never earn anything from God.

I take such great comfort in knowing that God has my life planned on his timetable. God wants what is best for me, and if I will relax and simply trust in God, I will discover that his plan will be so much better than mine could ever be.

Dear Lord, please grant me patience as I watch your plans for my future unfold in your perfect timing. Amen.

DECEMBER 31

MATURING IN CHRIST—READ COLOSSIANS 1:28-29.

New Year's Eve typically is a time for us to gather with friends and family and welcome the new year. We make some kind of New Year's resolution for the coming year, stay up until midnight, and think of the year to come. My resolutions usually include dieting more, exercising more, and spending more time in prayer and Bible study. Does that sound familiar? I wonder why it is the same thing each year. Why does it take a lifetime to improve a few things in our life?

We expect our students to give us 100 percent effort in all their work. For some students, that is earning an A in every subject; but for others, it is earning a C in every subject or just making a good-faith effort.

We never reach perfection because we are human. Jesus was the only perfect person who ever has or ever will walk the earth. But, we are expected to strive for perfection. God doesn't want us to give up; God wants us to depend on his strength to help get us through difficult situations.

As you make your New Year's resolutions, understand that you may not reach 100 percent perfection. Just keep trying hard to do what is right, and God will be honored.

Dear Lord, thank you for your power working in us, helping us become perfect in your sight. Amen.

JANUARY
Learning from the Master Teacher

Amy Maze

JANUARY 1
FAVORITE TEACHERS—READ JOB 36:22.

DO YOU HAVE A FAVORITE TEACHER FROM YOUR YEARS IN SCHOOL? Do you remember little things that one of your teachers did or said? We all have a favorite or memorable teacher in our past. Many of us have become and will be in the future the "favorite" of some of our students.

I love to see my former teachers around town when I am not expecting to see them. So many of them had huge influences on my life and my career choice; it is like seeing long-lost relatives. Whenever I have seen them unexpectedly, they have always remembered my name. What a major accomplishment! Despite the fifteen to twenty years that have passed, they still remember my name.

Jesus, our ultimate Master Teacher, knows every one of us personally by name. He knows every detail of our lives and has a perfect plan for each of us. During the month of January, we will take a look at many of Jesus' teachings found in the Gospels. He was a fascinating teacher, and we have many things to learn from him.

Dear Lord, thank you for the great teacher we have in Jesus. Help us strive for excellence as we follow his example and teachings and live our lives for him. Amen.

JANUARY 2

PLANTING SEEDS—READ MATTHEW 13:3-9.

I discovered early in my career that I had to surrender the dream of "reaching every child." For years I battled with myself about what I could actually accomplish. I was my own worst enemy, staying at school until dark, rising early in the morning to get paperwork done, and working all weekend on my never-ending "to do" list.

The truth is, we cannot be consumed with our work. It's a difficult realization for us, because there is always something to do, and our instinct is to do whatever it takes for our students to succeed. After a few years, I reprioritized my career and expectations. I realized I wasn't enjoying my students because I was consumed with meeting goals and deadlines and increasing test scores. I also realized I am only one important piece in their individual educational experiences. They are not going to pass or fail solely because of me.

In Jesus' parable of the four soils, he tells how the farmer sowed many seeds, but only some of the seeds sprouted; and those that sprouted grew at different rates. We should not be discouraged if we do not see immediate results as we faithfully plan, prepare, and teach. Regardless of what we can see and measure, our job does make a difference if we choose to do it with the right attitude.

Dear Lord, help me keep my priorities in order with your will. Remind me that I cannot be effective when I am overworked and burned out. Amen.

JANUARY 3

"IT'S NOT FAIR!"—READ MATTHEW 20:1-16.

"It's not fair!" Do those words make the hairs on your neck stand up? Sometimes I get so tired of my students telling me what is fair and unfair. I try to manage my classroom in the fairest way possible. I never want to intentionally be unfair to any student. Yet it never fails; by the end of the week I have been accused of being unfair, either by a student or a parent. Sometimes I want to scream, "Do you think that I stayed up last night dreaming up a way to be unfair to you?"

In the course of events, things sometimes do turn out to be unfair. It is a difficult pill to swallow. I tell my students and their parents that it helps them build character.

In Jesus' parable, I imagine that the workers in the harvest field thought that life was unfair after their full day of labor. Jesus quickly reminded his listeners that the only way anyone is saved is through God's grace. Not one of us deserves to enter the kingdom of God, but it is through the mercy of God that we are allowed to enter.

Are you ever jealous of what God has given to another person? Focus on God's gracious benefits to you, and be thankful for what you have been given.

Dear Lord, help me remember the importance of fairness in all that I do each day. Amen.

JANUARY 4
"WELL DONE"—READ MATTHEW 25:21.

As Christians, we are commanded to use our time and talents to diligently serve God in whatever we do. As teachers, we are blessed to have a real harvest field. We have the power to influence children's lives in positive ways. You see, God has called us into this profession of education, and we have a ministry with our students each and every day. We can choose to accept that assignment or deny it; yet we must remember that whichever decision we make will be judged by God.

One of the greatest ways we can minister to our students is to lift them up by name in prayer. As we do this, we are also changing our attitude toward some of those students who are especially difficult to have patience with.

We also can minister to our students by using our time and talents to share Jesus' love in our classrooms. I hope that when I meet him face-to-face one day, I will hear these words from Matthew 25:21.

Dear Lord, may I faithfully serve you each day and be a reflection of you for my students. Amen.

JANUARY 5

"WHAT ABOUT ME?"—READ LUKE 17:7-10.

Do you ever accomplish everything you set out to do in the course of a school day? Do you feel you are constantly "catching up" from yesterday's leftover work? It never fails that the day you plan to get a lot accomplished in the classroom, you have a fire drill, an unexpected assembly, and five kids who are dismissed early. You are left with yet another "to do" list for the next day. It's easy to fall into the trap of self-pity, feeling that too much is being required of you.

The same thing can happen in our Christian walk. Sometimes it seems that we have many things to do and not enough time to do them in, and we begin to feel persecuted or unappreciated. We take our eyes off the goal and begin to feel self-centered. It's really easy to compare yourself with others and think that you are more deserving than someone else because you have been a faithful servant. I have fallen into the "What about me?" pity boat many times myself.

The reality is that God does not reward or punish us based on merit. None of us is worthy of God's miraculous gifts, and yet he freely gives them to us. We need to remember that we are simply doing our duty as Christians when we obey God's commands.

Dear Lord, thank you for your continual blessings that I am not worthy to receive. Forgive me when I am self-centered and act selfishly. Amen.

JANUARY 6

BLESSED ARE THE POOR IN SPIRIT—READ MATTHEW 5:3.

When I finally get my class on schedule and ready for the year, I begin to really look into the eyes of my students. It is such an amazing thing to have twenty-five vastly different human beings in my classroom. As I speak with their parents and other family members throughout the year, I can see deeper into their personalities, interests, and lives.

There is always at least one child who rips at my heart. Robin was that student for me several years ago. From the day she entered my room, I could see pain in her eyes. She had been through so much at only nine years of age. She had a horrible family life, suffered abuse, and had no desire to be carefree. She *couldn't* be carefree because her life didn't allow for such things. I wanted to take her home with me and adopt her as my own, but, of course, that could not really happen.

I only had Robin for a few months until she moved away, yet again. I truly believe that she was the epitome of "poor in spirit." I prayed for her for a long time, and I still do when I think of her. I pray that someone will intervene in her life and help her feel worthy.

Dear Lord, help me be extra kind to those students who are poor in spirit. Amen.

JANUARY 7

BLESSED ARE THOSE WHO MOURN—READ MATTHEW 5:4.

Experiencing the death of a loved one is a tragic experience for anyone. I was introduced to the process of mourning and grieving as a teenager when I lost my father, and then, a few years later, my grandfather. When my father died, I was overwhelmed by the support of friends and family members. I was a senior in high school at the time, and I had one teacher who actually cared enough to seek me out and talk with me about my feelings. She comforted me in a way nobody else did.

It is difficult to know what to say to those who have lost loved ones, but simply praying for them and lifting them up to Jesus' care provides comfort.

I have had several students who have lost a parent or sibling, and they continue to mourn the loss of those family members long after they are gone. As teachers, we help comfort those students through our concern and the promise of Jesus' words.

Dear Lord, thank you for being my comforter in times of mourning. Help me know how to comfort others also. Amen.

JANUARY 8

BLESSED ARE THE MEEK—READ MATTHEW 5:5.

Many teachers struggle with power and control because we are accustomed to being in charge of our classrooms. I struggle with this because sometimes I think I can still "be in charge" outside the classroom. Periodically, I give my opinion to someone who never asked it. When I see something done in a way I think it shouldn't be done, I get distressed. I can't seem to understand why everyone doesn't have the same thought processes, rationale, or organizational skills that I have! In addition to having control issues, I have a problem with change. I prefer to know what is going on and what will happen next.

God wants us to be meek, not powerful. I think *meek* means kind, patient, and willing to adapt to new situations. Meek people take life one day at a time and move to the rhythm that each day brings. They are not threatened by change but realize that change brings growth and new experiences. When I am around meek people, I feel calm and peaceful. In contrast, when I am around people who are on a power trip, I feel uneasy and unsure.

God's promise to the meek is that they will inherit the earth. Isn't that perfect? People who are truly meek would never desire such an incredible gift.

Dear Lord, help me be meek in a world that is chaotic and out of control. Amen.

JANUARY 9
BLESSED ARE THOSE WHO HUNGER AND THIRST FOR RIGHTEOUSNESS—READ MATTHEW 5:6.

Doing what is right—that philosophy has been lost today. Instead, we would rather say, "What will I get out of it?" or "What will it hurt if I do such and such?"

In schools all across America, we are teaching character education, morals, and values. I tell my students that doing what is right is not always popular and that what is popular is not always right.

We come across students each day who have not been taught right from wrong. Though it's true that good values should be taught in the home, we also can do our best to help instill good values in our students. For example, I stress to my students that they should choose to do what is right even when nobody is around. I hope I will always make that same choice when I am faced with the temptation to do or say something rude or dishonest.

Jesus Christ was the ultimate example of someone who hungered and thirsted for righteousness. I believe he grieves our mistakes and bad choices. He wants us to have the best for our lives. We must choose to be righteous each day, and righteousness can only come from Jesus. He promised our lives will be full if we do what is right.

Dear Lord, thank you for filling my life with joy and contentment when I try to live as you want me to. Thank you for being my righteousness and helping me do the right thing. Amen.

JANUARY 10
BLESSED ARE THE MERCIFUL—READ MATTHEW 5:7.

In previous years of teaching, I would have been considered strict, harsh, and uncaring. I thought that being strict was a strength, and, to some degree, it is. However, I took it to the wrong level. I didn't grant students second opportunities or chances. One strike and you are out! I soon discovered that parents are quick to judge when teachers are not merciful to their children, and that this is a normal reaction.

So, I began to study child development, and my thought process changed. I also thought back to my childhood and school experiences, including my school experiences as an adult; and I realized that I have been granted mercy many times! It's easy to get caught up in the expectations of our curriculum and our discipline and lose sight of the fact that we are dealing with children. Of course, you know what is age appropriate for your grade level; I certainly am not promoting complete "free will," which turns into chaos in the classroom. However, I am challenging you to give mercy to those students who deserve another chance.

When I became more merciful, my classroom atmosphere became more positive and uplifting—for students, parents, and myself. Starting today, let's work on being merciful to our students, parents, and administration.

Dear Lord, thank you for the unlimited amount of mercy you pour on me each day. May I, in turn, give mercy to my students when they need it. Amen.

JANUARY 11

BLESSED ARE THE PURE IN HEART—READ MATTHEW 5:8.

Do you know someone who is pure in heart—someone who always does good things for others and who sees the good in everyone? Such people are truly few and far between. Our human tendency is to pass judgment and be selfish with our time.

My grandmother is pure in heart. She is a feisty eighty-three-year-old woman who is constantly "doing" for others; baking cakes, breads, and entire meals for people out of the goodness of her heart. Instead of expecting anything in return from the people she helps, she simply wants to do good for them. Some people have described her as being their guardian angel because she obeyed a prompt from God to visit or call or make something for them. On many occasions, the persons she has helped have stated that they were in the midst of some traumatic experience or event, and her kindness comforted them in an extraordinary way.

Jesus' promise for the pure in heart is that they will see God. I wonder if that means that they will see God in this lifetime because they were able to see the best in people. I wonder how many times I have missed seeing God in a situation because I did not have a pure heart.

Dear Lord, help me see things purely and not rush to judgment. May I always be obedient to your voice. Amen.

JANUARY 12

BLESSED ARE THE PEACEMAKERS—READ MATTHEW 5:9.

As a child, I would have been considered a peacemaker. I was not a loud and boisterous child but, rather, quiet and obedient—at least most of the time. My brother and I spent a lot of time with our cousins, especially in the summertime. One of my cousins was very bossy, and she loved to give orders when we played together. Usually I would do what she said or let her be in charge because I was a peacemaker—and because I looked up to her. As adults, my cousin and I recall these memories and laugh.

As teachers, we see personalities manifest in our students. We usually can identify the peacemakers and the dominant personalities early in the school year.

As an adult, the peacemaker holds his or her tongue, doesn't engage in petty matters, isn't rude or selfish, and puts aside self for the betterment of others. I am finding that it is harder to be a peacemaker as I get older. Somehow I assume the privilege to speak my mind freely without regard for others. These kinds of actions, however, are hurtful to God.

I'm challenging myself to become more of a peacemaker in all that I do, especially as I relate with students, parents, coworkers, and administration.

Dear Lord, thank you for the ultimate example of a peace-maker you have given me through Jesus Christ. May I strive to be more peaceful each day. Amen.

JANUARY 13
BLESSED ARE THOSE WHO ARE PERSECUTED— READ MATTHEW 5:10.

I experienced a horrible parent conference many years ago. The child had been making poor grades all year, and despite my phone calls and attempts to meet with his parents to discuss the problems and possible solutions, they never expressed interest. Now, it was the end of the year, and the student had failed third grade. His parents were furious at the thought that I had failed their son.

The father stood before me and shook his large hand in my face as he told me that it was entirely my fault. *Sure,* I thought. *Blame it all on me!* At the end of the meeting, the mother said that her son had always been a "margarine" student. I think she meant marginal. My principal and I had to exercise restraint in our reaction to her word choice.

When they left the school, I was able to laugh a little, but I also felt terrible. I honestly had given my best efforts to my students, and to be accused otherwise devastated me. I felt mistreated and even persecuted.

Most of us have never been victims of religious persecution, and we are fortunate to live in this time and place. Jesus understands personally about persecution. He has promised the kingdom of God to all those who are persecuted for righteousness.

Dear Lord, give me the strength to withstand persecution in whatever form I experience it. Thank you for being persecuted to save each of us. Amen.

JANUARY 14
THE SECRETS OF THE HEART—READ PSALM 44:20-21.

Students love to be in charge, and they take that position seriously. If I say, "Emma, you are taking names while I step outside," she enthusiastically gets out paper and pencil to begin writing the names of unruly students. The students are much stricter than I am!

From time to time, the classroom monitor will select a door monitor, unbeknownst to me, and that person will stand by the door and keep watch for me down the hallway. This always makes me laugh because they think they are being so sneaky, unaware that Mrs. Smith across the hall will tell me everything they have been doing! As I approach the corner, I will hear some students scrambling for their seats and the unison harmony of twenty eight-year-olds saying, "Shh! The teacher is coming!" Thinking they have really got by with something sly, they all have large grins on their faces.

Have you ever tried to outsmart Jesus? Is there something you are embarrassed about and think he doesn't know? Are there times when you think he cannot see you? He is an omniscient God. He knows all, sees all, and hears all. Yet, he loves us beyond all we can even imagine. Do not be afraid to bring the secrets of your heart to him. He already knows and sees, and he loves you.

Dear Lord, thank you for always being there for me. Forgive me when I try to hide from you. Amen.

JANUARY 15
SUPPORTING YOUR PRINCIPAL—
READ COLOSSIANS 3:22-24.

Through the years I have worked under many different styles of leadership. Some school administrators manage as a business owner, some manage as a coach, and some manage as a tyrant. To be sure, there are strengths and weaknesses to be found in each of these leadership styles. Despite the differences in leadership styles, all school administrators have one thing in common: They have the hardest job in the school!

Everything lies on the principal's shoulders. He or she must build up the teachers regularly, discipline the students effectively, work with parents calmly, observe the janitors constantly, and keep up with the mounds of paperwork continually. It's a tremendous burden!

Though I have not always agreed with my administrators and even have succumbed to the temptation to make negative comments about them on occasion, I have come to believe that it is my rightful duty to offer my full, undivided support to my principal—regardless of my personal preferences. I must be an encourager and a peacemaker in the workplace. I must pray for my principal daily. I must regard all aspects of my career as an act of worship and service to God.

The next time you're tempted to complain about your school administrator, think about this: If we treated our job problems as the cost of discipleship, we would have no right to complain.

Dear Lord, thank you for hardworking administrators. Help me encourage and support my principal in all areas of his or her job. Amen.

JANUARY 16

REWARDS—READ MATTHEW 16:27.

I'm a strict disciplinarian in my classroom. We don't have time for students to misbehave and distract the entire class. Recently, however, I have begun to think about all the good students who have come through my classroom doors. Carly was always on task and never did anything unruly. Arden was a true joy each day. Brandon obeyed all the rules, and I could go on and on. How many times did I praise these students? How often did they hear their names called in class because they were on task?

I have chosen to revamp my discipline procedures to reflect a more positive plan. Instead of calling the names of students who are off task, I will call the names of students who are doing the right thing and give them an immediate reward. I wonder how the change will impact my classroom. I think the difference will be huge!

Though there are rewards on Earth for following Jesus, the best rewards of all will be given to us in heaven. Jesus will look at how we handled our gifts, talents, and opportunities in order to determine our heavenly rewards. In the meantime, we know that Jesus sees our every act of obedience and rewards us with "unseen" spiritual rewards. And who knows—maybe he is calling out our names in heaven!

Dear Lord, thank you for all the earthly rewards I do not even recognize. Open my eyes to see more opportunities to serve you. Amen.

January 17

God Supplies Our Strength—Read 2 Timothy 4:17a.

I love snow days! It is the best feeling in the world to wake up on winter mornings to the announcement that "schools are closed today because of snow." Yes, there is a God! I truly believe I get more excited than the students.

In the past several years, we have not experienced many cold winters where I live and, therefore, have not had many snow days. But, for some reason, the Lord was looking favorably on me one winter a couple of years ago. You see, I was in the middle of the worst year of my career. My students behaved terribly, and their parents were even worse. I was unmotivated, and I wanted the end of May to come more quickly than ever. We went back to school in January after our two weeks off for Christmas, and I think I cried all the way to school that morning. I'm telling you, I didn't want to be with those students all day, and they felt likewise, I'm sure.

Amazingly, over the next three months, we missed ten days of school because of snow! We did not go a full week of school until after spring break! What a miracle!

Dear Lord, thank you for the miracle of snow days and other unexpected blessings that help us through the tough times. Amen.

January 18

No Substitutes—Read Exodus 20:3.

Children are creatures of habit. They prefer routine, sameness, and order. They especially misbehave with substitute teachers. I feel for substitutes as I pass them in the building because I know the students are constantly challenging their authority. I think students behave differently with a substitute because they aren't confident in the sub's ability to control them, and they aren't sure if they can trust this individual.

How many times have you placed your trust in persons or things only to be disappointed? In my early days of teaching, I put my trust in my own strength and abilities. I would spend countless hours working in my classroom, which eventually led to burnout and the realization that I could no longer function in my own strength. Likewise, I have put my trust in others only to be equally disappointed.

God is the only one we can truly trust. We must prioritize our time and energy according to God's priority list found in Exodus 20. God expects to be the first on our list of priorities, for he created us to worship him and fellowship with him.

Dear Lord, help me not substitute other things in my life for you. May my choices always begin with putting you first. Amen.

January 19

Controlling Anger—Read Matthew 5:21-22 and 2 Corinthians 10:5.

Have you ever been proud of yourself for not physically harming someone during the course of a day? If I start the day out wrong, bad things follow throughout the day. Have you noticed that, too? Consider a day like this:

My alarm clock didn't go off, and I'm running late. I get behind a construction truck going ten miles per hour, and a rock flies from his truck and strikes my windshield, cracking it. At school, I realize I have left my classroom keys at home; the janitor takes twenty minutes to get to my room to open it. My morning work isn't prepared for the day, and all the copy machines are broken. Joey's angry mom is waiting for me at the door, my students are out of control in the hallway, and the principal decides to do the morning announcements from my room! All of this happens before 8:00 A.M., and so it continues throughout the day.

On days like that, anger, rage, and fury can build up inside; and we can take it out on our students, families, or other innocent people. Expressing our anger violates God's command to love. It hinders us from developing a spirit that is pleasing to God. We must learn to practice not only self-control but also thought control, refocusing our negative thoughts by taking every thought captive to Christ.

Dear Lord, help me take every thought captive to you so that I do not unleash my anger on others. Amen.

JANUARY 20
CLEAR INSTRUCTIONS—READ MATTHEW 5:33-37.

My mother always amazed me when I was a child by consistently knowing when I was lying to her. She could read my face like a book. I thought she was some kind of prophet or something, and I learned that I could not get away with lying to her or keeping something from her. Even today she can look at my face and know what is happening in my life.

I now amaze my students each year as I, too, have discovered the gift of reading children's faces. In an instant I can decide whether they are telling the truth or a lie. Oftentimes, the younger the child, the more dramatic the lie seems to be.

As adults, we tend to see issues that are black and white as if they were gray. God has given us very specific instructions in the Word on how to live our lives. There are no gray areas. But, somehow, with age and experience, we think the "little white lies," the broken promise, or the occasional curse word is acceptable. Jesus says let your yes be yes and your no be no. Wouldn't life be so much simpler if we abided by his instructions!

Dear Lord, thank you for giving me clear instructions for living. Forgive me when I do not apply them to my life. May I be an honest and forthright person, faithfully serving you. Amen.

JANUARY 21

WHEN WE ARE WRONGED—READ MATTHEW 5:38-42.

"But, Ms. Maze . . . he did it to me first!" This is a common problem I deal with on a daily basis. "I pushed him because he pushed me first." "I stole from her because she stole from me first." Similarly, when I try to get the children to pick up trash from the classroom floor, they say, "But I didn't do it" or "It's not mine." I usually say, "It's not mine, and it's not the janitor's either, but we are usually the ones cleaning up your messes!"

Of course, adults are the same way. We are tempted to be rude when someone is rude to us, to take part in road rage when someone cuts us off on the road, to take the law into our own hands when we are victims of a crime, and so forth. Our human response is to get even when something happens to us that we consider wrong or unfair.

Jesus said we should do good to those who wrong us. Wow, that is really difficult to understand. Our desire should be to constantly love and forgive others, regardless of what they have done to us. This can only happen through the supernatural love we receive from God.

Dear Lord, thank you for not getting even with me each time I wrong you. Please give me the power to forgive others as you have forgiven me and to do good even to my "enemies." Amen.

JANUARY 22
PRAYING FOR DIFFICULT STUDENTS—
READ MATTHEW 5:43-48.

I don't think I have many enemies. I honestly cannot think of anyone that I would consider my enemy; it's a really strong word. However, I do have certain people that I really dislike. And, for that matter, I usually have a particular student or parent each year that I don't especially like. I think Jesus intended these verses to include even those students and parents. We should pray specifically for them.

Sometimes the hardest thing to do for people we dislike is to pray for them. I think it's because we know God will change our heart toward them. It is easier to dislike someone than to make things right. I especially love Matthew 5:46 because it reminds me that it is an easy job to teach the "good" students. Anybody can do that. However, it is a much greater responsibility to work with the discipline problems, lower-performing students, or disgruntled parents. These tasks require planning, patience, foresight, and self-control, all of which come only through prayer. It is in managing these situations that we have the opportunity to be Christlike, rather than like everyone else. I hope I choose to be Christlike so my parents, students, and coworkers see something different in me.

Dear Lord, be with the troubled student, the angry parent, and the off-task class. May I show them the love and grace you have shown me. Amen.

JANUARY 23
WHEN YOU PRAY—READ MATTHEW 6:5-8.

Jesus frequently taught about prayer, stressing its vital importance to our lives. He wants the best for us, and one of the best ways we can know his will is through prayer.

In these particular verses, Jesus asks us to determine our motive for praying. The Pharisees only wanted to be seen as holy. Jesus considered it abomination to do something in God's name for personal glory. He wants us to be honest with him. He already knows the desires of our hearts and the burdens we carry, but he is anxiously waiting for us to bring those desires and burdens to him through prayer.

When I try to have quiet time at home, something or someone usually interferes. There are two times when I am in complete solitude: in my car and during my daily walk. I usually listen to music during these times and pretend I'm a great singer—but that's beside the point! What I have discovered is that God wants me to give up some of that personal time to talk with him.

At first I thought *What? Walk with no music? Drive with no music?* However, it has been very fulfilling. As I walk, I share all of my confessions, burdens, and desires with God. It is as if he is walking right beside me. Actually, I think he is!

Dear Lord, show me the time in my day that you want me to set aside for you, and help me protect that time. Amen.

JANUARY 24
DO NOT WORRY—READ MATTHEW 6:25-34.

I once taught a mildly autistic girl who constantly worried about everything that happened throughout the day. She was smart and sweet, but she was consumed by fear. I really tried hard to earn her trust so that she would feel safe with me and understand that I had everything under control. I would let her know what was going on and warn her of any alterations to our daily schedule. She worked hard to improve that year, and I was so glad to have had the experience of knowing her and teaching her to relax and trust the people in charge.

I know of people who worry about every little detail of life. Some worry about the weather, money, health, the future, or the state of the world in general. What good does it do to worry about such things—about *anything?*

There is a difference between worry and planning. Planning for the future is something God expects us to do.

Careful planning is thinking ahead about goals and steps, and then trusting in God's guidance. Worry stems from fear. Do not be afraid to trust in God. He takes care of the entire universe, and he will take care of us, too. He has promised us so!

Dear Lord, thank you for your promise to care for me in every way. May your word be sufficient for me to trust you fully. Amen.

JANUARY 25

THE NARROW GATE—READ MATTHEW 7:13-14.

As a single Christian woman, I struggle with finding an honest Christian man to date and, perhaps, marry. It is very discouraging at times. I have met many men and have dated many throughout the years; some of them have been really good people, but they have not been strong in their faith.

I joined an online dating service one summer in hope of finding the perfect man, and I was shocked by the results. After I tirelessly completed the personality profile and chose all of my criteria for a man, the results said, "There are no matches for your criteria." I said, "You're telling me!" So I went back online and changed my distance preference from living within a twenty-five-mile radius of my city to a fifty-mile radius, and still no matches. I had to keep stretching my search until the limit was a five-hundred-mile radius of my home! Then there were a few people, but how would we ever get together?

Feeling completely defeated, I canceled my subscription and moved on. I told my mother about it, saying, "Can you believe that there is nobody on this particular service who meets those standards?" She quickly recited today's scripture verses and reminded me that those who really desire to follow Christ are few in number.

Dear Lord, thank you for showing me the way to the narrow gate that leads to life. Help me be willing to share this path with those I encounter each day. Amen.

JANUARY 26

SHOW AND TELL—READ PSALM 25:4-5.

My students have always loved show and tell. They love to bring something from home and share it with their classmates and teacher. This is one of those things that I do that will not raise my test scores, but it raises the confidence of the students and makes the entire class feel closer. They can relate to one another and discover that they share a common interest, sport, or pet. They really get excited when I bring in something from my house to share with them.

God wants to have "show and tell" with us, too! He desires to show us the direction for our lives if we will only come to him and ask for guidance. To receive God's guidance, first we must *want* to be guided by God. It is not our place to tell God what to do in our lives. Next, we must realize that all guidance is found through prayer and reading God's Word. God's answers can always be found in the Word. The Bible is an overflowing fountain of knowledge. By studying it, we glean God's direction for our lives, regardless of what we are going through.

Think of the many things God wants to show us if we will only ask!

Dear Lord, thank you for the wisdom I can find in your Word. Make my Bible study time and prayer time pleasing to you so that you can show me many things. Amen.

JANUARY 27

OUR HELPER—READ PSALM 124.

What ruins your day? What robs your joy as a teacher? What makes you cringe just thinking about it? I'll bet that I can list some annoyances that all teachers have in common: missing recess, losing your planning period, assemblies, lining up, bathroom breaks, new computer programs, table manners, pencil sharpeners, report cards, field trips, and unexpected parent conferences. There are a million things that interfere with our scheduled days. These events make us feel interrupted, ignored, and unappreciated much of the time. What gets you through the day? Where do you receive help, peace, hope, and comfort to start a new day?

God is our helper. He is always on our side. He is the Creator of the universe, and he certainly knows our frustrations. There is no problem, interruption, crisis, or circumstance that is too difficult for God to solve. Nothing is too great for him to guide us through. We can always turn to our Creator, Teacher, and Counselor in our times of need. We only need to trust him with our burdens and ask him to help us get through each day. Do you trust him?

Dear Lord, when I am overwhelmed by the daily trials of my job, give me the strength I need. Amen.

January 28

The Ultimate Authority—Read Matthew 7:28-29.

My dad was the final authority, the "buck stops here" guy, the "king" of our family. I never wanted to go against what he expected of me. I wasn't afraid of him; I just always wanted to please him. He was a wonderful husband and father who taught us to respect our parents and other authority figures. In return, we saw him respect my mother and ourselves. This mutual respect that I learned from my father helped me understand the authority Jesus has in my life.

Jesus was an amazing teacher, capturing the attention of great crowds of people. He did not have to quote other authorities of the day because he was the only true authority. Those who heard him noticed something different about his message. He explained exactly what the Scriptures said and meant like no other person had ever done before.

Jesus was and is the ultimate authority in our lives. As we go about the business of daily life, we should bring every decision before Jesus, just as we asked our parents for permission as children. He will never fail us.

Dear Lord, help me understand that you want to help me make the right choices. Thank you for having authority over me. Amen.

JANUARY 29

WHEN STORMS COME—READ MATTHEW 8:23-27.

I love to be in the water during the summertime. It can be the lake, the ocean, or the pool; as long as it cools me off, I'm happy.

My family had a small houseboat on a local lake when I was growing up, and we spent many Saturdays in the warm sun, enjoying the lake. During one afternoon, the sun faded and dark clouds encircled the lake. We knew what was coming: a summer storm. So we quickly began packing everything up, bringing in the floats, skis, and beach balls; but the storm was moving so quickly that we were caught in the middle of the lake, waiting it out. Storms are never fun, but they bring about a totally different level of fear when you are on the water! Lightning and thunder were all around, and rain was pounding our boat.

This experience gave me a whole new understanding of the disciples' fear when they were on the boat with Jesus. Just as Jesus calmly stopped that storm with his power, he can control the storms in our lives. He wants us to bring our fears to him so that he can show us his power over all our lives. We shouldn't want to hide anything from him.

May we always have faith that Jesus will intervene on our behalf when storms come.

Dear Lord, thank you for being the master of the sea and the master in my life. Help me turn to you with my problems. Amen.

JANUARY 30

READY AND WILLING—READ MATTHEW 9:35-38.

Do you know people who are really hard workers—people who don't stop until the job is finished? My grandparents are like that. They taught me how important it is to work hard and have a strong work ethic. They would go to work during the day and then come home and work for hours in their yard or around the house until everything was done. They did not wait for someone else to come and do it; they did what needed to be done, and now they are reaping the rewards.

Jesus needs hard workers for the harvest. Look around at your school staff. Do you see people who are waiting for you to tell them about Christ? Look in your community. Are there people living within walking distance of your house who need to hear from you? There is so much still to do that we cannot put it off on others. We must be ready and willing to be used by God.

Start preparing now by thinking about your personal testimony. What has God done for you this week or even today that you could share with someone? Confess any sins that may be holding you back from sharing with other people. Ask God to give you courage to be bold, and ask him to show you specific people you can witness to.

Dear Lord, I ask for boldness to share your love with those around me. Amen.

JANUARY 31

LISTENING FOR DIRECTION—READ PROVERBS 3:5-6.

Each year several teacher friends and I go to an amusement park before school starts. We love riding the tumultuous path of a roller coaster. When we began this yearly event, I hadn't been to an amusement park since I was a teenager. I had forgotten how thrilling each ride is and how anticipation builds as the roller coaster starts up the steep incline to dive into the curvy path ahead. As a teenager, I didn't experience any apprehension as the young employees strapped me in. However, as an adult, I suddenly became very uneasy about putting my safety in the hands of a teenager! I would check and recheck my safety belt and safety bar to make sure everything was working properly. Yet with each ride, I became less cautious about the safety and more eager to start the next ride.

Sometimes our lives resemble a roller coaster, though we would prefer them to look like a merry-go-round. Instead of the sudden and unexpected twists and turns, we tend to prefer the slower, calmer, more predictable life experiences. But Jesus promises that he is with us through everything. Sometimes he wants us to get off of the roller coaster and listen to his still, small voice giving us hope and encouragement for the ride ahead.

Dear Lord, thank you for the excitement that life with you brings. Help me stop and listen to your direction for my life in the midst of turmoil. Amen.

FEBRUARY
Students in Our Own Classrooms

Kellen Beck Mills

FEBRUARY 1
THE MASTER TEACHER OF MY CLASSROOM—
READ JOHN 8:12 AND MATTHEW 5:16.

I TEACH MIDDLE SCHOOL ART. AS A GIRL, I WANTED TO BE AN ARTIST or a child psychologist. So in college I took courses in psychology and then switched my major to fine art. I planned to get my master's in art therapy.

Instead, I got married and slowly traded my dreams of a career that would enable me to use my God-given abilities for a succession of stopgap jobs that would help pay the bills. Through the years, ongoing financial, health, personal, and marital problems took their toll. Not long after deciding to finally pursue my deep sense of calling to teach, my marriage ended. My heart broke open so wide that, in the chasm, I had to search for God.

I realized I had been relying on myself all those years. When I finally cried out to God, I was amazed to discover God's mercy. I began to study Scripture and to learn from my own life experiences. My greatest difficulties and my darling sons became my best "lessons." Then, one day, I read that I not only had God's permission to love and serve him with all my heart, but that Jesus said I *must* do so (Matthew 22:37).

Today I am an artist *and* a "child psychologist" of sorts as a teacher, and I'm at my best when I remember that I am a student of the Master Teacher of my classroom—Jesus. This month we will explore what it means to be students in our own classrooms.

Dear Jesus, thank you for being my Light so that I may be a light in my classroom as I help my students know your love. Amen.

FEBRUARY 2
COURAGE TO BEGIN—READ GENESIS 1:1-2, 4.

Our constitutional separation of church and state reminds us that we must not cause a child to feel that his or her faith tradition is "wrong" or "alien." Jesus included everyone, yet he never refrained from telling the truth. It can be a challenge to fulfill our legal duties and tell the truth, too. Many of us are afraid to ever mention God in our classrooms, and many of us find ways around the problem.

One day I was teaching my students about the process of drawing (contrast, using the whole space of the picture plane, and overcoming fears of beginning). I said, "First, you have a white sheet of paper, and you have to make a dark mark. If any of you are familiar with the Bible, in the very first chapter the ancient Hebrew poets told of God creating the heavens and the earth. According to the story, the first thing God did was separate the light from the darkness." Then I smiled and joked, "If that way to begin is good enough for God, it is good enough for you!" We all laughed, and I said a silent prayer of thanks to God for giving me a bridge.

If we look for bridges to values and meaning for our students within the subjects we teach, God will help us find them.

Dear Lord, thank you for all the faith connections you give us in the classroom and for the courage to begin. Amen.

FEBRUARY 3
GRACE'S LESSON—READ MATTHEW 6:8.

In my first job, I taught art at an "academically successful" school. When budget cuts came, my next job was at what everyone called "the F school." I looked forward to this challenge with hope and idealism. The reality became so much harder than I imagined.

That was where I met Grace, a very bright girl in one of my most behaviorally difficult classes. Daily she watched me tussle with the manifestations of poverty in my students' lives, which I lacked the skills to manage. I was determined that I was "gonna teach these kids," and I was failing miserably. Something in me had to change.

One day, as I was struggling to get my point across, I saw Grace sitting among the "detractors," smiling. I thought, *Boy, this must be amusing for her.* Then she interrupted and said, "Ms. Mills, you really got a lot of class!"

"What?" I asked. She repeated herself.

At first, I actually thought she was making fun of me. But I quickly discovered that she meant it. I was dumbfounded over such an unexpected gift of kindness. I was speechless. And, for the first time, so were the kids. Because of Grace's lesson to me, the tide began to turn right then.

It is important for us to remember the basic goodness in children.

Thank you, Father, for knowing what I need before I ask. Thank you for the wisdom of children and their gifts of generosity. Amen.

FEBRUARY 4
LOVE FIRST OF ALL—READ 1 CORINTHIANS 13:1-3.

When I began teaching, I was certain that I had some knowledge and skills that were of value to share, and that I had some life experiences I might be able to use in some way.

I hoped to teach high school or elementary school, but I definitely did not want to teach middle school—not the ones "in the middle," with their hormone changes, boundary testing, and mood swings. No, I did not feel like a very strong authoritarian, so I hoped to leave that job for someone else.

Of course, I have done nothing *but* teach middle school. God has a great sense of humor.

In middle school, I met myself. When I was young, it was where I took a wrong turn for a few years. Then, when I began teaching at-risk kids in middle school, I remembered *myself*. It was uncomfortable. But I discovered, or rediscovered, that the most important things I have to give my students are love and compassion—along with a good helping of fair guidelines and boundaries. When they really know I care about them, I have their ears. Then they will do what I say, in that order. Love, first of all, is what children are seeking from us.

Lord, please create in me a loving heart and the wisdom of discernment so that I may carry out your purposes. Amen.

FEBRUARY 5

THE WEALTHY POOR—READ MATTHEW 5:3.

We know the light by the dark; it forms the three-dimensionality of our experiences. In art, a composition must make use of both dark and light values to give a sense of depth. Similarly, God allows us to experience deep yearnings in our lives so that we may learn to depend on him.

Love conquers fear. It is more courageous to hope than to forecast doom. It takes more courage to notice what we did well than to shame ourselves or others for how we or they fell short. Noticing our successes, we have the courage to face our errors. Even the most seemingly stubborn child is just basically afraid of failure.

After each art project, my students must fill out a self-evaluation form, a chance for easy points. Among other questions, the most important ones they must answer are these: What did you do well? What would you change if you did this again? Their answers cannot be "everything" or "nothing";

they must be specific. In doing this, I hope they will gain the ability to see their strengths and to love themselves anyway, in spite of what they might perceive as their weaknesses.

It is important to learn to embrace the valleys in our lives as opportunities. When we are poor in spirit, we have the chance to grow wealthy in faith.

Dear Lord, thank you for loving us even when we don't love ourselves. Help us see the light so we can see the "whole picture." Amen.

FEBRUARY 6
THE REBELLION OF YOUTH—READ PSALM 25:7.

To begin teaching as part of a team of teachers of "gifted children" was a great blessing. I had a lot of support from my colleagues and, to meet certification requirements, I had to take three hundred hours of training in gifted education. I learned that gifted children have special needs, are not all the same, and do not necessarily feel successful just because they have the label of "gifted" and a special program. Many of them are rebellious, testy, and above all, questioning. I found that the more I allowed them to be themselves, while also "sticking to my guns," the more we were able to accomplish together.

I also began to truly believe that *all* children are gifted.

Each student we have is a gift to us from God. Some are God's gift to us because they are so "easy"; others because they are so "difficult." I was both when I was growing up, and so Jesus uses that to help me embrace both kinds of children as a teacher.

God forgave the sins of my youth and my own rebellious ways, but according to his love, he also helped me remember them. God helped me use the lessons of my own deep questioning, and my errors, to see myself in some of my kids who embark on that same road of rebellion.

Thank you, Lord, for my life lessons and memories, and for guiding me to use my experiences to understand others. Amen.

FEBRUARY 7
WALK A MILE IN MY SHOES, PART 1—
READ MATTHEW 5:41-42.

Dylan was surly with his peers and teachers. He was very intelligent but not doing well academically. He drew all the time in his classes, so it was suggested he enroll in art class. His parents had divorced recently, and his mother was very worried about him. His favorite—and only—subject to draw was demons.

He was testy and resistant to the assignments. It was obvious he had drawing skills, but he seemed to enjoy knowing that his drawings were disturbing. He was under the care of a psychologist. I decided not to make an issue of his pictures, but said one day, "If you want to really be a good artist, you will have to learn to draw more than just demons." It was an appeal to his pride, but it was a doorway.

He began to do the assignments. At home he continued his "demon" pictures. One day he showed me a detailed charcoal drawing of a screaming ugly face. I told him it was a very skillful picture and encouraged him to keep drawing with charcoal. The next picture he showed me was a landscape with a covered bridge. He began to open up and become a very cooperative student.

By year's end, Dylan and his mom felt he had discovered some direction. Jesus had walked the extra mile with us.

Dear Lord Jesus, thank you for all the times you help me hear a child's scream for help. Thank you for giving me your guidance to lend them, and the courage to not turn away. Amen.

FEBRUARY 8
WALK A MILE IN MY SHOES, PART 2—
READ PSALM 143:10.

Dylan's mom gave me a plaque that quoted Ralph Waldo Emerson: ". . . to know even one life has breathed easier because you have lived. This is to have succeeded."

The following two years were difficult ones. As I moved to a more challenging teaching situation, and toward acceptance that my marriage had failed, I struggled with depression and fear. Many days it took a lot of prayer to just get out of bed and start my day. I needed to read those words of affirmation often.

Dylan remained in my heart, and I often wondered about him. In the summer my divorce became final; I sought support at a few meetings for families of alcoholics in addition to my regular church activities. One day, there he was. Dylan was seeking help for his problems with alcohol, and we talked. He had grown heavier and did not look good, but we talked about his talents and his determination to not ruin his life. Seeing him again was a blessing for me. This tenth-grade boy was now courageously facing his "demons," and *he* became an example to *me* that day. If he could do it, so could I.

We cannot see where the roads we walk are leading, but we can have faith that the Lord will lead us to level ground.

Dear Lord, thank you that when I follow your will, the goodness of your Spirit leads me through rocky territory to level ground. Amen.

FEBRUARY 9
WALK A MILE IN MY SHOES, PART 3—
READ PSALM 51:10.

At my present school, I have the opportunity to teach kids of very diverse backgrounds and skill levels. My oldest son's desire to go there influenced my decision to apply there, and the job opened up just as I needed one again.

It also happens to be *the very same school where I took my wrong turn so many years ago.* It was where I decided it was "safer" to be street tough than a "goody-goody smart girl," and where I began to choose to fail. Now it is a place where God helps me to remember my own errors every day with precision, to integrate teaching with my life experiences, and to be present for my own sons through their middle school years.

At church one Sunday, the musician sang, "Before you abuse, criticize, and accuse, walk a mile in my shoes" (John Fogerty). After services, a very handsome, strong-looking young man came up to me and said, "Do you know who I am?" It took a few moments of looking into his eyes before I recognized Dylan. Now he teaches martial arts to kids at risk. He said he does not remember much from before he got sober; he just remembers that I was his art teacher.

As we follow in Jesus' footsteps, God renews our spirits.

Each day, dear Lord, create in me a clean heart, and renew my spirit as I continue to learn to follow you. Amen.

FEBRUARY 10

DIVERSITY AND UNITY—READ ISAIAH 65:25.

In 1969, the NAACP sued our local school board because the two African American schools in our community were profoundly underfunded. In response, the high school and the junior high school in the African American neighborhood were closed, and their children were bused all over the county. To use the two empty school buildings, all seventh-graders in the county were bused in to occupy them. This decision fanned the fires of anger instead of healing the wounds.

I was one of the seventh-graders who found myself far from home that year. My family valued equality, but I was too young to understand why I was the object of hatred by strangers. That was the year that acting tough began to look safer to me than succeeding in school.

A lot of time has passed. Now I teach at the school where I, and others, became victims of the inability of our leaders to act with justice and wisdom. After all these years, we are still one of the most racially segregated counties in the United States.

The stubbornness of humankind amazes me, but the faithfulness of God amazes me more. Every day I see examples of both, but there is an inherent wisdom and goodness in children that seeks resolution; and God always wins.

However long it takes, God always wins.

Dear Lord, thank you for weaving our adversity into the cloth of your will. Sharpen our vision so we may act within your purpose. Amen.

FEBRUARY 11

ADVERSITY AND GOD'S PRAYER SHAWL—READ MICAH 6:8.

I am so grateful that God uses adversity to make us look to him for direction. I am so grateful that Jesus shows us his boundless mercy and righteousness so that we have his example to follow. And I am so grateful for all the times God forgives us for our errors. We are all learners in the classroom of life, and when we see this clearly, we can look upon adversity as opportunity to follow Jesus and know we are not alone, or unique.

Yet each of us *is* unique. Our lives are all threads in God's prayer shawl, and the ways he weaves us together in the glorious fabric of his creation is truly wondrous and amazing.

Over the years, when I encounter a difficult situation in my classroom, I have learned to ask sooner and sooner for God to help me understand what the lesson is. I am still a very stubborn person, but when I remember God is a supremely loving teacher, I learn my lessons more easily and problems resolve, or else I understand that with some students, I am not the person empowered with a solution.

Remembering that I am not the only thread in God's prayer shawl helps me release feelings of failure. Students, parents, colleagues, and administrators—we are all in this together.

Dear Lord, thank you for empowering me with prayer to help me learn to act justly and mercifully. May I walk humbly, asking you what the lesson is when I encounter problems. Amen.

FEBRUARY 12

THIS IS THE LORD'S DAY—READ PSALM 118:24.

In the summer of intense changes and disarray in my life, I was invited to be a guest artist at a middle-school arts camp. I had never spoken to a group of kids before.

That day I had just enough time to gather slides of my art-work, along with pieces of my theme in the form of some poetry and loose ideas, and arrive at the school after only four hours of sleep! Knowing how important pop music is to kids, I chose a song to play during the slide show of my collages.

I hoped to show them creativity bridges between poetry, song lyrics, collage, and the origins of improvisation from Africa. The song I chose was "Standing in a Broken Phone Booth with Money in My Hand." I didn't know how I would tie all these loose ends together until I wrapped up my intro-duction, turned off the lights, and pressed the play button.

"The title means you might have the money, but the line of communication is broken. So you have to make this song."

Communication became my theme, and I realized God had made that day my debut as a teacher. Taking just "a bunch of stuff," he blessed me with perfect rhythm and timing. The whole day was a huge success, and I knew whose day it really was.

Thank you, Lord, for the days when your glorious improvi-sation shines through. Help me remember to rejoice in each day you give me. Amen.

FEBRUARY 13

SING A NEW SONG TO THE LORD—READ PSALM 33:1-3.

Kids love music. My generation also was shaped in large part by the music we heard, and many songs I listened to in my youth had spiritual messages in spite of secular origins.

John and Charles Wesley, founders of the Methodist Church, understood that "music of the day" spoke to the con-gregation when they used popular pub tunes for hymns. Today we sing these traditional songs, unaware of their pop origins from a different era. Just as Jesus joined in the expe-rience of the common folk of his time, the tunes of many Methodist hymns were appropriated from tunes familiar to the hearts of the common folk of the 1700s.

I incorporate music into my lessons often. If I play the Beatles, many caucasian kids know them; with Stevie

Wonder, my African American students perk up with recognition. There are many popular songs that have good "values messages."

Some of the music of today is singing "a new song to the Lord." The Lord speaks to us everywhere we listen. If we take the time to hear today's messages, we have another bridge for communication with our students.

Dear Lord, help me hear you in the voices of our times so I may build bridges for my students to experience the wonder of you—and understand the source. Amen.

FEBRUARY 14

LOGAN'S VALENTINE—READ 1 CORINTHIANS 13:13.

Logan was new to our school in his eighth-grade year. He was African American, but born in Germany. Even in a school as diverse as ours, Logan did not fit into any category.

One big division at our school is between the "rappers" and the "rockers." It is acceptable to be a "white rapper," but the tendency doesn't flow as readily in the other direction. Logan was a "black rocker."

He defied stereotypes. His peers did not know what box to fit him in, and they made him the brunt of their misunderstandings. Bigotry is ugly, but once in a while we meet kids who plow through the minefield of it with courage and wisdom beyond the capacity of many adults. The truth of inclusion of all within the love of God intersects in such children. We became close allies. Later that year, the rappers and the rockers came to an understanding in my class, and wonderful things happened; Logan's presence was a catalyst. Now he has gone on to high school, but he still calls me and always says, "I love ya" before hanging up.

Faith in who we are and the hope that this will carry us is great, but the greatest of all is the love that includes everyone.

Dear Lord, help me see my students for who they really are—beyond stereotypes. Amen.

FEBRUARY 15

THE RAPPERS VERSUS THE ROCKERS—READ ISAIAH 64:8.

Fridays are radio days for my classes who conduct themselves smoothly during the week.

I might not enjoy what I hear, nor do I enjoy the conflicts that emerge over musical tastes; and I immediately suspend "messages" I deem inappropriate. But the opportunity for lessons in accepting others' differences is worth meeting the fray, and the Lord shows up in the most unanticipated places sometimes.

The rappers and the rockers are the most sharply drawn line. Logan, who took to wearing earplugs during rap time, became the epicenter; but Aryanna and Shatoria faced off, and, in their dialogue over differences, came to an agreement as to fair amounts of time and which music to play when. Two girls, equally stubborn and entrenched in the outward appearances of the groups they thought they represented, managed to negotiate an agreement regarding a passion they both felt. One photo I have from that year shows the two of them: arms around each other, looking different as night and day in every way, and wearing smiles that shouted the value of the mutual acceptance they now possessed.

The sovereign Lord is the Potter, and we are all clay in his loving hands. When we seek to allow the Lord's solutions to resolve conflicts between our students, he creates outcomes beyond the ones we might create alone.

Thank you, O God, for shaping my life. Please help me allow you to mold my work with your hands. Amen.

FEBRUARY 16

ALVIN'S SKIN—READ PSALM 108:1-5.

Alvin shared a table with Melvira, whose outspokenness often got her into trouble at school. While painting their self-portraits, the issue of skin tone arose.

We were listening to an African musician, a recording of praises to God in Senegalese. Alvin expressed interest in the music, so I showed him the CD cover. Melvira saw the picture of the artist and reacted with some very unkind and loud words about how dark he was. There sat Alvin, his ebony skin inescapably covering the outside of his personage. Both had learned a certain pride in their ethnic background but still were captives to the myth of "lighter is better." Neither had heard this type of music before, and its sublime lyricism spoke in spite of its foreign tongue.

Alvin's eyes remained glued to the CD liner notes about Africa and the poetry by the artist. This opened up a fruitful discussion among the three of us about cultural perceptions and attitudes regarding skin tone. It also helped the kids with paint decisions. I made a tape of the music and gave it to Alvin. When the kids got their school photos, Alvin gave me one of his to keep.

We can make a difference in how our students perceive themselves. God is God of all nations and peoples, and beauty is a heavenly perspective.

Dear Lord, thank you for the unifying harmonies of your great love. Help me share the essence of this joy with my students. Amen.

FEBRUARY 17

BEAUTIFUL PEOPLE—READ GENESIS 1:27.

Scripture tells us that God created humankind in his own image. Being one who has dealt in images and metaphors as a teacher and an artist, I have pondered these words. *Image* is the root word of *imagination*. Some think of imagination as being "unreal," but imagination gives birth to the real. Einstein said, "Imagination is more important than knowledge." Imagination is one of our most uniquely human characteristics.

One lesson I always teach is how to draw an ideal human face. We go through proportions together step by step, and the kids finish the faces with details about themselves. One semester, we joined this lesson to the multicultural day being sponsored by the Spanish department. I used Melanie Safka's song "Beautiful People" to introduce the idea of cross-cultural unity. One boy who was a big talker kept interrupting, and I jokingly threatened to put tape over his mouth. Tape in hand, I spontaneously wrote "Beautiful People" on it and stuck it on his forehead. This led to a mass cooperative effort between us; and by the time class ended, everyone left wearing a "Beautiful People" sticker on their forehead or shirt. The momentum continued throughout the lesson.

Imagination is more spiritual than physical. God created us to feel connected in this way and to see his beauty within us all.

Dear Lord, help me see beyond the apparent real to the true real of your glory and splendor. May I imagine, and believe, how much you love me. Amen.

February 18
The Narrow Gate—Read Matthew 5:36-37.

Between willful passion and self-righteousness lies the narrow gate of simple "yes" and "no." When I don't choose the narrow gate, I always have a bigger mess to clean up.

One day a student played a deviously mean trick on me. I called her father and explained the situation. She was made to behave more respectfully, but it was apparent that this was superficial. Finally, I realized that I had lost my focus on the simple "yes" and "no" of the issue, and my personal anger had caused me to lose sight of her best interests—and mine. What she had done was not just wrong because it was hurtful to me, but such behavior would be hurtful to her in the long run. As the adult, it was my duty to guide us both away from further negativity.

We don't initiate these rebellious acts toward us as authority figures, but they are part of the job; and once they occur, what we say or do is part of the interaction. As I began to follow God's guidance in this, I was able to regain my objectivity. With anger out of the mix, and Jesus' guidance of a simple "yes" and "no" for our relationship, we parted in peace at year's end.

Awareness of the narrow gate of the higher good is essential to teaching.

Thank you, Lord, for being present for me when I turn to you for direction. Help me understand what you would have me do. Amen.

FEBRUARY 19
RULES, GUIDELINES, AND GRACE—
READ ROMANS 3:23-24.

Paul says we are justified freely by God's grace. The grace of God sets us free to behave justly.

On a computer, one can set the page for "justification" of the words on left, right, or both sides. Justification on both sides interests me as a metaphor for God's grace, justifying our alignment toward his purposes. Balanced in the middle, centering our thoughts toward God, we are free to act and speak more justly.

Students often question the need for rules: Why walk in a straight line? Why not speak any time one feels like it? Why do we have to learn about composition and color relationships?

One day I wrote on a piece of paper: *The purpose of rules is NOT "to have rules." The purpose of rules is to have guidelines so that we may have freedom.* I used the message as a hall pass. Elisa had really questioned my disciplined approach to art in her seventh-grade year, but as an eighth-grader she had become an exemplary student. One day, she returned with the hall pass and said: "Wow, this is really cool."

Rules are never the point; they only point in the right direction. Knowing this, we can free our students and ourselves from the sort of judgment and self-justification that prevent us from having permission to be learners.

Dear Lord, thank you for your precepts and guidelines for application to my life. Help me communicate the value of these to my students. Amen.

FEBRUARY 20
SEEDS, SOWERS, AND HEARING EARS—
READ MATTHEW 13:3-9.

Poor Mrs. Farmer, my seventh-grade art teacher, was old, with a large class of unruly kids. The only words of hers I remember are, "Shut up! You're rude, crude, and ignorant!"

Jesus' parable of the sower tells how the Word of God settles into us according to our receptivity. I used to think of the four examples as being fixed; the listener was one or another of the four. I have come to understand that in our lifetimes, we can be all four: the vulnerable path, the rocky shallow place, the thorny place, and the good soil. In our lives, the Word comes, and keeps coming until we are ready to hear.

It took me years of teaching to notice that Mrs. Farmer also left me with vivid memories of her lessons. I remember each and every project we did in her class. I cannot say I remember anyone else's assignments with such precision.

This realization humbles me. I can forgive her words now, and we probably deserved them! But by acknowledging how much I learned from her a full thirty years later, I am struck by how ungrateful we can be toward those who were our teachers. God rest her tired old soul.

For better and worse, what we do or say might matter to our students a very long time from now.

Dear Lord, thank you for the gift of influence. Please help me communicate clearly and with patience. Amen.

FEBRUARY 21

TEACHER GUIDEPOSTS—READ PHILIPPIANS 4:8-9.

My sixth-grade teacher, Mr. Jordan, was the first male teacher I had and the only African American teacher. Growing up fatherless in the Jim Crow South, I was apprehensive about being in his class at first. But his high standards and humor made us feel lucky to be his students. He had a talent for things like riling up the whole class during poetry recitations, turning a student's lack of preparation into a hilarious event that made even the lone forgetful performer laugh along with the audience.

Mr. Jordan made me take his advanced math class. I made my first ever D on a quiz. One boy made fun of me, and I was in tears. Mr. Jordan took me aside and said, "People have laughed at me all my life; do you know why?" I knew why, but I didn't dare admit it. "Because I'm black. You can't let things like this get you down." My mother told me she would rather I make a hard-earned B than an easy A, and she thought Mr. Jordan was right. And, of course, he was. He taught us all about honor, challenge, acceptance, and humor.

I am grateful for thoughts and memories of Mr. Jordan and other teachers from my school days. The excellence of his example is still a guidepost for me today.

Dear Lord, help me honor those who taught me the deeper values by putting their examples into practice in my own classroom. Amen.

FEBRUARY 22

THE LITTLEST ANGEL—READ MATTHEW 5:5.

Colby was small and thin. He appeared frail, and his innocence made him seem much younger than his peers.

Yet, he had a persistence I came to admire.

For example, the science department was selling environmental calendars for a fundraiser, and Colby asked if I would buy one. I said yes, but I didn't usually take cash to school with me; so I told him I would bring it the next day. Well, I kept forgetting, and Colby kept reminding me in his persistent but quiet way. Finally, after several days, I bought a calendar. That day the science teacher told me Colby was so proud that he was the *only* student in his class who managed to sell *any* calendars! He gave me a special gift he had made: a paper clip with a blue ribbon tied on it.

One story my own children and I enjoyed reading together was *The Littlest Angel,* which is about a little boy angel who gives a humble gift from his heart to the Christ child. God honors his gift by making it into the star of Bethlehem.

The only thing Colby got from selling me that calendar was the gratification of knowing he had helped the science department. And he was so grateful that he gave me something for it. What a bright little star!

Dear Lord, thank you for my students' eagerness to help for the sake of making a difference somehow. Please help me to be so meek. Amen.

FEBRUARY 23
POWERFUL SMALLNESS—
READ 2 THESSALONIANS 1:11-12.

*Dedicated to my mother, five feet tall,
and always powerfully loving.*

"Maybe I've been put on this earth to be an ordinary person. Not to do anything great, but to do something small that involves great love." These words by an anonymous adoptive mother, from a page in a book my own mother gave me, have helped me through the many times I judged myself to not be good enough, or successful enough.

The greatest gifts of my life have been motherhood and teaching. But if my youthful self could have visited my future, I think I would have been puzzled to hear my older self saying that.

Sometimes we look at our lives and compare them to those who seem to make bigger waves than we, who do great things that influence many people. In each of us is a yearning for purpose and meaning, and sometimes we try to measure our worth by comparing our accomplishments with those of others we might deem more worthy. But Jesus did not want us to feel dissatisfied if we occupy no position of great influence and power.

No matter how small our lives may seem, if we resolve to glorify the one who taught us to love God and love one another, we may be confident our lives have been great enough.

Dear Lord, help me remember to ask you to make me worthy of the purposes you give me so that Jesus may be glorified in me. Amen.

FEBRUARY 24
MUSTARD SEED METAPHOR—
READ MATTHEW 17:20 AND LUKE 13:18-19.

"Without faith nothing is possible. With it, nothing is impossible." Dr. Mary McLeod Bethune's faith echoed Jesus' words and made it possible for her to begin a school for African American children in 1904 with $1.86. The school grew into Bethune-Cookman College. Its students participate in fundraising for scholarships by giving inspiring musical performances ranging from classical to gospel.

When I was small, I was pilfering through my grandmother's jewelry box. I pulled out a small glass sphere with a tiny bit of something in the center. It had been a part of a necklace owned by someone in my family. When I asked Grandmother what it was, she said, "That's a mustard seed. The Bible says if you have the faith of a mustard seed you can move a mountain." I had never seen a mountain, but I knew they were large and fairly unmovable. I was amazed.

I can still see that tiny seed in my mind's eye and hear my grandmother's voice. The metaphor seemed planted in me for safekeeping until I would hear the words one day with greater understanding.

When we tell our students about those who overcame great obstacles through persistence and vision, we are planting seeds of faith in them.

Dear Lord, thank you for those whose faith in you gave them the ability to do the undoable. Help me plant seeds of their stories in my students so that they may also feel empowered by faith. Amen.

FEBRUARY 25
WALKING THROUGH THE DARK—
READ PSALM 119:130, 133.

I often finish my grading and planning late at night, when the rest of my household is asleep. I turn out the light in my workroom, gather my things, and maneuver my way through the dark. I began this habit originally to avoid waking up my sleeping babies, but at some point I began to do it just for the practice of walking in the darkness. It makes me have to remember and sense the placement of furniture and walls, and as I do so I think this is what it might feel like to be blind.

There are periods when we do walk through dark times, uncertain of an outcome or the future; yet still we trust what we know is true in spite of apparent change and disorder in our lives. "Order my steps in Your Word, Dear Lord," the gospel hymn sings.

Each dim moment we experience is an opportunity to trust God, turn to Scripture and prayer, and wait for the unfolding of his word and work in challenging situations.

Sometimes we have dim moments in our classrooms. Yet we may be relieved knowing that if we ask God to order our steps, he will and he does. The answer will come in the form of a new perspective, or a creative solution, or an idea from another person.

Thank you for the light of your word, dear Lord. Please grow my trust in you with each period of dimness I experience. Amen.

FEBRUARY 26

MERCY, MERCY—READ PSALM 86:5-6.

Kyrie eleison. Christe eleison. Kyrie eleison.
Lord, have mercy. Christ, have mercy. Lord, have mercy.
(ancient Greek/English hymn)

When I was very small, my grandmother would be working hard, cleaning house or cooking, and she would sigh, "Lord, have mercy!"

That "mercy" word was just a sound to me, but I knew that whatever it was, my grandmother wanted it. It seemed to have something to do with hard work, and asking for it didn't seem effective because the floor never did mop itself! I thought, *That's something grandmothers say.*

Years later, after a particularly long day, I was in the kitchen cooking dinner and let go of a "Lord, have mercy!" groan of my own. I felt better, even though I still had to cook dinner. I imagined my grandmother winking at me with a smile.

My grandmother had been talking out loud to Jesus, and at some point, I began talking out loud to Jesus, too. In my car, in my classroom, wherever I may be, I say it: "Lord, help me do this"; "Lord, help me make the most of this day"; "Lord, help me get done in time"; "Lord, forgive me for doing that."

"Lord, have mercy!" I suspect that well before I'm a grandmother, I might have one or two students who think: *That's something teachers say.*

Dear Lord, thank you for your near and present care for me. Please help me know that I can talk to you anytime. Amen.

FEBRUARY 27

MIRROR, MIRROR—READ GALATIANS 6:3-5.

Students give us feedback on our strategies and curriculum through their behavior and achievement. If a majority of students do poorly on a lesson, this is a mirror whose reflection we must examine to determine what characteristics of the lesson are flawed.

One semester I got carried away with trying to pack too much into one lesson. I realized this when the project was handed in. There were a few beautiful pictures made by the most artistically confident students. And many were late, or missing. As I was entering all the F's in my grade book, I acknowledged that the responsibility for so many failures was at least partially mine; yet this was a dilemma because the students knew they were responsible for trying.

The next day, many kids told me the assignment was too difficult. I acknowledged that the technique I asked them to use requires a lot of discipline and focus, but the fact was that more of my sixth-graders had attempted the lesson than my more complacent eighth-graders. I decided to let the grades stand and then offered an opportunity for them to do extra credit. The next semester I changed the technique.

This became a test for my students in the importance of trying, but it was a test for me in the importance of changing.

Dear Lord, thank you for the reciprocity of relationship with my students. Help me bend when the wind blows unmistakably in the direction of need for change. Amen.

FEBRUARY 28

THE SHOE ON THE OTHER FOOT—READ LUKE 6:38.

One day I miscalculated how much time I had left for lunch and ran an errand to the office, returning to my classroom about a minute after the bell. To my relief, my students were all settled in their seats. And they were delighted to see me hurrying through the door with my apologies for tardiness. It was obvious they weren't going to let me off easy, so I decided to come clean and ask them what I should do for atonement.

Several enthusiastic punishments were suggested before one student said, "You can't talk for the whole period." For some reason, this struck me as a great idea. So I agreed to give my instructions silently.

Miming and gesturing my way through the lesson, it was one of the funniest, and most engaging, classroom moments I've ever had. Everyone was on the edge of his or her seat, shouting interpretations and guessing. And they learned what I wanted them to know for that day in spite of the mute presentation—maybe even better!

A picture is worth a thousand words.

It's good for our students to know we are human, and laughing at ourselves is good medicine for everyone. If we make a mistake, we might as well seize the opportunity to demonstrate humor and humility.

Dear Lord, thank you for moments of laughter with my students. Help me demonstrate that I am not above the same standards I expect of them. Amen.

MARCH
Pilgrimage: Running Away and Coming Home

Kellen Beck Mills

MARCH 1
THE RUNAWAY BUNNY—
READ ACTS 9:3-6 AND PSALM 139:7-8.

ONE OF MY SONS' FAVORITE BOOKS WAS MARGARET WISE BROWN'S *The Runaway Bunny*. A little bunny keeps saying he is going to run away, and each time his mother says how far she will go to find him.

I had a wise and kind Bible study mentor. One evening we were studying Psalm 139, and she read *The Runaway Bunny* to our group to illustrate its common message with the verses. "We cannot run beyond God's love and safety," she said. That spoke to my "mother's" heart. It was a comfort to me, who had often been a runaway bunny myself.

Saul's experience on the road to Damascus is famous for its suddenness. But scholars say his actual conversion took years. This helps me be patient with myself because if it took Paul a long time to follow Jesus, I feel forgiven for how long it is taking me.

"'Shucks,' said the bunny, 'I might just as well stay where I am and be your little bunny.' And so he did. 'Have a carrot,' said the mother bunny."

All the roads we take lead to Christ, and he walks with us on every one, even when we run away. This month we will explore Jesus' appearance in our lives, and the "carrots" that he gives us in our pilgrimage toward him.

Dear Lord Jesus, thank you for pursuing me, one of your runaway bunnies. Thank you for the runaway bunnies you entrust me to pursue through your example. Amen.

MARCH 2

HARMONY LEARNING—READ 2 CORINTHIANS 13:11.

When we are living in agreement, we are living in peace. Strategies for cooperative learning helped me a lot in my classroom. I used to be proud of my ideals of independence and doing things myself. That says a lot right there; pride goes before a fall.

God gave me a great gift in teaching a "messy" subject. It is not humanly possible for me to clean up after thirty to thirty-five students, and I *must* depend on them to pitch in and be good citizens of the classroom. Each year I have learned a bit more about how to delegate duties, and this involves creating a classroom environment where everyone plays a part pitching in. As we practice cooperative discipline and learning strategies, we are modeling values that harmonize with scriptural teachings.

It is easy to resent the behavior of students who come from homes where life is chaotic. But when we look within the person, we see a very frightened child. The best thing we can do for them is give clear instructions and safe boundaries, and *include* them in the goals and purposes of harmony in the classroom. This is more important than the subjects we teach.

The more we facilitate agreement, the more enjoyable the learning experience is for everyone.

Dear Lord, thank you for ways you show me to enhance cooperation and harmony among my students. Please help me continually improve my ability to do so. Amen.

MARCH 3

THE FACE OF JESUS—READ MATTHEW 25:40.

History is filled with images of Jesus portrayed by different artists for the past two thousand years. Each portrayal is limited by the attitudes and cultural influences of those who created them. We still wonder: What did Jesus *really* look like?

I like Mother Teresa's idea of what Jesus looks like: the needs of others. The "face of Jesus" is in each of us—in our sorrow and need, and also in our compassion and joy. A heart that loves God serves humanity, not to earn points toward salvation, but because service is a natural result of loving God. We see more opportunities to serve as we grow in devotion. Opportunities to see the face of Jesus can come in simple ways.

Each school day begins for me with hall duty. My post is at the landing of the stairwell. One morning, I decided I would let the gum chewers and minor dress code violators slide, just for this moment. Instead, I chose to see "the face of Jesus" coming up the stairs in each of the students and to greet their needs to feel welcome and safe with a warm smile and a hello. Now I practice this regularly.

It is a small way to serve, but a great way to begin the day.

Dear Lord, thank you for revealing opportunities for serving you through my actions toward others. Help me grow in devotion and service in all my activities. Amen.

MARCH 4

UNDER CONSTRUCTION—READ 1 THESSALONIANS 5:11.

Each interaction is a network between us and within us. There are no accidents in God's universe; there are only points of discovery for our places within the fabric of the whole.

Susan was a social studies teacher who regularly extended her concern and compassion toward others, students and colleagues alike. At year's end when the students had gone, she was sharing her students' journals with me. One, by a girl named Gina, troubled her. Gina wrote: "Not all of us come from perfect homes." She said that she felt held to an academic standard that took domestic tranquility for granted. Tearfully, Susan said, "I try so hard to understand all my students; I had no idea she perceived me as so uncaring."

Sometimes teenagers seem to lash out toward the very ones who provide a safe relationship. Susan had provided a safe venue for this girl to vent her angry feelings about her parents' divorce and isolation from her peers. Gina's journey was under construction, and Susan's journal lesson was a point of departure for Gina—and valuable toward gaining insight into her feelings.

The Lord gives us to one another for his purposes. As we support one another, we can feel confident that the blueprint is in God's hands.

Dear Lord, thank you for your wondrous plan for my life. Please help me encourage others within the framework of your purposes. Amen.

MARCH 5
THE ALTERNATIVE KIDS IN THE MARGINS— READ LUKE 5:31-32.

Every school has its group of kids who dress in black and submerge themselves in a so-called alternative counterculture that "conforms to nonconformity." What I see are kids who value truth, but who are trading the easy security of "belonging to tradition" for "belonging to a place in the margins."

Many of them have a gift for seeing things differently. So I try to give them a safe place, and I seem to attract them. Art might be the only class where they succeed. Ashley was one of those.

One day she said, "No matter how hard I try to screw up, I always end up doing OK in your class; why is that?" Well, the reason was that her creative thinking always came through her work. Children like her are diamonds in the rough.

One day her friend Vicky, always a good student, was down and negative. Ashley complained, "Wait a minute! That's my line, and you see where it's gotten me! Stop that!"

Given a safe point of departure, kids experience freedom to realize things for themselves, and they teach one another. Jesus never turned his back on the marginal members of society. As Thomas Keating said, "He seemed to prefer them, actually."

Dear Lord, let me welcome the marginal kids into my class-room. Help me help them feel accepted and loved, so that they may grow in truth. Amen.

MARCH 6
MAKE MY DAY, LORD—READ PSALM 105:4.

As I begin my day each morning, I practice centering myself in prayer, a simple intention to focus my thoughts toward God.

No matter how I might diverge into cares and concerns, I know that as I gently come back to the silence deep inside, God will give me the peace I need to accomplish the day's tasks. I am grateful for this inner oasis of strength and balance. It is a great relief to understand that Jesus still heals us with his advice to live one day at a time. Long before psychology came into being, Jesus was a healer of anxiety and fear—of both past and future events.

One morning, I spontaneously thought of Clint Eastwood's famous vigilante threat to the cinematic villain: *Go ahead, make my day!* This thought juxtaposed simultaneously with: *This is the day the Lord has made, let us rejoice and be glad in it.* The equation led to: *Go ahead, Lord, make my day!* Though it was an unlikely connection, the humor of it stuck with me; and it became a personal joke. It's not a dare, but a surrender of the day's concerns to the Lord's strength and wisdom.

This kind of centering silence and surrender can be infectious. When I practice it while standing before a noisy distracted group, silence predominates. Go ahead, try it!

Dear Lord, thank you for supporting my needs each day. Help me remember to look to you for my source of strength. Amen.

MARCH 7
REAL COLORS IN THE EYES OF BABES—
READ PSALM 139:14.

When my youngest son was in preschool, he described his friends as shades of orange or brown. At four years old, his accurate observation seemed to surpass the culturally based perceptions of most of us. This helped me later in teaching my students about skin tone.

We are not black and white; not at all. Those words are grossly inaccurate. When I teach my kids to draw portraits, I hold a white sheet of paper up to my face and say: "There is no such thing as a white person" (or a black person), and my students can easily see that I am telling the truth.

"Value" in art is the quality of lightness to darkness. In art, "light" and "dark" are not "good" or "bad," they are just parts of a continuum of shades. All have their place, like high notes and low notes on a musical scale, and they contribute to contrast, which describes form.

Judgment about skin color is a learned attitude. We are blessed to live in a time when the edges between the colors within the spectrum are becoming blurred, and when we can see the evidence of hope for harmony in the generation we are guiding into maturity. We are all wonderfully made.

Lord God, thank you for our rainbow race. Help me see clearly the beautiful faces and hearts of all of the children you have made so wonderfully. Amen.

MARCH 8
AFFLICTIVE LEARNING—READ PSALM 119:71-72.

Affliction is a great teacher. If we could personify affliction, it would be the teacher we feared and hated as students but from whom we ironically learned the most. One pastor of our church was fond of saying his mission was to comfort the afflicted and afflict the comfortable. I can think of teachers I had who "afflicted" me, some of whom with which I might still take issue, and some toward whom I can only now feel gratitude—and relief for having survived the experience!

Affliction comes inevitably in our lives, whether through a person or a set of circumstances. Affliction is the teacher of hard lessons. Some lessons might be the obvious result of our own actions; some might seem to have come from nowhere and be beyond our control. Yet, regardless of causes, our best recourse is humility. Humility breeds receptivity for solutions. There are many situations where bending and surrendering to change within ourselves is more effective than standing firm in inflexibility.

In my classroom, when I am faced with a conflictive or afflictive situation, the sooner I humble myself by putting aside defensiveness and surrendering to precepts of faith, bending receptively in prayer, the sooner the situation passes into resolution.

Thank you, Lord, for each time you offer me an opportunity to learn from trying circumstances. Help me seek your precepts for each small and large affliction I encounter. Amen.

MARCH 9

FOCUSING ON THE UNSEEN—READ 2 CORINTHIANS 18.

Nelson Mandela was in prison for more than twenty years. When a journalist came to visit him, a guard accompanied Mr. Mandela for the interview. As they greeted each other, Mr. Mandela respectfully said, "I would like to introduce to you my guard of honor." The journalist reported that this introduction caused a visible change in the guard's demeanor. He straightened his shoulders and stretched out his hand for a warm handshake with the reporter; then he took his place on the sideline for the interview.

This generosity toward the prison guard was a part of the character in Nelson Mandela that eventually led South Africa out of apartheid. He chose to see decency in his captor, and behaved as though he expected it.

Our expectations of others influence our behavior toward them. When we choose to see the best in them, the child of God in them, it is a generosity cultivated by the spirit. This does not mean we should ignore destructive behavior, but we must keep our main focus on the inner person. This is correcting the behavior but loving the child.

One girl, ironically named Angel, was in trouble often at school. One day she hung her head and said, "I am not my name." Would the Lord have us give any other response than, "Yes you are"?

Dear Lord, thank you for your eternal love and care. Help me see the unseen best of you in others and in myself. Amen.

MARCH 10
ABBA'S CHILDREN—READ GALATIANS 4:6-7.

Jesus called God *Abba*. It is the Aramaic intimate word for Father, like *Daddy* or *Papa*. This helped me understand a missing piece of myself—missing "peace" within.

My mother raised the four of us on a secretary's salary with our grandmother's help. Our family was a loving one, but worry and anxiety were familiar companions. In my mother's Sunday school classes, the teacher focused on the sin of divorce in the lessons. Mom had tried for nineteen years to live with my father's bipolar illness, but eventually she divorced him to protect us from the chaos of his behavior. This judgment each Sunday left her in tears, so we quit going to church. I did not learn why she had left the church until she returned with my own children and me.

It took me years to understand that I have a heavenly Father. Today, more than 50 percent of our students live in single-parent homes. Missing pieces in them—missing peace in them—they come to school each day with a hunger they cannot name or describe. Maybe the law prevents us from saying, "Abba loves you dearly." But we can show them they are loved and treasured; and we can pray for the Holy Spirit to reveal this through our actions and words.

Dear Lord, thank you for your loving personal concern for each of your children. Please make me an instrument of your peace and comfort. Amen.

MARCH 11

FEAR AND FORGIVENESS—READ JOSHUA 1:9.

Franklin Roosevelt said, "The only thing we have to fear is fear itself." When we are in the grip of fear, it seems infinitely large. But it is an illusion. John said that love is the opposite of fear. Love neutralizes fear.

Anxiety is fear. Jesus taught us to avoid anxiety and worry. He said, "Consider the lilies of the field . . . they neither toil nor spin" (Matthew 6:28 NRSV). There are many things that cause us to worry: What should we wear? What should we say? What do people think of us? A whole range of menacing thoughts plague us if we choose to listen to them.

The big lie is that we deserve to feel fearful. There is a thin line between guilt and repentant conscience. The former binds us; the latter frees us. Jesus performed many miracles of healing that included body and spirit simultaneously. Again and again, he said, "Your sins are forgiven." Sin and fear divide us from God. Forgiveness and love bring us back to remembering that God is with us and for us, not against us.

When we are tempted to worry about our lesson plans, the receptivity to our ideas, our performance, or any of the myriad concerns we have as teachers, let us deliver them to God and ask for his guidance. We have no use for fear.

Dear Lord, help me come back to remembering to trust every time I step off the path into worry. Amen.

MARCH 12

THE INNER COMPASS—READ PSALM 46:10.

Grace had an easy smile and a straight-spoken honesty. In an inner-city school, she was an enthusiastic A student, even when others around her manifested results of not having enough stability in their lives. Grace had an inner compass.

187

One day she told me that her mom was never home, and that her mom's boyfriend supported the family by dealing drugs. "But my auntie watches out for me. Well, that's my story. How about yours?" Matter-of-fact and uncomplaining, she talked about her hope to become "one of those doctors who takes care of babies, so I can take care of my own babies when they get sick."

Wanting to give her a chance to be in an academically exciting environment, I encouraged her to audition for the high school that specialized in the arts. Her application was rejected. She was the only student I had ever recommended who did not get in. She was disappointed, and I felt terrible for exposing her to this disappointment. Clearly, God had other plans for her, and Grace had already told me months before that she wanted to be a doctor.

God gives each of us a still, inner compass to follow the path he wills. If he says no to a plan of ours, we can be certain he has a greater one.

Dear Lord, help me be still and know you're in control when I feel disappointed for my students. May I speak words of encouragement. Amen.

MARCH 13

THE CALM IN THE CENTER—READ MARK 4:39.

As I've been writing these devotions, our area has been visited by two hurricanes. The first came three weeks ago. The second approaches as I write this. Several days before we knew about the first one, the one whose eye passed directly near our community, I kept hearing the scripture in my mind about Jesus and the storm. I kept thinking of metaphorical storms and metaphorical boats, and of Jesus rebuking metaphorical winds.

Then a meditation on it appeared in one of the devotionals I read each day. I thought, *There must be an application here I should explore.* Then, the next day, news came of the first hurricane headed for our area in forty-four years. The application was more real than I imagined!

Hurricane warnings are common in Florida. We even have hurricane days built into the school calendar. Usually everyone prepares, and the kids get a free day off and the storm blows by. This time even my students were saying: "We would rather come to school tomorrow!"

In this awesome force of nature, whirling winds and rain surround a completely calm center. The hurricane itself is a model of how to respond to it. With a hurricane blowing outside, it is a great blessing to hear Jesus saying on the inside, "Peace! Be still!"

Dear Lord, thank you for the safety of your reassuring words in turbulent times. Help me apply your teachings to all of the events in my life. Amen.

MARCH 14
PRAYER RESORT—READ ISAIAH 48:17
AND 1 THESSALONIANS 5:17.

How often we wait to pray until things get really tough. We wait until we have exhausted our abilities and resources to solve problems. Finally, we resort to prayer.

The word *resort* is defined as a resource, as in "this is my last resort." It also is defined as "a much visited place, to go to frequently or in great numbers," "to turn to for help," and finally, "to have recourse to."

Paul tells us to pray at all times about all manner of things. Prayer can be "a much visited place," where we go frequently and in great numbers—great numbers of us, and great numbers of prayers. God hears them all, and the more we connect and cultivate the connection in ourselves, the more we see the difference it makes in our lives and the lives of those within our concerns. Suddenly a corner is turned, a resolution found, a conflict deflated.

Imagine the influence to be had on education by teachers praying regularly for students, colleagues, administrators, and support staff! I have several prayer buddies at my school, and we link up regularly. We see the difference it makes.

Prayer is our first, middle, and last resort. As a favored, much visited place, it's a vacation for the spirit that rejuvenates the vocation of our hearts.

Thank you, Lord, for the gift of prayer and for directing us to pray continually. Help me remember to pray for and with others often. Amen.

MARCH 15

MY FATHER'S EYES—READ ISAIAH 58:8.

One evening, as I was listening to Eric Clapton's *Pilgrim* CD, the song "My Father's Eyes" caught my attention; then I noticed the title of the album. Several years ago, Clapton had to endure the greatest nightmare of any parent; his four-year-old son died when he fell out of a window.

The song is a poignant picture of pain and redemption. He tells of his joy in fatherhood, his devastating loss, and his discovery of the Father's supreme mercy. There's no mistaking where Clapton turned for comfort. "As my soul slides down to die . . . I've realized that he was here with me." The "father's eyes" in Clapton's song is a vision of God's omnipotent compassion for him.

Clapton is using his platform of fame to teach about his experience of grief and the transforming comfort of God in his life. In *Pilgrim* he sings about a journey toward redemption.

Rembrandt painted a beautiful picture, *The Return of the Prodigal Son*. The son kneels before his father, and his head seems to melt into his father's bosom. All of us returning to the Father in our greatest times of need have stories to tell and teach about his grace.

As teachers, we have a platform for sharing stories of redemption. For me, choosing music to play and artwork to show are ways to share subtle messages.

Dear Lord, thank you for the examples in art and literature where your purposes and message intersect with the mediums. Help me find many to share with my students. Amen.

MARCH 16

THE INNER OLDER BROTHER—READ LUKE 15:31-32.

I began our devotions this month mentioning *The Runaway Bunny*. The archetypal ancestor of the story is the prodigal son. Henri Nouwen, a great spiritual writer of our time, recorded his meditations on Jesus' parable of the lost son. He said that he discovered within the parable "the whole gospel." His words appear in *From Fear to Love: Lenten Reflections on the Parable of the Prodigal Son*. It is a deep application of the parable to our inner lives.

Nouwen says that our Father freely loves us whether we stay or leave, whether we are the prodigal son or the older brother, and that we might see one or both types within ourselves. Through deeply understanding our sin that separates us from the Father, whether through squandering our inheritance or harboring self-righteous resentment, we return to the Father, whose essence of boundless love and forgiveness is received in the journey back to him.

Resentment is the downfall of the faithful, obedient, hardworking people who do what's right, according to Nouwen. The self-righteous older brother is simply the flip side of the runaway brother.

Sometimes we resent some of the things we experience as teachers. Here the *inner older brother* in us needs the Father's forgiveness and needs to extend forgiveness so that we can grow beyond destructive resentful feelings.

Dear Lord, resentment is not how you would have me feel about my hard work. Forgive me for my transgressions, and help me forgive others. Amen.

MARCH 17

SAINT PATRICK'S SOUL FRIENDSHIP—READ PSALM 95:7.

Christ be with me, Christ before me, Christ be after me, Christ within me, Christ beneath me, Christ above me, Christ at my right hand, Christ at my left.

—Saint Patrick's Breastplate

Saint Patrick was the missionary who spread the word of Christ to the people of Ireland. Celtic theology teaches about the goodness of God's creations in the world and of the nearness of God's presence both within and transcending his creation.

Patrick spent years in slavery, living as a herdsman in the green open borders of God's creation. His word for God became *Anam Cara,* which means "soul friend" in Irish.

The portion of the prayer above, written about a century after his time, bears Patrick's name because it expresses the way his faith manifested in his life. This prayer bespeaks the *anam cara,* the intimate relationship Patrick found with Jesus. What more could we hope for than to be so essentially surrounded by Christ's presence?

Today we might put on green to honor Saint Patrick's Day and teach a lesson on its history. We might also envision ourselves surrounded by God's green pastures, and Christ within and around all of us. This gives a new meaning to "the wearin' o' the green."

Thank you, Lord, for your presence with me, within me, within others, and all around. Help me see that I belong in your green pasture as part of your flock. Amen.

MARCH 18

LOVING THE WORK OF OUR HANDS—READ PSALM 90:17.

When we turn the glory for everything that we do well over to God, we are relieved of the inflation of ourselves that eventually proves burdensome. When we turn our disappointments in projects that fall short of our hopes into prayers for help, we begin again sooner with renewed focus.

We might feel stressed with many cares and concerns that take our attention away from the moment, causing us to miss opportunities to communicate with our students that would enhance their learning and our enjoyment.

For myself, I sometimes notice that if I have a certain agenda for the day that doesn't go as I had planned, I respond with frustration that causes me to lose my focus on the current picture. If I make a choice to let go of frustration and focus again on the moment, asking for guidance, I am free to proceed with creative solutions.

Anyone who has seen clay formed into a beautifully shaped vessel on a potter's wheel sees that the potter, clay, time, and motion are in synchronicity with the creation. Alice Coltrane, the great jazz pianist, said once, "Everything I do is an offering to God, and that's the truth."

As we allow God to shape each moment in our work, participating with enthusiasm and calm, we are constantly refining the craft of faith and surrender.

Dear Lord, help me see that every moment is an opportunity to experience joy and enthusiasm—your favor for the work of my hands. Amen.

MARCH 19

FEATHER AND STONE—READ MATTHEW 11:28-30.

Clinging to a concept of "me" is an inherent stubbornness of living this journey. The more I let go of "me," the easier my life is. The more I choose to be enthusiastic about whatever is set before me, the richer and deeper is the reward. The more I choose to learn and change from my experiences, the greater is my gratitude and joy.

I had the great blessing of doing many types of work before I became a teacher. In each scenario, I found that the more of myself I put into my work, the more enthusiasm I had for doing it well and the better I felt. And I observed this in others. The ones who worked for the sake of others had an enthusiasm and joy that was absent from those who put little of themselves into their jobs.

Service: it is a paradox of our existence. The more we serve with a joyous heart, the lighter we are: feather versus stone. If we serve resentfully, we serve heavily and our hearts are heavy. The more we serve joyously and enthusiastically, the lighter we feel and the freer we are to skip from one ripple to the other, like a stone shot from a child's hand—feather free, with forward momentum.

Dear Lord, thank you for the experiences that help me understand that your burden is light. Yoke me together with others so we may see that your call to service lightens and enlightens our lives. Amen.

MARCH 20

UNBENDING INTENTION—READ 1 CHRONICLES 28:20.

When we embrace paradox, we realize that often truth is one thing and the other simultaneously. For instance, consider trees in a great wind. On one hand, bending in the direction of the gale ensures survival and integrity of form. On the other hand, there is a center of gravity and rootedness that prevails over the circumstances of weather. Stand firm *and* bend.

Listen to Maya Angelou, a poet who did not speak at all in her formative years because of personal trauma but who became a great communicator with a gift for expressing grace and faith:

> As for me, I shall not be moved. . . .
> I go forth. . . . Alone, and stand as ten thousand.

In our peripheral concerns, we can bend with the flow of the moment, and we should. Lesson plans, daily agenda, and specifics of accomplishing our objectives we can and should bend with the moment at hand. In our central concerns, the values at the center of our consciousness—loving God first and foremost and loving others as ourselves—we can stand firm in unbending intention.

The paradox is resolved as we realize our smaller and greater purposes. Unswerving in the greater ones, we can bend in the smaller ones, knowing that the greater take precedence.

Dear Lord, thank you for the unchangeable, unmovable center of your wisdom. Help me bend when I should, and fortify me with firmness and clarity of purpose on matters you would have me uphold uncompromisingly. Amen.

MARCH 21
TOUGH SKIN, GOLD HEART—READ JOB 38:22-23.

I had an art professor in college who was known for his critical eye and tongue. He seemed to take pride in being a curmudgeon, but we knew he had a heart of gold.

His was the only opinion that ever mattered enough to reduce me to tears. He devoted himself to teaching, and his hopes of being an artist had been nudged aside. He tried to discourage me from choosing a path he himself had found frustrating. "You can't be an artist *and* a teacher," he had said.

Ironically, it was his example and passion for teaching that shaped my career desires. Years after graduation, I gathered courage to write to him for a reference, and he took the time to write an in-depth letter. He did not have to do that, but he probably couldn't help it. Underlying his demands for excellence was always a concern for us that went beyond obligation.

He used to say, "True learning is a change in behavior and a change in thinking." He changed my thinking so much that his influence still shapes my curriculum today.

We never know the true value of what students might learn from us, or the treasures they will find in the process of effort, frustration, failure, and success.

Dear Lord, thank you for the treasures within and beyond what I teach. Help me support my students through the sometimes painful struggle to learn. Amen.

MARCH 22
JOY CAN BE YOUR COMPASS—
READ MATTHEW 6:33 AND MATTHEW 7:8.

Each church that opens its doors to working families is serving a very great purpose in caring for small children. Out of necessity, my sons attended a church daycare down the street from where I worked. When my youngest was three, he learned a little song there called "Seek Ye First" which included these words:

> Seek ye first the kingdom of God, and his righteousness,
> and all these things shall be added unto you.

As his cherubic voice sang this simple hymn, so sweet and pure, he awakened a joyful memory deep inside of me and long forgotten. I had loved that song, and its tune, in my own childhood.

Joyfully, my little one's voice now revealed a compass in my hand, and I cherished the message in my heart. I realized that I had wondered and wandered for years, had forgotten to ask for help in finding my way, and had not understood my priorities.

That little school played a very important role in our family's return to church. The preschool teachers taught my sons many songs and values that are now little compasses stored inside of them.

Dear Lord, thank you for those who care for infants and small children of working parents. Bless them with knowing how important their service is to us. Amen.

MARCH 23

GOODNESS AND LOVE EVERY DAY—READ PSALM 23:6.

Each week on the way to Sunday school, my little boys picked flowers from the front walkway to give to me. Each time I placed the flowers in my Bible. These simple gifts of joy and love are still there, dry and beautiful memories—God's bookmarks. Now my sons are teenagers and are beyond the age of picking flowers for Mommy.

Recently, I had this cherished memory in mind, as well as some concerns, as I was going to church. After worship I saw, framed through a picture window streaming with brilliant sunlight, a small boy picking flowers in the butterfly garden to give to an elderly man—probably his grandfather.

It was a humble and sacred moment, and I was grateful to witness this event as though it was my own. Whatever my worry or concern for my children as they grow through adolescence, I know that they possess an inner compass of joy to guide them, because they have a foundation in scriptural teaching and love.

God communicates to us in the everyday. Whenever we experience joy in small and simple things, we know God is in the very fiber of it.

Sometimes our students are inspired to give us a simple gift of a picture, flower, or note. These are sacred gifts that give to the receiver and the giver.

Thank you, God, for the inner compass of joy you give us. Open our eyes to the simple gifts that contain sacred and miraculous messages from you. Amen.

MARCH 24

GIVING AND RECEIVING—READ ACTS 20:35.

We've all seen the excitement of children at a birthday party. "Open mine first!" they shout. Each child wants to see the birthday boy or girl's happy surprise in opening the gift he or she has chosen.

It *does* feel good to give. True giving comes with no strings attached, no fine print, no expectations.

If we're comfortable with giving but not with receiving, it may help to realize that it's also important to give others the "gift of receiving" so that they may know we value their efforts and interactions with us. Then we can relax, knowing that the time we have given to others—listening to what they have to say—is a gift. Gratitude, or graciousness, is a gift to others as well as to ourselves.

Jesus said it is more blessed to give than to receive. He was not talking about the sort of giving that earns us points or power in the material plane of human interactions. He was talking about giving grace—just as God gives us grace freely, with no strings attached.

Every day we give our knowledge to our students. Every day we also have the opportunity to receive their insights and perspectives. If we are willing to receive their insights, we are giving them the gift of participation. The reciprocity is symbiotic and benefits us all.

Dear Lord, thank you for the unearned free gift of grace. Help me live graciously in the reciprocity of giving freely and receiving gratefully. Amen.

MARCH 25

HEARTS OF STONE—READ LUKE 7:31-35.

We played the flute for you, and you did not dance, We sang a dirge, and you did not cry.

Our hearts harden in the face of fear. Our chests tighten defensively, blocking out what we perceive as threatening: a difficult personal interaction, a problem that seems beyond our abilities, a risk of being wrong.

The Pharisees hardened their hearts toward John the Baptist and Jesus. They could neither hear with humility nor respond with sincerity. Neither joy nor sorrow entered their hearts because they rigidly clung to a need to be "right."

Today, we are not so different from them, nor are our students. A hardened heart sinks like a stone in a river of tears. But before that, it treads water indefinitely.

Better to dive right in and swim than debate the pros and cons of immersion in the fluid and dynamic business of living. Better to live fully and freely than to sit on the sidelines fearing failure, making a mistake, or being wrong.

Each student who chooses failure is treading water within a heart of stone. These students present a special challenge: We might see that our own hearts risk becoming hard through our fear of not being successful in reaching them.

And Jesus is whispering to us: "Dance! Cry! Dive right in, *and swim!*"

Dear Lord, thank you for sincere feeling, passion, and courage—which help me take the risk of trusting you. Help me encourage my students to risk making mistakes, knowing that each step in the right direction is progress. Amen.

MARCH 26
TURNING THE OTHER CHEEK BOLDLY—
READ LUKE 10:36-37 AND MATTHEW 5:39.

Any teacher who has experienced a power struggle with a student knows that the more you attack or defend, the more you both lose. The more attention you give to negative behavior, the worse it gets.

I know this because I've resisted and struggled and found myself wishing I could rewind the tape. "Cut! Take two!" *Practice, practice, practice.*

We often don't know what circumstances a child is living in that are causing him or her to act out. Yet our fear can make us look the other way or become defensive. Fear can even cause us to go on the offensive.

If a student's words or actions get under my skin, I notice that it's mostly because I fear losing control of my classroom. But I am not in control in the first place. God is. And I know I can turn again to Jesus to help me become better at turning the other cheek calmly and boldly.

Nonresistance is both a choice and an action. In education, this means letting the negative stuff go by, standing firm in the standard, *and* having mercy on the transgressor. It means delivering the consequence for the negative behavior without using inflammatory, judgmental words, and welcoming the child back to the positive flow of guidance as soon as possible.

Dear Lord, help me apply your teaching, and help me understand that this involves skills I improve in as I practice them, for I am your student. Amen.

MARCH 27

BROKEN HEART, OPEN HEART—READ LUKE 13:33-35.

You'll never break—this Heart of Stone.
—Rolling Stones
My heart broke: Open.
—Ancient Haiku

Jesus' heart broke for us. He made himself vulnerable— open in every way—in his Passion and compassion because he loved us dearly then and loves us dearly now.

"'O Jerusalem! . . . Look, your house is left to you desolate. I tell you, you will not see me again until you say, 'Blessed is he who comes in the name of the Lord'" (Luke 13:34, 35).

We are in Jerusalem. We are not so different than the characters and personalities we read about in scripture. The ancient words and stories transcend time and place.

Human stubbornness and hard-heartedness are with us still today. Still we do not listen and we choose paths that lead to heartbreak. Our merciful Master meets us in the cracks and crevices, in the tears and sorrow, and restores us to wholeness. Then we do see him clearly: Blessed is he who comes in the name of the Lord.

When we see young persons embarking on the trail that leads to tears, and then graduating into the next year beyond our influence to help, it can be heartbreaking. In these instances we can pray for them and be confident that the Lord will continue to keep going with them—today, tomorrow, and the next day.

Dear Lord, thank you for the hope you give me to carry on. May I continue praying for the ones I know need your special care. Amen.

MARCH 28

AS THE WORLD TURNS—READ EZEKIEL 18:31-32.

Repent means literally "to turn around."

Every day the world spins around. Yesterday is gone; tomorrow will come in its time. Today we return to prayer and begin again anew.

Rhythm and time: Process and cycles in the continuum.

When students recognize their progress in their work, they can tune into the process of learning and understand that, although there are moments of epiphany where leaps and bounds are made, much of learning occurs gradually and imperceptibly. Then a time comes when one looks back and sees the record of point A in the past heading toward point B in the present, ideally gaining a vision of future possibilities and growing confidence and trust.

When we point out our students' progress to them, they can see for themselves how they solved a problem differently, and with more expertise, than previously. This evidence is a gift we can give them: "You really did get better. You really do know more now than you did then."

Learning is a process of walking through the rhythm of dark and light.

Repentance is turning toward the light and finding one's way. It's a gradual, lifelong, and worldwide process.

Dear Lord, help me nurture my students' confidence in their progress over time so they may turn toward the light of learning to live their lives in the patience of process. Amen.

MARCH 29

THE TRUTH—READ EPHESIANS 4:25.

The events at Columbine deeply underscored the reality that the ones who inflict pain on others are in pain themselves.

After Columbine, I wanted to give my students a chance to respond to the horrible events and distance themselves from some of the negative generalizations about teenagers that were being made. They were to think of a positive value message and design a poster that they would want to see on a billboard. I wrote words on paper such as *blessings, tolerance, integrity, truth;* and the kids drew them randomly from a bowl.

Lenny was a boy who picked on other kids. He stole things and lied all the time. He lived with his grandmother because his mother was in prison for killing his father. We had many private discussions about living honestly.

Lenny drew the word *truth*.

He looked me in the eye and said, "I'm not supposed to get this one."

"That one's got your name on it," I said.

He never did the assignment. He was arrested for stealing his grandmother's car. Some of those posters still hang in my classroom; they remind me to pray.

The reality is, the story doesn't always come out the way we hoped. But we don't see the whole story, either. Hope is still justified, and we can pray. And that's the truth.

Dear God, help me see the deeper truth in troubled kids, and hope for them when they have no hope for themselves. Amen.

MARCH 30
NO FEAR, NO BULLIES, NO VICTIMS—
READ 1 PETER 5:7 AND MATTHEW 5:44.

And I for winking at your discords too,
Have lost a brace of kinsmen. All are punish'd.
— William Shakespeare, *Romeo and Juliet*

Bullying, whether on the delivery or receiving end, should not be accepted as normal.

A former student of mine named Logan was hated in high school by a group of boys for his nonconformity. They taunted him daily, called him racist names, and goaded him into conflict. Finally, they pushed and hit until he hit back. He had lacerations and some fractured bones in his face. He was suspended, along with them, for fighting. Fortunately, the school's video cameras recorded the event, and he was exonerated and allowed to go back to school.

Usually there are no cameras, and children are left to defend themselves. That's why we have to be in the hallways, on the bus ramp, and present wherever students are moving en masse around our schools. We have to listen to the talk that goes on in our classrooms and advocate zero tolerance for nontolerance.

Everyone deserves to come to school free from fear—the victims *and* the bullies, whose aggression originates in their own fears.

Even if we think home is where safety and respect for others *should* be established, it often isn't. So this is real, and this is ours. And we know where to turn.

Thank you, Lord, for teaching me to love my enemies and to love others as myself. Amen.

MARCH 31
DINOSAURS, PIRATES, AND ETERNITY—
READ JOB 26:13-14.

One evening, when my oldest son was very small, I was tucking him into bed and he said, "Which came first, the dinosaurs or the pirates?"

"The dinosaurs," I said.

"And did you come before or after the pirates?"

"After the pirates."

"So, first dinosaurs, then pirates, then you."

A mystery solved. The simplicity of his time line and his satisfaction in putting me in my proper place was one of those moments parents live for.

As I sat in his room after he'd fallen asleep, I marveled over the continuum of God's creation. We begin in wonderment; then we organize things into ways we can understand them: time lines, categories, tables, graphs, species, elements, principles, metaphors, subjects, predicates, color wheels, comparison, contrast, countries, states, maps, measurement, and on and on.

In the Smithsonian Institution there is a totemic obelisk that is a geological time line of our planet, perhaps a couple of stories high. Humankind appears at the top few inches. Eternity is beyond the boundaries of our understanding; the more we know, the more we know we don't know. And in our attempt to understand the parts of the whole, we encounter a glimpse of the holy countenance of our awesome God.

Dear Lord, thank you for giving us some knowledge and understanding of your awesome universe. Help us share this basis for amazement and wonder with our students. Amen.

APRIL
Lord, Teach Me . . .

Cindy M. Bradley

APRIL 1
LEARNING FROM THE MASTER TEACHER—
READ LUKE 11:1.

"LORD, TEACH US . . ." (LUKE 11:1). THE DISCIPLES MADE THIS request of Jesus. While on this earth, Jesus, the Master Teacher, taught his closest friends many things, and he will teach us many things as well if we will only ask: "Lord, teach me how to . . ."

As teachers, we teach a variety of subjects. We may teach math, English, spelling, science, history, art, music, or several of these subjects—perhaps even all of them if we teach in elementary school. We study our subject areas, write our lesson plans, use the best practices and the latest research. These practices are important as we enter the classroom so that we may convey all of this knowledge to the students.

However, we also bring ourselves—our beliefs, our values, and our ideals. In addition to the curriculum, we are teaching principles of living. Every day we need to call upon the Master Teacher to teach us first. In doing so, we are inviting Jesus to accompany us into our classrooms. We are acknowledging our dependence on the Master Teacher.

Over the next month, we will spend time asking Jesus to teach us how to see, speak, hear, think, laugh, and so on, as we acquire the skills necessary in this course we call Life.

Lord, teach us what you want us to learn. We want to learn from you. Amen.

APRIL 2
LORD, TEACH ME HOW TO SEE—
READ MATTHEW 9:20-22.

I try to picture myself as this sick woman who has been bleeding for twelve years. I can't conceive of being so ill for that length of time, day in and day out, with no relief. She took a chance. Scripture tells us she came up behind Jesus and touched the edge of his cloak. "Jesus turned and saw her."

I imagine the woman was nervous when Jesus turned to her. She may have thought she was in trouble. Yet Jesus' eyes must have been kind because he addressed her as "daughter." Jesus saw her pain, her years of suffering, her loneliness, and her loss; and he healed her.

Lord, teach me how to see. I look at my students every day, but do I see them? I gaze at them as they come into my classroom. I observe them as they interact with one another. I examine their work and their projects. I watch them as I teach. But do I *see* them?

When I look at my students today, I want to see them the way Jesus saw this woman. When my students look into my eyes, I want them to see my heavenly Father and the way he looks at them.

Dear Lord, teach me how to see. Please help me see my students today with your eyes. Amen.

APRIL 3
LORD, TEACH ME HOW TO HEAR, PART 1—
READ 1 SAMUEL 3:9.

As a teacher, it's easy for me to speak, but sometimes it's hard for me to hear. In order for me to hear my students, I must stop talking, stop my thoughts from wandering, and stop thinking about my response. Likewise, in order for me to hear God, I must stop talking, stop my thoughts from wandering, and stop thinking about my response.

When I take time to listen, I may hear a child's story about his or her day, a teenager's questions about God, or the real reason behind a student's poor grade. When I take time to listen, I may hear how to pray for a coworker, a reason to rejoice with a friend, or the laughter of a child. When I take time to listen, I may hear something seemingly insignificant to me but very important to someone else. When I take time to listen, I may hear God speak to me about a problem I have prayed about, a situation I am facing, or the answer to a decision I need to make.

Eli taught Samuel the importance of hearing God. When I take time to listen, I am modeling an important life skill. God will speak to me if I take time to hear.

Lord, teach me how to hear. I want to take time to hear you today—and to hear others. Amen.

APRIL 4
LORD, TEACH ME HOW TO HEAR, PART 2—
READ REVELATION 5:11-13.

I love to hear voices reciting the Pledge of Allegiance and singing the national anthem in unison. In worship, it thrills my heart to hear voices singing hymns of the faith and contemporary praise choruses, proclaiming the creeds, and praying the Lord's Prayer together.

But sometimes I take these sounds for granted. I hear the words of the prayers, songs, and creeds; but somehow their meaning is lost. In times like these I need to stop myself and pray, "Lord, teach me how to hear."

When I stop and listen, my ears discover that I can still hear. I can hear a young man with Down syndrome saying the Lord's Prayer. I can hear a youth choir singing a praise chorus. I can hear a group of Korean children singing a hymn of response in Korean. I can hear a group of Chileans proclaiming "Vivé Jesus!" What a beautiful sound!

I can only imagine what it will be like to hear every creature in heaven and earth singing,

"To him who sits on the throne and to the Lamb
be praise and honor and glory and power,
for ever and ever!" (Revelation 5:13)

Lord, teach me how to hear. I'm so thankful I can hear your children of all ages, nations, and races speaking, singing, and praying in your name. Amen.

APRIL 5
LORD, TEACH ME HOW TO SPEAK, PART 1— READ MATTHEW 25:21.

In the parable of the talents, Jesus says, "Well done, good and faithful servant!" (Matthew 25:21). These are the words we desire to hear.

Recently I read a book that challenged me to be more encouraging in my words and to catch people—especially my students—doing something "right." The truth is, I spend too much time catching students doing "wrong" and too little time catching them doing "right." Of course, we must address the "wrong," but how many times do we overlook the "right"?

Today, I want to compliment my students when they are doing the right thing. I desire to see their faces light up when I tell them I appreciate them. Today I hope to be specific in speaking words of praise to my students and to others. Sometimes when I call them by name, they have a look of fear, wondering if they have done something wrong. Then when I compliment them, it is just like a breath of fresh air.

I've heard it takes about ten compliments to outweigh a negative comment. It is important for us to take the time to stop and say, "Well done."

Lord, teach me how to say words that bring out the best in the people I meet today. Amen.

APRIL 6
LORD, TEACH ME HOW TO SPEAK, PART 2—
READ EPHESIANS 4:29; 5:19-20.

It happened again today: I let some unwholesome things come out of my mouth. Occasionally when this happens, the person I was speaking about appears from out of nowhere; and I find myself in an awkward spot, wondering if he or she overheard my careless words. Even though I try not to let this happen, especially in front of my students, I realize that I need to be more careful.

Have you ever heard a child repeat a phrase that you have spoken? Sometimes it is cute or funny, but other times it is embarrassing. Paul's letter to the Ephesians reminds us that we should speak only what is "helpful for building others up according to their needs, that it may benefit those who listen" (Ephesians 4:29).

There are days when I speak negatively about situations or other people, and it is a bad habit to fall into. I really need to guard my words. Once they are out, there is no taking them back. When I speak carelessly, it is usually on a day when I rushed out the door without spending time with the Lord before going to work. Taking time with the Lord first will help me to speak in ways that are pleasing to him.

Lord, teach me how to speak "in living echoes of thy tone." Amen.

("Lord, Speak to Me," Frances R. Havergal, 1872)

APRIL 7
LORD, TEACH ME HOW TO REACH OUT, PART I—
READ MATTHEW 8:1-4.

"Jesus reached out his hand and touched the man" (Matthew 8:3). Human touch is so important to us. Psychologists have performed studies on the effects of physical touch and the problems created by the lack of touch.

Leprosy is a disease that inflicts people in such a way that others avoid contact with them. That is why this story is so meaningful. Jesus was not afraid to reach out and touch this man with leprosy.

Sometimes you and I treat others as if they have leprosy. There may be students in our classrooms or in our realm of influence that we avoid. Can you think of people like that in your life? I know I can see their faces in my mind. Picture Jesus reaching out and touching these persons through you.

Every day we have opportunities to reach out and touch others. A pat on the back or a hug may be just the thing that will brighten a student's day. A "thumbs up" or "high five" can show support in a way that positively makes a difference. A kind word or a smile can bring healing to someone who is often avoided. How will Jesus use you and me to reach out and touch others today?

Lord, teach me how to reach out and touch others in ways that bring your healing. Amen.

APRIL 8
LORD, TEACH ME HOW TO REACH OUT, PART 2—
READ MATTHEW 14:22-33.

Peter had been walking on the water and suddenly found himself sinking. "Immediately Jesus reached out his hand and caught him" (Mathew 14:31). Jesus could have merely commanded Peter to stop sinking, but instead, Jesus chose to reach out with his own hands to save him.

Some of my favorite memories of working with children and youth are when our hands have ministered together to assist others. We have reached out by singing at nursing homes and giving hugs to the residents; building a Habitat house with our adult mission team; gleaning apples and broccoli to give to those in need; visiting people who have difficulty leaving home; shopping for families in need; serving hot meals and packing shoebox gifts for children; taking our puppets to the hospital or to Head Start; placing our hands on a person needing prayer; and picking up trash from an older person's yard. In doing so, we have reached out and let the love of God touch others.

Mother Teresa said, "When we touch the sick and needy, we touch the suffering body of Christ" (*Mother Teresa: In My Own Words*, Jose Luis Gonzalez-Balado [New York: Random House, 1996], p. 26). This is an amazing thought we should take to heart. What an opportunity we have when we reach out.

Lord, teach me how to reach out—how to have the courage to touch others with my own hands. Amen.

APRIL 9
LORD, TEACH ME HOW TO CELEBRATE—
READ LUKE 19:28-40.

Every year on Palm Sunday our church reenacts Jesus' triumphal entry into Jerusalem, signifying the start of Holy Week. The children excitedly wave palm branches and walk down the aisle as the people sing *"Hosanna."* There is electricity in the air as we approach worship on this day.

When Jesus entered the city riding on a donkey, the people did not hold back in restraint. They threw off their cloaks, waved the palms, and joyfully praised God in loud voices. There was excitement and energy as shouts of praise were raised.

Sometimes when we approach worship, we forget that it is a celebration. We sing the songs, but we lack the intensity. We say the words, but we forget what they mean. We go through the motions, but our heart is not in it. I wonder how different it would be if we had to worship in secret. I wonder how different it would be if we did not have the freedom to go to church any time we want.

Some Sundays, I confess that I have not prepared myself for worship. Forgive me, Lord, for taking worship for granted.

Lord, teach me how to celebrate and worship you in spirit and in truth. Amen.

APRIL 10

LORD, TEACH ME HOW TO PRAY—READ LUKE 22:39-46.

I pray. I pray because I am supposed to. I'm the teacher, the leader, the pray-er. It's part of my job, but is it part of *me*?

Trying to make it easy, I tell the children, "Let's talk to God." Reminding them that Jesus is our friend, I say that we can talk to him anytime. Sometimes I'm spontaneous when praying with adults, but oftentimes I plug into the formula of ACTS: Adoration, Confession, Thanksgiving, and Supplication. This is a good place to start and a good pattern to follow, because we are human and our prayers can become one-sided. So, my mouth forms the words, and God hears.

My students teach me a lot about prayer. Their words are simple. Their tone is natural. Their meaning is sincere.

When Jesus prayed to his father, he was honest in sharing his true self. He offered Thanks and praise. He cried out in desperation. He spoke out of the depths of his soul. I need to pray like that.

"Prayer is then not just a formula of words or a series of desires springing up in the heart—it is the orientation of our whole body, mind and spirit to God in silence, attention and adoration" (Thomas Merton, *Thoughts in Solitude* [Boston: Shambhala Publications, 1986], p. 44).

Lord, teach me to pray, to call on you about all things and in all things. Amen.

APRIL 11

LORD, TEACH ME HOW TO HUMBLE MYSELF— READ JOHN 13:1-17.

"Humble yourself in the sight of the Lord, and he will lift you up." I learned this verse as a chorus based on James 4:10.

Jesus, creator of the universe, humbled himself first by coming into this world as a baby, born in a lowly manger. This life of humility continued as Jesus lived a simple life among the people, demonstrating God's love for everyone. It continued in the final days of his life and completed itself in this: "He humbled himself and became obedient to death—even death on a cross!" (Philippians 2:8).

Jesus showed great love for his friends when he took on the role of a servant and washed their feet. We too are called to humble ourselves and take on the role of a servant. As teachers, sometimes this means wiping a nose, tying a shoe, or hugging a smelly body. It also can mean saying, "I'm sorry. I was wrong. Can you forgive me?" It might involve washing dishes, sweeping the floor, or taking out the trash. It may reveal itself in giving a drink of water, clothing the naked, welcoming a stranger, visiting those in prison, or sharing a hot meal.

How can you be a servant today?

Lord, teach me how to humble myself and be obedient to you by serving others, no matter what it may involve. Amen.

APRIL 12
LORD, TEACH ME HOW TO REMEMBER—
READ LUKE 22:7-20.

We have seen the artists' renderings of the Last Supper. Some churches reenact the meal and the conversations around the table. Even though Jesus had prepared the apostles for the events to come, it must have seemed so unreal at the time.

My view of Holy Communion has been transformed over the years as I have received the elements in different ways, with different people, and in different circumstances. As we approach the table, we do so with reverence and thankful hearts. It is always an event that requires much thought and reflection. We remember Jesus' body was broken and his blood was shed for you and me. We receive the elements with grateful hearts, and we celebrate God's grace and forgiveness.

213

We may be using the formal ritual of the church to recite the liturgy or using our common everyday language. We may be taking thin wafers with wine or homemade bread broken and dipped in grape juice. We might receive the elements in unison in the pew or alone at the altar. It could be in a small group fellowship or a large crowd gathering. Each time is unique and special.

Take some time to think back and recall moments you've had at the Lord's table. Remember and be thankful that you have a place at the table.

Lord, teach me how to remember and be thankful, especially at your table. Amen.

APRIL 13
LORD, TEACH ME HOW TO FORGIVE— READ LUKE 23:32-34.

"For it is in pardoning that we are pardoned."
—St. Francis of Assisi

They stood staring each other down, each one waiting for the other one to say, "I'm sorry." I watched them and wondered why it was taking so long for them to say these simple words, and yet there are times when I find myself not wanting to say them. Instead, I choose to wait it out, allowing my heart and mind to stew. I determine to wait until the other person says it first, or I continue to recall the event in my mind over and over again.

Aren't you glad God is not that way? He made the first step in restoring us to himself. God didn't wait for you and me to say "I'm sorry" first. No, forgiveness was granted even before we understood how desperately we needed it. "But God demonstrats his own love for us in this: While we were still sinners, Christ died for us" (Romans 5:8). Even while hanging on the cross, Christ said, "Father, forgive them, for they know not what they are doing" (Luke 23:34).

214

Our minds need to know forgiveness, our hearts need to feel forgiveness, our souls need to receive forgiveness, and our mouths needs to speak forgiveness.

Lord, teach me how to receive your forgiveness and extend that forgiveness to others. Amen.

APRIL 14

LORD, TEACH ME HOW TO DIE—READ LUKE 23:44-49.

"For it is in dying that we are born to eternal life."—
St. Francis of Assisi

Death is never easy. It never comes at a good time. We try to prepare for it, but it always comes unexpectedly. There are many different kinds of deaths we face while on this Earth. The end of a relationship can feel like a death. Leaving a career can be like a death. Moving to a new place can seem like a death. Then there are the actual physical deaths of family and friends. Each one hurts. Each one grieves the heart. Each one overwhelms the spirit.

Jesus died on a cross for you and for me. This death had to take place for our redemption to be complete. And our old nature must die as well. Paul tells us in his letter to the Colossians to "put to death . . . whatever belongs to your earthly nature"—in other words, our fleshly desires (Colossians 3:5). So as we reflect on the death of Jesus, let us take time to consider what needs to be "put to death" in our lives. It could be a habit or an attitude; it might be an unforgiving spirit or an unloving heart. It might be a friendship with the world or an old lifestyle. Whatever it is, Jesus died on the cross so that you and I might be born again and become new creatures in Christ.

Lord, teach me how to die—how to put to death the old life, the old nature, and put on the new. Amen.

APRIL 15

LORD, TEACH ME HOW TO WAIT—READ PSALM 27:14.

We do not like to wait. We want everything from our food to our faith in a moment. It is hard for us to wait.

We wait in line; we wait in traffic; we wait for the computer, the doctor, the phone list of options—we wait.

We wait for students to learn, teenagers to mature, children to listen, adults to understand—we wait.

We wait for the healing to happen, the relationship to be restored, the wrong to be made right, the fear to turn to faith—we wait.

Try to imagine what it must have been like for the followers of Jesus. They did not know the outcome of his death. They did not know that he would rise again three days later. They did not know that the wait would end.

It is hard to wait. Yet this scripture tells us that we are to wait for the Lord. It doesn't say we are to wait for ourselves or for other people; it says we are to wait for the Lord. We can trust the outcome to him. We may have to wait a long time, but remember: We are waiting for the Lord.

Lord, teach me how to wait on you in every area of my life. Amen.

APRIL 16

LORD, TEACH ME HOW TO LIVE—READ LUKE 24:36-49.

We had gathered on that first day of the week. We were outside, and it was still dark. We stood huddled together (Easter in Virginia can be very chilly). We were on a hill in a cemetery, a place of death, of sorrow. We had been to this place before and had laid our friends and family to rest there. We had come on that Easter Sunday. We began to sing some of the favorite hymns of the faith, of the Resurrection: "Because he lives, I can face tomorrow." And the sun rose again on that Easter morning.

The miracles of nature remind us of the resurrection of Jesus. Spring flowers remind us that life springs from the dead and buried bulb. The caterpillar spins its chrysalis, and there is a long period of stillness until, one day, a beautiful butterfly emerges. These images remind us of the message of resurrection.

Only after we die to our sins and the old nature can the new life come forth. That is the message of the Resurrection and the message of God's grace. The tomb is empty. Death has been defeated. The victory is won. It is a message to celebrate every day of the year.

Lord, teach me how to live, because I know you hold the future. Amen.

APRIL 17
LORD, TEACH ME HOW TO WRITE, PART 1—
READ JOHN 8:1–11.

There are many opinions about what Jesus wrote in the sand. Whatever it was, it must have had some influence because of the outcome.

As teachers, we write—a lot. From good morning messages to assignments, notes on papers, notes for parents, monthly newsletters, and personal correspondence, we write. It takes time to write, but it is worth the effort.

One day a young lady from my youth group told me how much a card I had sent meant to her. In it I had included a Bible verse for her to look up. She told me that ever since that note, she also included a Bible verse in her cards.

Think about the influence of written words in your life. Do you have a "rainy day" file, a place where you have collected notes from students or other people in your life? Whenever I have had a difficult day, I pull out that file. In it I find a card of thanks, a note of encouragement, a crayon-colored picture, or just a scribbled message that brightens my day.

You and I may never know the impact of our written words.

Lord, teach me how to write. Help me find the time to write that note of encouragement or thanks. Amen.

APRIL 18
LORD, TEACH ME HOW TO WRITE, PART 2—
READ 2 TIMOTHY 3:16.

As teachers, we understand the power of the written word. For centuries, reading and writing were reserved for only the most educated or the wealthiest. Today it is a privilege that we sometimes take for granted.

In our classrooms, we expend a lot of energy improving our students' reading and writing abilities. They are important skills that need to be developed. We introduce the concept of journal writing at a young age. Students devote time to writing about various subjects. But what happens to our reading and writing as we get older? We may focus on our writing when we have a lesson to prepare or when we are taking a class, but what about in our personal lives?

I have kept journals off and on throughout my life. It is not a well-developed skill for me. Nevertheless, it has helped me in my study of Scripture and in examining my Christian life. Writing about my faith helps me develop my understanding, and it requires discipline. God's Word is a gift that is new every morning, and it speaks when I take the time to read and reflect and respond to it. Journal writing is one way to trace my thoughts and record my growth.

Lord, teach me how to write and reflect on what you are teaching me through your Word and through all the ways you speak to me and direct my life. Amen.

APRIL 19
LORD, TEACH ME HOW TO LAUGH, PART 1—
READ JOHN 10:10; 15:11.

Have you seen pictures of Jesus smiling or laughing? I grew up with images of Jesus looking rather serious, having his face buried in his hands, or suffering on the cross. While these are important to the life of Jesus, I am pleased that there are now illustrations of Jesus smiling and laughing. Scripture shows us that Jesus' life was also one of joy. In fact, he came to bring us joy.

As teachers, we have so much to do that sometimes we fail to let go and laugh. Recently I went through a stressful situation in my life. Looking back, I realize that I was out of balance. I spent most of my time working and being anxious over my job, and there was little time left for joy. Unfortunately, often we do not realize when we are living this way.

So, think for a moment: When was the last time you *really* laughed? Take a minute and listen to the laughter of your students; and then give yourself permission to laugh with them. Their laughter is contagious. It is a beautiful sound. Join in on the laughter. There is a time to work, but there should also be a time to be joyful and laugh.

Lord, teach me how to laugh and let your joy fill my life. Amen.

APRIL 20
LORD, TEACH ME HOW TO LAUGH, PART 2—
READ ECCLESIASTES 3:4; MATTHEW 19:13-15.

We laughed in church today. The young and old, the rich and poor—we laughed together. It was a beautiful sound. We laughed in class today—boys and girls from many different nationalities. It was a beautiful sound. There is a time to laugh.

Children know when someone loves them, and they want to be with that person. I cherish the story of Jesus with the children. The children loved Jesus and wanted to be near him. I can picture Jesus laughing with the children. There is a time to laugh.

Sometimes in our churches and in our classrooms we expect children to be serious all the time, instead of allowing them to be children. We need to teach them that laughter is okay too—not at the expense of others but just for the sake of laughter. There is a time to laugh.

I'm sure Jesus laughed many times with his disciples. Similarly, I want to be able to laugh and enjoy life with my students. I want to allow them to laugh and be filled with joy. I want them to know that I love them and want to be with them. They *need* to laugh. Many times their world is filled with pain, suffering, anger, or fear. There is a time to laugh.

Lord, teach me how to laugh and to spread joy to your children. Amen.

APRIL 21
LORD, TEACH ME HOW TO CRY, PART 1—
READ JOHN 11:33-35.

His mother had fought breast cancer for several years but finally lost the battle. I cried when I saw him and hugged him.

She had a fight with her parents and called me in tears. My eyes welled up with tears, which spilled over as I listened.

We watched the events of 9/11. Later, as we gathered at a candlelight vigil, the emotions flowed.

Many times as teachers we try to keep our composure. We want to be in control in the midst of difficult situations that face our students. But there are times when it is okay to cry with them. When we do, we are teaching them that tears are part of the process of grieving, of repenting, of feeling, of loving. We are showing them that Jesus is with us in our pain.

Jesus knew that Lazarus would live again, yet he allowed himself to be "deeply moved" and to weep. Jesus experienced every emotion we do. "For we do not have a high priest who is unable to sympathize with our weaknesses. . . . Let us then approach the throne of grace with confidence, so that we may receive mercy and find grace to help us in our time of need" (Hebrews 4:15-16).

Lord, teach me how to cry, knowing that you cry with me and with those I cry with, as well. Amen.

APRIL 22
LORD, TEACH ME HOW TO CRY, PART 2—
READ LUKE 19:41.

Jesus wept over Jerusalem.

There is a lady in my Sunday school class who is a public school teacher and has a heart for children. She prays for them every week. I admire her passion. There are times when I let myself weep over the children.

I weep over their broken homes and the nights they cry themselves to sleep. I weep over the angry words spoken to them and by them. I weep over physical acts of violence and neglect. I weep over diseases that take over their bodies, bringing pain and suffering and zapping their very lives. I weep over their lack of education, medical care, food, and clothing—things I have always had. I weep over wars that ravage their countries and fighting that displaces them from their homes. I weep over natural disasters that destroy their families' way of living and fill them with fear and uncertainty about the future. I weep over the way they are being raised, because many have no knowledge of Christ or his love for them. I weep over those who have been taught distorted ideas of God and Jesus. I weep over their feelings of depression and hopelessness. I weep over _____ (you fill in the blank). I weep over the children—your children, our children.

Lord, teach me how to cry over your children throughout the world, and show me where I can help ease the pain and suffering. Amen.

APRIL 23
LORD, TEACH ME HOW TO THINK, PART 1—
READ PHILIPPIANS 4:8.

This scripture gives quite a list. Oftentimes it stands in direct opposition to what we see on the big screen and the little screen, what we hear over the airwaves, and what we read from the printed page.

The world says white lies are okay. God's Word says, "Whatever is true. . . ." The world says offensive language is acceptable. God's Word says, "Whatever is noble. . . ." The world says cheating is part of life—just don't get caught. God's Word says, "Whatever is right. . . ." The world says impure thoughts are going to fill your mind. God's Word says, "Whatever is pure. . . ." The world displays disgusting ways of treating others. God's Word says, "Whatever is lovely. . . ." The world endorses acting mean. God's Word says, "Whatever is admirable. . . ." The world says get by doing as little as possible. God's Word says, "Whatever is excellent. . . ." The world says make yourself look good in the eyes of others. God's Word says, "Whatever is praiseworthy. . . ."

"As [one] thinketh in his heart, so is he" (Proverbs 23:7 KJV). We need to guard our thinking because our thoughts will express themselves in one way or another. We can think, say, or do either according to the world or according to God's Word.

Lord, teach me how to think, not as the world but according to your Word. Amen.

APRIL 24
LORD, TEACH ME TO THINK, PART 2—
READ MATTHEW 7:24-27.

Maybe you grew up singing the children's song about the wise man and the foolish man. As a child, I didn't understand the depth of meaning of this parable Jesus told, but I had fun singing the song—complete with hand motions. I remember it to this day, though now there is more meaning attached.

My state of Florida experienced four hurricanes in the summer of 2004. For me, this parable took on added significance at that time. I was privileged to help with disaster relief after the first storm, and I saw firsthand the devastation brought on by the wind and the rain. I saw homes that fell with a great crash, and I saw homes that stood firm. It was an object lesson I will never forget.

Jesus says that whoever "hears these words of mine and puts them into practice is like a wise man who built his house on the rock. "I want to think like the wise man, the way God wants, and thus build my life on the rock, as opposed to thinking like the foolish man, the world, and build my life on shifting sand.

Lord, teach me to think as the wise man and thus build my life on you. Amen.

APRIL 25
LORD, TEACH ME HOW TO "WALK," PART 1—
READ 1 JOHN 1:6-7.

What is your testimony? How did you come to follow Jesus and walk in the light? How does your pilgrimage continue today? Do you remember when you first heard the words of Christ: "Come, follow me"? The call continues. Step by step, he leads us. It is a daily journey, not a one-time event. It is a lifelong marathon, not a single race.

Our children and youth need to see and hear our testimonies of faith—of what it means to walk in the light and follow Jesus every day. As we are living, eating, sleeping, working, driving, playing, competing, or whatever we are doing, we should do it as unto the Lord.

There used to be a T-shirt with this message: "You can't talk the talk if you don't walk the walk." As a teacher, I have always tried to be careful of my actions, my dress, and my conversations because I know little eyes are watching me and little ears are listening. Children and youth are very good at noticing hypocrisy. They know when we are being sincere and when we are faking it. Scripture warns us against doing anything that would cause one of these little ones to stumble.

Lord, teach me to always walk in the light—for my sake and for the sake of those watching. Amen.

APRIL 26
LORD, TEACH ME HOW TO "WALK," PART 2—
READ JOHN 8:12.

We walked together, side by side. We talked about a lot of things: school, friends, parents, God. Today, many years later, we walk together again, side by side. She is married now and finishing graduate school. We talk about school, friends, parents, her husband, God. What a privilege it has been to walk with this young woman, to be part of her journey of faith.

Albert Camus said, "Don't walk behind me; I may not lead. Don't walk in front of me; I may not follow. Just walk beside me and be my friend" (www.quoteland.com/search.asp).

I believe we need to find a way to join others on their walk of faith. We should seek a common connection point and first be a friend. When we start there, sometimes we will see them follow us as we follow God. We cannot push, and we must not drag them along the way. After they spend time following, we must give them an opportunity to lead. It requires patience, prayer, and perseverance.

What a blessing to join others on this walk of faith with our God. Along the way, we walk beside in friendship, we walk ahead in leadership, and we walk behind in companionship.

Lord, teach me how to walk beside, before, and behind your children as you lead me. Amen.

APRIL 27
LORD, TEACH ME HOW TO LOVE, PART 1—
READ MARK 10:13-16.

We tell them the golden rule: "Do unto others as you would have them to do unto you." We teach them the greatest commandments. But do we live these things before them?

As I often told my youth-worker volunteers, not every young person is going to like you and me; but we can hope that every young person will connect with at least one significant adult. In our classrooms, not every student is going to like us, but we have to find a way to love each of them. We cannot do it in our own strength; we can do it only in God's love.

I picture the disciples standing with their arms crossed as they tried to keep the children away from Jesus. It angers me to think that they would do that, but I am afraid I do it too at times. I do it when I avoid eye contact with a child or pretend I don't hear a child or breathe a sigh of relief when a child is absent. Forgive me, dear God.

Mother Teresa said, "Are we not by definition, messengers of love?" (*Mother Teresa: In My Own Words*, p. 38). Jesus always welcomes children. Jesus always welcomes me.

"Tell the children I love them."—God

Lord, teach me how to love by welcoming the children with open arms. Amen.

APRIL 28
LORD, TEACH ME HOW TO LOVE, PART 2— READ JOHN 3:16.

Many of us memorized this verse at a very early age. It is one we can recall without much difficulty, but at what point do we understand its meaning?

Before we can pray, "Lord, teach me how to love," we have to experience that love for ourselves, personally. Place your name in the blank. "For God so loved _____ that he gave his only begotten Son, that if _____ believes in him, _____ should not perish but have everlasting life."

Think about a time when this verse came to life for you personally. I had the privilege of going to Chile on a missions trip. While on this trip, John 3:16 became so real to me. Hearing our Spanish-speaking brothers and sisters worshiping our Lord in song, crying out to him in prayer, and sharing the promises in God's Word, I realized the meaning of this verse. God so loved me. God so loved the people of Chile. God so loved the world. Wow, what a beautiful picture of the character of God and the depth and breadth of God's love.

The next time I have a hard time loving someone, I will put the person's name in "the blanks" of John 3:16.

Lord, teach me how to love by understanding the enormity of your love for me and for others. Amen.

APRIL 29
LORD, TEACH ME HOW TO TRUST, PART 1—
READ JOHN 6:1-14.

This is one of my favorite Bible stories. It has been dramatized in Sunday school and vacation Bible school, and even in our daily lives. I sum it up this way: Trust God with all you have, and God will provide.

It is an overwhelming dilemma. There is a crowd of hungry people and no money to buy food. You and I face similar situations. Maybe the cupboard is getting bare, the bank account is running low, the job is ending, or the relationship is fading. Perhaps your patience is ending, no ideas are coming, or your energy is waning. We can add an entire list to these desperate situations.

Then a boy appears with his "lunch bag." The disciples ask, "How far will that go?" The story continues. After Jesus gives thanks and all have had enough (I love that part), they collect the leftovers. Wow! What a miraculous sign! Groceries last through the month, a check arrives, a job opening appears, a relationship is restored, patience endures, ideas develop, energy is renewed.

Whatever you and I have, when we give thanks and commit it to God, it is more than enough.

Lord, teach me how to trust you with all that I have and all that I am, knowing that it will be enough. Amen.

APRIL 30
LORD, TEACH ME HOW TO TRUST, PART 2—
READ PROVERBS 3:5-6.

These are my life verses. I hid them in my heart at an early age and continue to come back to them. Their words provide reassurance and hope.

How do these verses apply to you, and how has the promise been fulfilled? From life-changing decisions to the smallest details, we are called to trust God, taking steps of faith.

Here are some memorable steps of faith from the Bible:
- The children of Israel placed their feet in the riverbed as God held back the waters.
- The disciples placed their nets on the other side of the boat after a long night of catching no fish.
- The man who was paralyzed picked up his mat and walked, praising God.

I recall some of my own steps of faith:
- I decided to go on a mission trip and trusted God to provide the money.
- I moved to a new town without a job and found one at just the right time.
- I changed careers and believed God would continue to meet my needs.

Relive *your* steps of faith and remember how God has directed your paths. Share them with those you teach, and encourage them to practice trusting God in their own lives.

"Trust the past to the mercy of God, the present to his love, and the future to his providence."—St. Augustine

Lord, teach me how to trust you, to continue to claim your promises for my life. Amen.

MAY
Remembering

Cindy M. Bradley

MAY 1

PRECIOUS REMINDERS—READ 2 PETER 1:2-11.

I WEAR THREE RINGS. ONE IS MY BIRTHSTONE. IT REMINDS ME OF my parents and their love for me. The second is heart-shaped and was given to me by a group of tenth-grade girls in the first Sunday school class I taught many years ago. The third is a diamond. My grandfather gave it to my grandmother on their fiftieth anniversary when they renewed their vows. Each holds unique memories of special people.

In my home I have treasured mementos that remind me of incredible times, places, and people. I also have keepsakes that prompt me to remember "whose" I am. I belong to God. I am a follower of Jesus. The Holy Spirit lives in me.

A cross says, "As for me and my house, we will serve the Lord." Praying hands symbolize the importance of this act. A picture of Jesus holding a lamb shows me who is my Shepherd and reminds me that I am his sheep. The books on my bookshelf explore topics on the Bible and how to live out my faith in the world. My cross necklace is a constant reminder that Jesus died for me.

This month we will be considering and celebrating precious reminders of the faith—reminders of who and whose we are, and of what we are called to be and do.

Lord, help me to remember to celebrate all you have done in and through my life. Amen.

MAY 2
REMEMBERING TO REST—READ EXODUS 20:8-11.

The calendar says May. Where has the year gone? The clock says 3:00 P.M. Where has the day gone? There is a rhythm to life. There is ebb and flow—a time to work and a time to rest. God built this into creation. There is a season when everything rests and waits.

We need to practice this in our lives too. Every *year* we should find some time to stop and rest and wait. Every *week* the sabbath is there for us to stop and rest and wait. Every *day* we need to take a moment to do the same.

We are busy, you and I. We are pressured by the demands of administration and paperwork. We are overwhelmed by the voices of students, families, and friends. We are kept awake at night by thoughts of problems, plans, and procedures. The busyness never seems to stop for us. *We* have to stop for us. Our students need our help in building rest into their schedules as well. It is important to provide them an example of what that rest looks like.

Remember to stop and rest and wait in the middle of each day. Remember the sabbath day each week. Remember to set aside a couple of retreat days each year to stop and rest and wait. Our bodies, minds, hearts, and souls need it.

Lord, help me remember to rest in order to be and do my best. Amen.

MAY 3
REMEMBERING GOD'S WONDERS—
READ 1 CHRONICLES 16:12.

At the end of last year, I heard a message about "remembering stones." After the nation of Israel crossed the Jordan, Joshua told the leaders of each tribe to pick up a stone from the middle of the river and place it in their camp. These stones were to be a memorial to the people (Joshua 4:1-9). Just like the children of Israel needed to remember this awesome miracle, we need to remember the wonders of God in our lives.

What remembering stones will you place as a sign of God's miracles in your life for others to see? What wonders has God done in the lives of your students?

Perhaps you were there when a young person reached out to Jesus in a prayer of salvation. After what seemed to be an eternity, a student understood a difficult concept you have been teaching. It could have been when parents finally showed up for a child's performance or a sporting event.

Miracles, wonders of God, happen. At the time they are important, but sometimes they fade into the background of our memories. This year I am making a conscious effort to write down these "stones" to remember them as signs of God's faithfulness. And when the doubting comes, I will point to these stones, these wonders of God, and my faith will be renewed.

Lord, help me to remember the wonders you have done in my life and in the lives of others. Amen.

MAY 4
REMEMBERING OUR CREATOR—
READ ECCLESIASTES 12:1.

Psalm 139:14a proclaims, "I am fearfully and wonderfully made" (NRSV). When the children come to school in the fall, I ask them to draw a self-portrait. It's fun to see how they picture themselves. Though we tend to focus on the outside, we need to remember that God is working on the inside as well.

Sometimes when I look in the mirror, I forget my Creator. Instead, I complain about certain features and worry about others. But what about the inside? How much time do I devote to that created part of me?

If I am honest, I occasionally do the same with my students. I forget their Creator. There are days when I see only the outside and don't take the time to do the hard work on the inside. Whether we are having a good day or a bad day, we are to remember our Creator.

Praise God—he is not finished with me yet! The Creator of the universe made me, formed me, breathed into me, and wants to continue creating in me and through me. My Creator is able to create in me a clean heart and a right spirit, to renew my strength, and to purify my thoughts. I need that when I look in the mirror. I need that when I look at my students.

Creator Lord, help me to remember that you created me and my students, and that we are wonderfully made. Amen.

MAY 5
REMEMBERING WE ARE FORGIVEN—
READ PSALM 103:12.

Our memory is amazing. The mind holds so much information, and we can recall facts, figures, people, places, and other information fairly easily. But sometimes I remember things I don't want to remember and forget things I do want to remember. Like the time I . . . or when I said. . . . You fill in the blanks. Those images flash back into my mind just when I want to forget. Satan tries to bring up past mistakes and convince me that I cannot overcome those problems or be forgiven of those sins. That is when I need to reread this promise from Scripture that says God will remember our sins no more.

I need this promise from God for myself, and I need to practice it with others. Children are much better at forgetting than we adults are. One minute they are arguing and deciding not to be friends; the next minute all is forgotten and the friendship is restored.

Sometimes I recall what others have done to me and choose not to forget; in doing so, I also choose not to forgive. At those times I must pray for forgiveness, asking God to remember my sins no more. Then my forgiving God can help me to extend that forgiveness to others. Even now I pray. . . .

Lord, thank you for remembering my sins no more. Just as you forgive me for _____, I forgive _____ for _____ (fill in the blanks). Amen.

May 6

Remembering the Poor—Read Galatians 2:10.

Most of my ministry as a teacher has been to those of the middle and upper-middle class. These children and youth have always had food on the table, clothes on their backs, a roof over their heads, and money in their pockets. Together we have had some good experiences of sharing with the poor. After we do, we are a little more helpful, a little less complaining, and a lot more thankful.

I currently minister at a school where most of the students are on free or reduced lunch program. I am also involved in a food distribution ministry to migrant families. Both are meaningful to me. I am fortunate in that my family has always had enough, and even more than enough, to meet our needs. I need to remember the poor.

It must be difficult if you are uncertain of your job future, of when your next meal is coming, or of where you will sleep for the night. I cannot imagine what that must be like for children and families. But poverty takes on many forms. Mother Teresa once said, "It is possible that our children, our husband, our wife, do not hunger for bread, do not need clothes, do not need a house. But are we equally sure that none of them feels alone, abandoned, neglected, needing some affection?" (Jose Luis Gonzalez-Balado, *Mother Teresa: In My Own Words*, [New York: Random House, 1996], p. 27)

Lord, help me to remember those around me each day who are poor in body, mind, or spirit. Amen.

May 7

Remembering the Covenant—Read Genesis 9:12-16.

Rainbows have always fascinated me. Their appearance surprises me every time. I keep my eyes on the sky after the storm clouds form, but I never can predict where or when one may develop. Suddenly against the backdrop of darkness the vibrant colors brighten the sky. Each time I see one, I remember that it is a sign of God's covenant with his people.

I need to be reminded of God's covenant. It extends from generation to generation. I love that part because it means God's covenant encompasses me! And I have an opportunity to extend that promise to others.

I do not have any biological children of my own. Instead I have been blessed to be a part of the covenant in the lives of several young ladies. The first young woman was part of a small-group ministry to middle-school girls. The second was a born leader in her youth group and church, of which I served on staff after I completed seminary. The third and fourth currently attend college. Each of these young women of faith is an example of God's covenant to the next generation. Their lives, which are as different as the colors of a rainbow, remind me that God's promises continue.

How have you seen God's covenant at work in the lives of your students?

Lord, thank you for rainbows, one of many reminders of your covenant from generation to generation. Amen.

MAY 8
REMEMBERING THOSE WHO HAVE INFLUENCED OUR FAITH—READ PHILIPPIANS 1:1-11.

Several years ago I started a list of people who have influenced my faith journey. Throughout my life many have crossed my path, and I am grateful to God for their encouragement and example.

Included on my list are Sunday school teachers, youth leaders, and pastors. Most are people I met in school, in youth group, and at work. Some I still keep in touch with; several are now with our Lord. Others I have lost track of, but the memories linger. Some are up in years; others are like parents to me. Some are my age, and a few are a lot younger.

What do I remember? I remember Bible studies, prayer meetings, and worship services. I remember hard work, laughter, road trips, and tears. I remember campfires and commitments, retreat weekends, and responses. There have been potlucks, car washes, puppet skits, and face painting. I remember living rooms, outdoor chapels, seashores, kitchen tables, backyards, mountainsides, kneeling rails, and dorm rooms. There have been bus tours, van excursions, carpools, airplane trips, neighborhood walks, and boat rides. I remember nursing homes and hospitals, rooftops and front porches.

It is good to remember. It is good to give thanks to the Lord for those who have influenced my faith. Yes, I remember; and I am thankful for their partnership with me on this journey of faith.

Lord, thank you for my brothers and sisters in the faith who have made an impact on my life. Amen.

MAY 9

REMEMBERING THE LIGHT, PART I—READ GENESIS 1:1-19.

Since I am a morning person, I enjoy starting my day with a walk. As the sky begins to brighten, I watch as the light gradually appears and the colors change to fill the space. Every morning there is a different breathtaking scene to take in—another of the Creator's masterpieces as the new day begins. It is one of my favorite times of day.

The evening scene is no less spectacular as once again the vibrant colors splash across the sky. The final streaks of sunshine disappear, and the light fades into the night. It is my other favorite time of day.

I have always enjoyed gazing up at the sky, watching the sunlight and the clouds of the day and then the moonlight and the stars of the night. Whenever there is a storm and darkness covers the sky, I look forward to the streaks of sunlight finding their way through the clouds. It is such a breathtaking sight.

On retreat weekends, I take pleasure from the outdoor services in the early morning light and the evening hours spent around the campfire. In worship services, I relish the lighting of the candles as they flicker and shine on the altar.

Light: We can't live without it. The Light of the World: We can't live without him.

Lord, thank you for creating light and for shining your Light into our lives. Amen.

MAY 10
REMEMBERING THE LIGHT, PART 2—
READ PSALM 27.

This is a favorite psalm of mine. I especially like the first verse. My name, Cindy, means "bearer of light." I pray that I live up to its meaning because our world needs the light to shine in the darkness.

I ask the children to answer this question by raising their hands: "Who is afraid of the dark?" A couple of them do, but most won't admit it. The darkness is scary. It's one thing to stumble around in the dark in your own room; it's quite another to do so in an unfamiliar place.

When the light shines in the darkness, you have more confidence to take a step. We need the Light of Christ to shine on the darkness in our lives. As the light shines, we have courage to move ahead.

The darkness may represent the sin in our lives, the places where we have chosen to disobey God. *Light of Christ, shine on me.*

The darkness may be the uncertainty of a decision we need to make. *Light of Christ, shine on me.*

The darkness might be a fear that we need to overcome. *Light of Christ, shine on me.*

The darkness could be a mistake that we can't forget. *Light of Christ, shine on me.*

Whatever the darkness, remember the Light.

Lord, thank you for being my light and my salvation, taking away my fear. Amen.

MAY 11
REMEMBERING THE LIGHT OF GOD'S WORD—
READ PSALM 119:105.

When I was younger, Communism was a threat. We were encouraged to learn Bible verses because one day we might not have access to a Bible and would need to rely upon those scriptures we had memorized. Many of those passages I can still recall. I am so thankful that I hid them deep in my heart because they are a source of encouragement and wisdom today.

Every year when our church gives Bibles to our third-graders, I get excited. Because I have always had a Bible nearby, I sometimes forget what it is like for young children learning to find books and verses. It is such a privilege to own a Bible and to have the opportunity to read and study it whenever I want to.

One day a young person asked me, "How do you know where those verses are that you share with us?" Part of it stems from my familiarity with certain passages and books of the Bible, yet I wish I knew more verses by heart.

It's hard to picture ourselves living without access to a Bible or trying to worship in secret. We can talk about this with our children and pray for our brothers and sisters around the world who are suffering for their faith.

Forgive me, Lord, for taking your Word for granted. It is a lamp unto my feet and a light unto my path. Amen.

MAY 12
REMEMBERING TO SHINE THE LIGHT—
READ MATTHEW 5:16.

We sang the chorus together, complete with hand motions. *"This little light of mine, I'm gonna let it shine. . . . Hide it under a bushel, NO! . . . Shine all over (name of town). . . . Don't let Satan blow it out. . . ."* It is fun to watch the children sing this song, but let us not miss its meaning.

My light is important; yours is, too. We can help children and youth and adults understand the importance of shining the light of Christ within them. How? It happens when we shine the light of truth into the darkness of dishonesty. It happens when we shine the light of faith into the dark places of doubt. It happens when we shine the light of love into the bleakness of hatred. It happens when we shine the light of caring into the sea of skepticism.

We sat in the dark in a circle. It was the last night of our mission trip. We laughed about occasional blackouts, which also meant no fans or running water. One by one, each person turned on his or her flashlight, and the lights shined in the darkness.

When you and I shine the light of Christ, we encourage others to shine; and together we brighten the dark places in our lives and in our world.

Lord, give me the courage to shine your light into every corner of this dark world. Amen.

MAY 13
REMEMBERING TO REFLECT THE LIGHT—
READ 2 CORINTHIANS 3:16-18.

His eyes squinted, jaws clenched, lips pressed together as we stared face to face. It was definitely a confrontation. As I looked at this five-year-old before me, my first thought was, *I'm the teacher and you are going to do as I say.* Suddenly I wondered, *What is my face saying to this young boy—one of God's creations, a son, a child, my responsibility at this moment?* I prayed for wisdom, smiled, and tried to look more pleasant. Not surprisingly, his features gradually relaxed a little too. We still had an issue to resolve, but I think the changes in my demeanor helped the situation.

There is a children's song that says, *"When you're happy and you know it, then your face will surely show it."* We have all been in the presence of a person who loves God so much that his or her face brightens the room. It is a beautiful thing.

Did you know that it takes more muscles to frown than it does to smile? A smile can turn a heated argument into a friendly discussion. A smile and hug can make a booboo bearable. A smile and a wave can turn someone's boring chore into a pleasant experience. A smile can turn a frown upside down.

Lord, help me to remember to reflect your glory, your light, as I interact with others today. Amen.

MAY 14

REMEMBERING OUR MOTHERS—READ EXODUS 20:12.

Each year on Mother's Day, I invite the children to bring their moms—or someone who is like a mom—forward for the children's message. We talk about moms and the special place they have in our hearts.

After talking about moms, we hand out different "gloves" to the children to symbolize some of the many things moms do for us: a kitchen mitt for cooking; rubber gloves for cleaning; a garden glove for helping us to grow; a driving glove for taxi service; a baseball glove for playing games with us. The children enjoy wearing the gloves and talking about all the things moms do. We close our time together by giving mom a hand and praying a blessing over her.

My biological mom has always been a blessing; she is a strong Christian who prays for me and encourages me in every area of my life. (I am blessed with a godly father, as well.) I am also thankful for those who have been my adopted "moms" when I was living far away from my own mom. They too have supported and cared for me.

Though I do not have any biological children, I have "adopted" many children along the way in church and school. What a privilege it is to have a mom and to be a mom, sharing God's love.

Lord, thank you for a special day to remember moms. Bless my own mom and/or others who have been like a mom to me. Amen.

MAY 15

REMEMBERING TO LOVE—READ JOHN 13:34-35.

One of my favorite choruses from youth group was *"They'll Know We Are Christians by Our Love."* I never attended summer camp when I was a child or youth, but my last summer in college I worked at a retreat center. It was a great experience. Ever since that time, I have served as a camp counselor or children's camp leader most summers. Some of the reasons I like camp include being outdoors, enjoying nature, and getting away. It is amazing to watch a group of people who are strangers on the first day turn into best buddies by the last day. I believe it is because of God's love. After a week of eating, sleeping (very little), running, sharing, laughing, crying, playing, competing, singing, jumping, and kneeling together, you feel part of something bigger. You once called each other stranger; now you call each other brother and sister.

It has happened to me as an adult, too, during various weekend or weeklong retreats or camps. It happened for me again in August 2004 as we joined together from across the country to do hurricane disaster relief work. We were strangers one day, friends the next. And the people knew "we were Christians by our love."

Lord, help me remember to bear love so they'll know we love you. Amen.

MAY 16

REMEMBERING TO BE JOYFUL—READ PSALM 16:7-11.

"I've got the joy, joy, joy, joy down in my heart. . . . Where? . . . . Down in my heart to stay. . . ."

I grew up singing that song in Sunday school. Now years later, I sing it again as I lead vacation Bible school. We sing it with excitement as our voices fill the room.

I love vacation Bible school. Even though it is tiring and even though it is hard finding volunteers, the effort is worth it. We held VBS in the evenings, beginning with a family meal and ending with a closing time together. What a blessing to have our youth, men, and senior adults serving our children this special week.

One evening a thunderstorm threatened to put a damper on our joy. Over halfway through the evening, lightning flashed, thunder boomed, rain poured, and lights flickered. It was time to go to the fellowship hall for our closing. The children would have to walk into the rain to get from one building to the next. We came around the corner, prepared to get wet, and we saw the men of our church holding a tarp so that we would be protected. When we entered the fellowship hall, others were standing there, clapping and cheering us on! What a beautiful picture of the church looking out for one another, caring for and protecting our children, cheering them on in the faith. My heart overflowed with joy!

Lord, thank you for joy that is down in my heart; let it overflow today. Amen.

MAY 17
REMEMBERING TO BRING PEACE— READ COLOSSIANS 3:15-17.

Most days people come in and out of my life, and things go fairly smoothly. Today is different. My heart and mind are heavy. It has happened before. There was the day I learned a friend's mother had died; and there was the phone call from my best friend, telling me she had been diagnosed with multiple sclerosis. Today I've learned that another friend is facing divorce.

One of our students will not be decorating for Christmas. She is living in a hotel room. Another child spends weekends with different parents. A young man's father died after complications from a car accident. A little girl and a little boy have parents in prison. The list could go on and on. You could add your own to this list.

Yes, my heart and mind are heavy. So today, especially, I pray for peace. When I worry about children and their families, I need peace. When I think about my friends and their needs, I need to remember that Christ gives us the "peace of God, which surpasses all understanding" (Philippians 4:19 NRSV).

People of all ages know when you are a person of peace. They will come to you, bearing their problems and concerns. You and I are bringing peace when we listen and offer to pray.

Lord, thank you for your peace; may it rule in my heart and in my mind. Amen.

MAY 18
REMEMBERING TO BE PATIENT—
READ COLOSSIANS 1:9-14.

I have cafeteria duty thirty minutes every day. My job is to watch over the first-graders. As they finish eating—or picking at their food—they dump their trays and line up in order to return to their classrooms. Every day I find myself saying the same things: "Clean up your area," "Don't run," "Stay in line," "Wait your turn," "Keep your voices down," and so on. Some days I admit I find it hard keeping my patience.

It seems that God often says the same things to me: "Don't worry," "Ask me for wisdom," "Pray without ceasing," "Don't judge," "Give thanks always," "No," "Wait," and so on. There is never a time when God says, "That's it; you have used up your allotment of patience. There is no more grace for you." I am so thankful that God is always patient with me.

Maybe you have seen the bumper sticker that says, "Please Be Patient. God Isn't Finished with Me Yet." In the same way, I need to be patient with the children in the cafeteria. I need to be patient with the people in my life. Patience is a fruit of the Spirit. Just as God is patient with me, God will give me patience to bear with others.

Lord, thank you for being patient with me. Help me to be patient with others. Amen.

May 19

Remembering to Be Kind—Read 2 Timothy 2:22-26.

Be kind to everyone.
But he cut in line. . . .
Be kind to everyone.
But she sat in my seat. . . .
Be kind to everyone.
But he looked at me funny. . . .
We tell the children, "Be kind," and "Treat others the way you want to be treated." Sometimes we make it sound so easy. I know that I am not naturally kind because the same things that bug my students and make them unkind make me want to be unkind, too. Then there are all the "adult" annoyances that make me want to be unkind.
Be kind to everyone.
But he cut me off in traffic. . . .
Be kind to everyone.
But she always gets into other people's business. . . .
Several years ago there was a lot of talk about "random acts of kindness." Kindness is a fruit of the Spirit. The only way kindness comes out of me is if the kindness of God is in me. If I'm connected to the vine, Jesus, then my life should be filled with kind deeds for others. My mouth should be filled with kind words for others. My mind should be filled with kind thoughts toward others.

My students need to experience kindness in my life. The hymn lyrics *"Jesus' hands were kind hands, doing good to all"* is the example we need to follow.

Lord, help me to be kind to everyone. Our world needs a lot of kindness. Amen.

May 20

Remembering to Do Good—Read Galatians 6:7-10.

When I was growing up, we always ate supper together as a family. It was a special time of sharing around the table. My parents have the gift of hospitality, so we regularly invited many into our home. I often said to my friends, "We can go to my house." Whether it was dinner after church or Friday nights after the game, people always felt welcomed at our house. Breaking bread together, fellowshipping with one another, inviting others in—these are all important acts.

I find myself trying to do the same today. It is a joy for me when friends come over to my house and sit around my table—the same one I sat around when I was growing up.

What about your home? Your classroom or office? Is it a place where others feel welcome? I always enjoyed when people would come by my office to see me. Sometimes it can get tiring being available to others, but as the scripture says, "Let us not become weary in doing good" (Galatians 6:9).

People need places of rest and peace and goodness. Is your home, classroom, office a place where others feel welcome? Do you invite others to share around your table and fellowship in your home?

Lord, help me to bear goodness today as I welcome others in your name. Amen.

MAY 21
REMEMBERING TO PRESS ONWARD—
READ PHILIPPIANS 3:12-14.

Each year about this time my congregation celebrates our high-school and college graduates. We join with their families and friends in recognizing their accomplishments. Sometimes we have had the opportunity to follow these young people through the years of childhood to these monumental occasions. What a privilege to see them succeed. The years of disciplined study and our many prayers have paid off.

Like our students, we teachers continue to study and grow as well. It is important that we take advantage of opportunities to read and attend seminars that will challenge us and stretch our minds. We are always "in process." Paul encourages us to "press onward," never becoming stagnant at any one point on this journey of faith.

Sometimes our reading and continuing education focuses only on our work. We also need to spend some time expanding ourselves in all areas of our lives. So, as you and I study and press onward, let us strive for balance in every area: physical, mental, relational, and spiritual.

Lord, help me to remember to press onward in every area of my life, never becoming stagnant in any area but always looking toward you. Amen.

MAY 22

REMEMBERING TO BE FAITHFUL—READ ROMANS 12:10.

I have lost track of the times people have said, "I'm praying for you." Thank you, God, for faithful parents, family, and friends who have been prayer warriors in my life. Whether I was making a decision, needing discernment, facing a difficult situation, or struggling in any way, these pray-ers were there for me. Their faithfulness on my behalf has been such an encouragement as they have surrounded me and upheld me.

Then there are those people who have said, "Let me know what I can do to help." Thank you, God, for faithful friends who have been the do-ers in my life. Whether it was buying groceries for a retreat, preparing supplies for VBS, cleaning up after a big event—whatever the need—these do-ers were there for me. Their faithfulness on my behalf has been reassuring to me.

Faithful in prayer and faithful in service, consistency is hard to find in our world today. Our children and youth need to hear our prayers for them and see our commitment to be with them and do for them. Unfortunately, many people to will them down by breaking promises and not following through on their responsibilities. Our faithfulness is a witness to God's faithfulness and unchanging character.

Lord, thank you for faithful pray-ers and do-ers in my life; help me to return their faithfulness to others. Amen.

MAY 23
REMEMBERING TO BE GENTLE—READ PHILIPPIANS 4:5.

When I think of gentleness, many things come to mind, like the intricately formed petals of a flower. There is gentleness in the breeze blowing through the trees and the waves lapping onto the shore. I feel gentleness in a warm blanket on a cold night. I hear it in the call of the morning dove. I see gentleness in a mother caring for her child or a father holding his child close. I hear gentleness in a whispered, "I love you." I feel it in the hug of a friend.

The way Jesus interacted with people can be characterized as gentleness. When Jesus reached out to touch the sick, comfort the grieving, smile on the elderly, and welcome the children, it was with gentleness.

God deals with us gently and tenderly, not as we deserve. He is always reaching out to us, calling us to himself. His mercies are new every morning. The way God calls people throughout the Scriptures display his gentleness.

Do my students see gentleness in the way I look at them? Do they feel gentleness in the way I interact with them? Do they hear it in the way I talk to them and to others? Gentleness is something we all need, no matter what our age.

Lord, help me to remember gentleness in my interactions with others today. Amen.

MAY 24
REMEMBERING TO BE SELF-CONTROLLED— READ TITUS 2:1-12.

This passage challenges older men, older women, and young men to be self-controlled. Clearly, it is a trait that is needed in our society today. As teachers and leaders, we have many people who look up to us. They listen to what we say, they watch what we do, and they follow where we lead. What are we saying, wearing, watching, supporting, and doing?

Unfortunately, there are many reports of people in leadership being caught doing something they shouldn't. As adults, we are free to do as we please, but Scripture reminds us not to do anything that would cause a little one to stumble (Matthew 18:5-6 and 1 Corinthians 8:9). It also says that we are to set an example "in speech, in life, in love, in faith and in purity" (1 Timothy 4:12).

So, I have to ask myself the hard questions. Am I reading anything I wouldn't want my students to ask me about? Am I surfing the Internet regarding anything I wouldn't want my students to know about? Am I watching anything I wouldn't want my students to watch with me? *Who Are You When No One Else Is Looking* is the title of a book by Bill Hybels. It is something I have to think and pray about. Am I setting a good example in every area of my life?

Lord, help me to be self-controlled in speech, life, love, faith, and purity. Amen.

MAY 25

REMEMBERING TO FILL OUR CUP—READ ROMANS 15:13.

This verse speaks of overflowing with hope. I like the imagery of being filled to overflowing.

On a shelf in my living room there is a pottery mug that says, "Fill My Cup, Lord." It is a daily reminder that I need to be filled with God. In order for me to be filled, though, my cup first must be emptied and cleaned out; otherwise, there won't be room for what needs to go in. Think about it: If I fill my half-empty coffee cup with pure water, that water will become impure. First, I must empty and clean my cup so that when it is refilled, the contents will be uncontaminated.

Every day I need God to cleanse me as I confess my sins and receive his forgiveness. Then I can offer my cup—my life—to be filled by the Holy Spirit. So I ask God to empty me of pride and pour into me humility, to clean me of anger and overflow me with love and peace, to wash me of impure thoughts and fill me with holiness. We can alter the prayer however we need as we lift up our cups—our lives—to God and pray, "Fill my cup, Lord." Then God can clean us and fill us with all that he is so that we can overflow to others.

Lord, thank you for cleaning my cup, my life, and for filling me up again. Amen.

MAY 26

REMEMBERING THE YEAR—READ EPHESIANS 4:1-13.

It's teacher appreciation time at our school—an opportunity to say "thank you" to teachers. The end of the school year is here. A lot has happened since the fall.

Whether you teach every day or once a week, your calling is an important one. You give of yourself to your students every time you teach. You give your heart, soul, mind, and strength. There are moments and days when you may wish you were someplace else or had a different class of kids, but you keep coming back. Your effort shows. The students have changed and grown, and you find it hard to say good-bye. You touch the future when you teach a child or young person. You make a difference. There may be a few that you feel you have lost along the way, but overall you have influenced the lives of many. You have stirred the hearts and minds of most, and they will never forget you.

So, thank you for staying the course, persevering under trial, striving to win the battle, and going the extra mile. Thank you for your willingness to be called teacher.

Lord, thank you for teachers who have taught me many things. Thank you for another year of teaching your children. Amen.

MAY 27

REMEMBERING GOD NEVER SLEEPS—READ PSALM 121.

One of my favorite psalms is Psalm 121. Each verse is a source of help and strength, reminding me that God is there for me, even as I sleep. God is there for me everywhere I go.

It is almost summer—time for vacations, getaways from the hustle and bustle of life and work. But sometimes for leaders in the church, things seem to get much more hectic in the summer. There are camps and mission trips, outings, vacation Bible school, and preparation for fall. I need to remember where my help comes from as things get so busy.

Because of all these activities, sometimes it is hard to take the time for a vacation. But vacation days are important for the renewing of our strength. This psalm reminds me that God watches over all these things while I get away to rest.

I enjoy visiting other churches while on vacation, seeing other believers worshiping, praying, and serving in other parts of the country. It is an encouragement to see others making a difference for our Lord. I need to remember that God watches over my coming and going and is big enough to watch over others too. What an awesome and mighty God we serve.

Lord, help me to take time for vacation as I remember that you never sleep and you watch over me. Amen.

MAY 28

REMEMBERING TO GROW—READ ROMANS 8:28-39.

My grandmother cross-stitched a pillow that says *Grow Where You Are Planted*. This is good advice, no matter what your age. Sometimes we want to hurry up our days and get to the next year of life. Other times we want time to stop so we can slow things down. Or we want to turn back the hands of the clock to return to a simpler day.

But nothing is ever wasted in God's economy. Nothing can ever separate us from God's love. We may not understand every situation we face or the reason for every struggle, but we can trust God. There will be times when we will look back and see that because of an experience, we are better people. There will be days when we realize that a certain struggle helped our faith mature.

So, let us be thankful with where we are planted today. The children in our classrooms may not be there next year or even tomorrow. We do not know where we will be this time next year. Let us grow in grace at our jobs. Let us grow in joy with our friends. Let us grow in love in our families. Let us grow in mercy with the people we meet.

Lord, help me grow where I am planted, knowing that all things work together for good and nothing can ever separate me from your love. Amen.

MAY 29

REMEMBERING TO BREATHE—READ GENESIS 2:7.

Take a deep breath. Breathe in and breathe out. We do not think a great deal about breathing unless we have a cold or suffer from asthma or a lung disease. It seems to happen naturally, without much effort. Our breath—in fact, our very life—comes from God. I love reading this passage about Almighty God breathing life into Adam. Breathe in again and think about this verse. Without breath, the breath of God, we have no life.

Take another deep breath. After the Resurrection, Jesus appeared to his disciples and "breathed on them and said, 'Receive the Holy Spirit'" (John 20:22). Without the Holy Spirit, we have no life. The Holy Spirit guides, intercedes, protects, comforts, and so much more. This breath of God gives us everything we need for life.

I learned this exercise at a seminar I attended:

Breathe _____(insert your name) out, and breathe Jesus in. Exhale your sin and all that is in you that is not from God, and inhale forgiveness and all that you need from God. Say, "_____ (your name), out" (while exhaling), and say "Jesus, in" (while inhaling).

Practice this spiritual breathing during the day and see what happens.

Lord, thank you for the breath of life. Help me to remember to breathe you into my life. Amen.

MAY 30

REMEMBERING GRACE—READ EPHESIANS 2:8-10.

Has anything good come from our lives? We have touched many lives. Prayers have been answered, grades have been raised, concepts have been mastered, skills have been gained, faith has been experienced, and lives have been changed. Our hard work and long hours have paid off.

What are we good at? We teach, read, listen, plan, respond, question, and so on. Our attention to work and the effort we put forth shows as we achieve in our profession.

Where are we on our walk of faith? We call out to God; we study and grow; and we seek to love God with all of our heart, soul, mind, and strength. Our faith has deepened through the years.

The scripture from Ephesians should be a familiar one. It is because of grace that any good comes from our lives. It is because of grace that we develop the gifts and talents we have received. It is because of grace that we have been saved and continue on this path.

We can fill in the blanks: For it is by grace that I _____ (teach, give, love, serve, and so forth)—and this not from myself, it is the gift of God—not by works . . . so I will boast only in God and this gift of grace.

Lord, help me remember that it is only by grace that I do anything of any good. Amen.

MAY 31

REMEMBERING OUR CLOUD OF WITNESSES— READ HEBREWS 10:19-25.

I received some wonderful advice from a professor. He encouraged us to find a "soul friend"—someone to pray with often, hold accountable, and meet with at least once a year for a spiritual retreat. My soul friend and I met in college. Our paths have crossed and our lives have paralleled in amazing ways. She lives in New Jersey and I live in Florida, but through the years we have found a way to meet someplace at least once a year. She prays for me and helps hold me accountable. One spring when I was facing a difficult decision, she reminded me of my convictions and helped me correct my thinking. I am thankful she is part of my cloud of witnesses.

We need people in our lives who will encourage us to do the right thing. I have a T-shirt that says, *What's right may not always be popular, but what's popular may not always be right.* Children, youth, and adults need to be surrounded by others who will do the right thing and who are willing to stand alone if necessary. The letter to the Hebrews reminds us that even when we feel alone, we can be assured that we are surrounded by a cloud of witnesses (12:1-3). Give thanks today for your cloud!

Lord, help me to remember my cloud of witnesses, and thank you for my soul friend(s). Amen.

JUNE
Life Passages

Cathy Howard

JUNE 1

LIFE PASSAGES—READ ECCLESIASTES 3:1-8.

FOR SOME OF US, SUMMER BREAK HAS ALREADY STARTED; FOR OTHers of us, it is almost here! The kindergartners will soon be first-graders; the juniors will take over as top dogs in the high school. June is a time of life changes: of graduations, confirmations, weddings. In June, people move to new cities, new jobs, new lifestyles. June is a time of passage for teachers, especially. Some celebrate their retirement; others interview anxiously for their first job. In June, the teacher down the hall plans to finish his degree so he can be a principal next fall.

Many life passages are bittersweet. Moving to new opportunities means leaving friends behind. Each graduate has to say good-bye to childhood; to each bride and groom, a family will have to say good-bye.

These passages aren't always easy; we do like our ruts. But the world of creation is dynamic, always in a state of flux. This month brings to mind these changes we all undergo— these tunnels we have to pass through to move on. Some transitions are life changing in a major way; others are much smaller. But all changes can move us closer to the Lord if we let them.

Dear Lord, let me use life passages, no matter how difficult they may be, to become closer to you. Amen.

JUNE 2
THE GIFT OF OUR WEAKNESSES—
READ 2 CORINTHIANS 11:30.

By the end of the school year, we teachers are really getting on one anothers' nerves! Frank always leaves the copy machine clogged with burnt paper and blinking for help. Melissa sprays so much air freshener in the staff restroom that I have to hold my breath as well as risk slipping on the wet floor. Kim is seething with secret anger at George because he makes fun of Mrs. Benson behind her back. And on and on.

Lord, we are so petty! So careless! So unkind! Sometimes I think putting up with the shortcomings of others is one of the hardest things we ever have to do. Sometimes I feel like the cross that the pastor displayed last March, the one we put nails into on Ash Wednesday. And every nail has somebody else's name on it: Frank, Melissa, Kim, George. Ouch!

And then it came to me: even our weaknesses are a gift. Yes, a gift from you, Lord. Without these "weaknesses" in others, we'd never have a chance to learn tolerance, patience, and forgiveness. Without our own weaknesses, we'd never learn humility.

Lord, help me use the gifts of human weakness—those of others as well as my own—to grow in love. Amen.

JUNE 3
OVERWORKED—READ MATTHEW 11:28-30
AND PSALM 68:19.

Lord, I can never get through this pile of paperwork! By Friday, I must have grades averaged and report cards made out; by Thursday, a list of overdue and lost books together with the replacement costs; by Wednesday, a list of students who are failing as well as what they can do during the summer to make up credit; by Tuesday, a time line for the curriculum committee; by Monday, a final exam for each class, plus the numbers of all the state standards it covers.

Somewhere in all this, I still have to teach classes from 8:15 to 3:30 every day, use up a couple of "free" periods to substitute for coaches going to the state track meet, and take my turn at bus duty after school. Will there be any time left for my family? Which will I have to give up, eating or sleeping?

Whoever said that we teachers have it easy because we get off work at 3:30 every day never had to spend a day in my worn-out shoes! Whoever said we have it easy because we have summers off doesn't realize that the taxpayers more than get their money's worth during those other nine months! How can I ever get this all done?

Lord, sometimes it's difficult to see the light at the end of the tunnel. Help me give my burdens over to you. Amen.

JUNE 4

CALMNESS—READ JOHN 14:27-28.

It's cloudy outside, and the dampness permeates the not-quite-heating, not-quite-air-conditioning system. Girls wear sweatshirts over their skimpy summer outfits, and paper doesn't feed properly through the copy machine. But all that's OK. In these last days of school, I'm grateful for anything that has a calming effect on the students. Warm sunny days bring out their jumpiness—beckon them to the lake, the pool, the playground, the ball field.

If it stays cloudy, maybe we can still cram their minds full of those last chapters in the history or algebra book. Maybe we can have one last shot at making them understand the periodic table of the elements or intransitive verbs. Maybe they'll forget for a moment about water guns, Frisbees, and their raging hormones. Maybe we can still teach them something.

Or maybe not. At least they don't beg to have class outside. At least it doesn't take half a class period to get them settled down. But how am I going to get them excited about the beauties of great literature and the importance of their final exams?

Lord, thank you for the gift of serenity. Amen.

JUNE 5

CARING FOR GOD'S LAMBS—READ JOHN 21:15-17.

In the halls littered with the remnants of the year, emptied lockers gleam from fresh polish. Students and teachers alike have fled into the budding summer, but my first-grade friend sits slumped and alone on a bench in the lobby, waiting for his mother. I almost make a wisecrack about being sad on the last day of school, but instead I ask, "Are you OK?" Turning away, he whispers, "Yes." But something's wrong. I ask if he has a headache or tummy ache.

"I said I'm OK!" he answers, almost angrily. "Well, you don't look OK." I put my hand on his shoulder. "You look sad."

I feel his little body tremble, fighting the tears he doesn't want me to see. "I'm going to miss school." I'm glad now that I didn't make that wisecrack. Patting his back, I remind him that he'll see his friends all summer at the pool, at T-ball, in Cub Scouts. Still slumped and turned away, he waits, sniffs again, and replies, "I'll miss my teacher."

I hug him and make a mental note to tell this to Becky, who doesn't let any kid leave her classroom without high fives and a personalized comment about the day. I'll tell her what a difference she's made in this first-grader's life. But maybe she already knows.

Lord, thank you for the people who guard young children along life's paths. Amen.

JUNE 6

WORKING TOGETHER—READ ROMANS 12:4-11.

It was time for the spring music program. Soon after lunch, custodians folded out the bleachers and set up risers in the high-school gym. Later, dads and brothers hauled arm loads of child-size chairs from classrooms. The art teacher supervised the stabilizing and decorating of backdrops. I snagged a couple of eighth-graders to help set lights while the choir teacher checked the sound system.

Finally, it was time to start. A multicolored sea of parents filled the bleachers as one by one, each grade filed up to sing their four or five selections. Kindergarteners and first-graders, dressed lovingly in frills or little suits, lisped their songs through newly gapped teeth. Sixth-grade girls, noses high, clomped past in shoes huge in proportion to their spindly legs. Fourth-grade boys with tousled hair and ornery grins tried unsuccessfully to stand still.

With each change of classes on the risers, there was a corresponding change in the "Video Mom" lineup on both sides of our tech table. Babies cried, and restless toddlers led frazzled parents noisily up the bleachers and out into the commons where they could run free. Finally, everyone breathed a sigh of relief. The marathon was over until next year. It would take at least two hours to put it all away, yet we all went home with a sense of having participated in something important.

Lord, thank you for the other people whose work and support help us mark important occasions in our school life. Amen.

JUNE 7

THE TIME IS SO SHORT—READ PROVERBS 31:10-31.

Of all people, don't let it be her! Susan had cancer. For years, our classrooms were next to each other. My English students wrote essays and read Shakespeare, all the while wishing they were in her Spanish or French class singing songs or eating tacos and éclairs—and laughing, always laughing.

When she left teaching to start a business with a longtime friend, we lost touch. But whenever I passed through her town, I visited her store. We shared stories of our aged mothers who were slipping into dementia. We remembered our mothers' saying they would never be like that. Sadly, we agreed that, in spite of our promises to our children, we, too, would slip into our nineties bereft of memory.

I'd planned to visit her after school was out, when we'd have more time. Now, only days before, she's dead. Did she ever know how much she enriched my life, how much she inspired me?

Lord, thank you for friends who have traveled through the last passage into your love; thank you for all those who help and inspire us. Amen.

JUNE 8

SEEING CHRIST IN OTHERS—READ LUKE 6:37-38.

Crunch time! It's the last week of school, the director of the sixth-grade operetta is ill, and a group of teachers and moms are trying to salvage the show. My job is to aim, focus, and gel all the stage lights. Mrs. Salter has agreed to take into her study hall my last-period sophomores—an immature, undisciplined bunch. I plan to cull out a select few to help me.

I give the sales pitch: this study hall will give them time to prepare their best possible final exam speeches. Only three take me up on the offer; the other sixteen want to help me. As we head for the auditorium, I pocket a red pen and a pad of back-to-study-hall passes.

As it turns out, I can't keep up with them! With the skimpiest of directions, they're aiming and focusing lights, cutting and installing gels, making paper palm trees. Three of the orneriest sit in the darkness. "We're done," they say, not moving, hands folded politely in their laps. I draw a little halo around my head, point to them, and give them thumbs up. They smile.

Dear Lord, help me be able to see your face in all your children, even the ones I think are most unlike you. Amen.

JUNE 9

FAITHFUL SERVANT—READ MATTHEW 24:45-48
AND 1 CORINTHIANS 4:1-2.

Today is the last day on the job for Bob the custodian. All teachers and staff are invited to join him for cake and punch in the cafeteria after school to celebrate his retirement. Too bad there won't be any kids there. For twenty-five years, he's wiped their fingerprints off the glass lobby doors and scraped their gum from the undersides of desks. He's cleaned their littered halls and classrooms; he's unclogged their toilets.

Every day, we're greeted by a waving American flag, glistening tile floors, and warmed or cooled air because Bob came to work at 6 A.M. Walls are freshly painted, fluorescent lights don't blink, and doors don't squeak because Bob and other custodians work summers. Lunch tables are set up and taken down daily. Paper product and soap dispensers are kept full. Copy paper is moved out of storage.

A new man will be hired, but will he smile and lay down his mop when I've forgotten my keys and need my door unlocked? Will he come to school during Christmas break and unlock a classroom so a child can get the shoes she forgot to take home?

Lord, thank you for the faithful service of others; help me notice life's "invisible" people and thank them for their service. Amen.

JUNE 10

A TIME OF MIXED EMOTIONS—READ JOHN 15:1-7.

Around here, they still take graduation very seriously. Grandparents, aunts, uncles, and cousins started arriving four hours early to save seats, so now the school is closed until two hours before. Solemn-faced graduates try to keep their balance as they struggle with the hesitation step they probably still won't have mastered at their weddings in a few years.

The packed gym is usually too hot, the speeches too long. The PowerPoint presentation showing past and present photos of each graduate seems interminable. As cap-and-gown-clad seniors take their places in the band for one last number, we can see where they'll leave holes. When they take their places in the choir, everyone becomes teary-eyed at the nostalgic song.

We send out a new batch every spring, all filled with optimism for a bright future. Some don't go far: They'll be here snapping photos of their own kids graduating. Some we never see again, whether because of great success or great tragedy. Graduation is boredom, excitement, fear, anticipation, joy, and sadness all wrapped up into one. We never think they're quite ready, but somehow, they always are.

Lord, help these young people starting off on their own remain connected to their roots, to you. Amen.

JUNE 11

A CHILD IS MISSING—READ LUKE 15:4-7.

Ryan didn't get on the bus this afternoon. Sherri in the office calls the dispatcher, who radios the other drivers to see if anyone has an extra child. No one does. A quick call to Mom confirms that Ryan is, indeed, supposed to ride. An intercom call to his classroom yields no response, nor does a school-wide page.

Now everyone is worried. Sherri calls Mom at work to get a list of friends, looks up the phone numbers in the school records, and starts dialing. We check the restrooms, the playground. Nothing. It's a small community, so nothing can happen, we tell ourselves. We hope.

The office staff is so busy calling and paging that no one notices Mrs. Schultz waiting at the counter, probably to pay for her child's lunch ticket. "Excuse me," she says. "If you're looking for Ryan, I saw him going down the hall past the gym with Danny Peabody."

Mrs. Peabody was Ryan's former baby-sitter! A quick call ascertains that Danny and Ryan are coming up her front walk. Child found! Life can return to normal.

Lord, thank you for people who watch over children; thank you for watching over us, even when we don't "get on the bus" like we're supposed to. Amen.

JUNE 12

THE SAVING POWER OF GRACE—READ LUKE 15:11-33.

I shook his hand at graduation today. He has come so far since last year when he sat in the back of my class, eyes reddened and mind befuddled from whatever he'd been high on the night before. He'd look at me only for a moment, and only if we were alone in the hall. But today the old Chris was back. He's been back all year. He passed all his classes and wrote a deeply moving essay.

English isn't easy for him, but he wrote a powerful story of how he began drinking in sixth grade and graduated to marijuana in junior high. That was when we first noticed. He doesn't remember much about his sophomore year, when he was into all kinds of things he didn't specify. As a junior, he had several minor brushes with the law. Then he met Lisa coming out of the library. She smiled and invited him to the church youth group she and her husband sponsored.

The rest of the story is a testament to the saving power of God's grace and of Christian witness. The old Chris is back! He greets me with that little grin and even let me hug him at graduation. He cut his hair and has gone to work as an assistant manager. Praise God!

Lord, thank you for the saving power of your grace; help us keep our arms open to welcome all your straying children back to their home. Amen.

JUNE 13

TWISTING PATHS—READ ISAIAH 40:3-5.

Summer is a time for vacations, so I decided to take my children to Yellowstone Park before we moved away from Wyoming. I rented a tent-trailer and we practiced setting it up. Two highways cross the Big Horn Mountains from the east; local postcards featured a spectacular photo of the northern route with its thirteen switchbacks. Clever me: I chose the southern one.

The car labored more and more as we approached the summit. The engine didn't sound good, and I began to doubt the wisdom of pulling a trailer—of taking the trip in the first place. At the top, we looked into the valley—straight down! There weren't thirteen switchbacks, but there must have been at least ten. "How will we get down?" my worried children asked. My motto must be "God protects the stupid," because more times than I can count, I've gotten myself and others into situations like this. The only way out is to take a deep breath, trust God, get in the car, drive, and pray.

We have children looking to us for answers to questions we can't answer, depending on us to smooth out the path for them. Sometimes we're not sure we're up to the job. Only by placing our trust in the Lord can we lead them safely on the right path, even if it has thirteen hairpin turns.

Lord, I place my trust in you; help me guide your children on right paths. Amen.

JUNE 14

MINISTERING TO THE NEEDS OF OTHERS—
READ LUKE 9:12-17.

Death struck our family. Out-of-town relatives began to gather the next day. That's when the food began coming in. Before long, the kitchen was filled with casseroles, hams, rolls, and cakes brought in by friends and neighbors. I never had occasion to find out whether this custom exists anywhere else, but here in the rural Midwest, this carrying in of food is repeated whenever someone dies, goes to the hospital, graduates, gets married, or has a baby.

We've all read about the generosity of people to victims of natural disasters; it's amazing how much stuff we find we don't need when someone else needs it more!

As we see in the miracle of the loaves and fishes, nothing is impossible with God. If we live in faith, live in the Spirit, miracles can happen every day.

Lord, thank you for providing for our needs; help us follow your lead and minister to the needs of others. Amen.

JUNE 15
BEING READY FOR THE LORD—
READ MATTHEW 24:42-44.

The news raced through school in hushed, horrified whispers. A student was killed in a car wreck the night before. We teachers were notified via calling tree at 6 A.M. and briefed by the crisis team at a meeting at 7:30. But what can we say? How can we teach English, math, or science to these youngsters who are overwhelmed by grief?

It's a public school, so we're not supposed to touch students or teach religion, but today the rules are suspended. Hugs abound; shoulders are wet with tears. We whisper, "I'll pray for you," or "She's with God now."

She was bright, beautiful, and invulnerable, just like them. But today, no one's invulnerable. The bell rang. My wounded class waited dully for their assignment. "We can't bring Cassie back," I told them. "We'll never have a chance to tell her how much she means to us. So let's spend the period writing letters to those still living, telling them what we appreciate about them, forgiving them their weaknesses, telling them we love them."

They wrote silently until the bell, then filed out slowly, clutching folded papers in their hands.

Lord, help me make the most of the time you have given me. Amen.

JUNE 16
GRATITUDE—READ LUKE 17:11-19.

Kendrick was that rude little junior-high kid who walked out in the middle of every concert and play, slamming the door behind him. When he was in high school, I had him in two required classes. Intelligent but undermotivated, he certainly kept me on my toes. Then, he took my class as a senior elective and joined forensics and drama, both activities I coach. At graduation, I shook his hand warmly and breathed a sigh of relief.

Several years later, he showed up at my classroom. After floating in and out of college, he'd decided to become a teacher. He wanted me to know that my class had helped him "KLEP" out of an English class and save money. A few years later, he surfaced to get suggestions for a play. Though he still had no degree, he was teaching in a small Christian school, and part of his job was to stage a school play. I loaned him a script. Later, I heard he'd quit college and was working as a youth minister.

Then I received an invitation to his wedding. I'm glad I went. Because of the size of the church, he'd invited only two teachers, one from grade school and one from high school—me.

Lord, help me accept the gratitude of others; help me remember to express my gratitude toward them. Amen.

JUNE 17

GOD GIVES US WHAT WE NEED—READ LUKE 12:22-31.

The RIF letters came out months ago, yet we're still edgy around our friends who didn't get a contract for next year. It's hard to look for a job when you're piled high with uncorrected papers, unfinished curriculum revisions, conferences with desperate parents, and endless committee meetings. At least they have the summer. They could end up taking jobs in this small community for which they're vastly overqualified and underpaid; if they're lucky, they'll find a teaching position in a neighboring town.

When it happened to me, I wasn't lucky. Twice I had to move my children to a new home, a new school, a new life far from friends. So I know how my colleagues feel. There's a knot of uncertainty in their stomachs; the road ahead is suddenly blank. To add to their ignominy, the school is holding a farewell reception for them in the lunchroom today! We all tiptoe around them. What can we do? What can we say?

But looking back, I can see that the life we have is better than the one we would have had. We survived the painful transplant and bloomed. I'm grateful for the man my daughters met here and married, the friends I've made, the opportunities to take up my music again. Maybe I can tell that to my RIFed friends.

Lord, help me let go of my uncertainties and place my trust in only you. Amen.

JUNE 18

JOYFUL MUSIC—READ PSALM 150:1-6.

I kind of miss the piano. It had been stored in my classroom at the old school long before I came; no one knew why. I turned it to the wall so the kids wouldn't be pounding on it all the time. Instead, it collected dust and gum wrappers. But sometimes, long after the building had cleared, I'd pull it out a little and slide onto the wobbly bench. My fingers would search the stiff keys for fragments of Scott Joplin's "Solace," a Mozart sonata, or the theme from *Pink Panther*.

Sometimes students preparing for a music contest would shyly ask if they could use my room to practice, the music rooms being already filled. How many teachers get to correct vocabulary tests to a live performance of a Mozart flute concerto, or a soaring Puccini aria? When we used my classroom to do makeup for the spring play, Shane treated us to his renditions of Beach Boys favorites, which he played by ear.

What would a wedding be without music—or a graduation, funeral, baptism, or class reunion? So many of life's passages are enriched by music. Yes, I do miss that piano.

Thank you, Lord, for the gift of music, and for the people who bring it to us. Amen.

JUNE 19

WORTH OF A PERSON—READ 1 CORINTHIANS 13:1-3.

The paper I return to her is only a C minus. "I'm not very good at English," she admits. I know she struggles. I also know that Cody, who has a lot of friends but is still too shy to ask out a girl, is expecting her to find him a prom date. She has less than a week.

"I know," I answer her. "But you're good with people." She looks at me quizzically. "There's a reason," I add, "that people come to you for prom dates." She brightens. "People know they can trust you, know that you won't make fun of them, know you'll be there for them." She pauses, then smiles. "I guess so."

I hope she realizes there's more to life than school. I hope that even if she struggles with math, spelling, and achievement tests, she'll find a niche where her gifts are valued. Sometimes we teachers tend to forget that the measure of a person's worth is so much more than her report card.

Lord, help me look beyond their schoolwork to see the real value of all my students, your children. Amen.

JUNE 20

ACCEPTING DIFFICULTIES—READ MARK 14:32-42.

"I hate it here," wailed the voice on the other end of the line. "I want to come home." She was my student for two years, and then she lived with me her senior year. Enlisting in the Navy was no whim. She'd thought long and hard about this decision, not allowing herself to be swayed by the recruiter's pressure. Now, after less than a week of boot camp, she was ready to quit.

"Give your body time to adjust to the new climate, schedule, altitude, and food," I advised. She cried. "The worst thing is that everybody yells all the time." She'd always had a tough time with conflict, caving at the slightest hint of disapproval from authority figures and friends. "Yell back," I suggested.

266

"The next time they yell at you, yell, 'Yes, Ma'am!' just as loud as you can. It'll help relieve your stress, and they'll think you're the most enthusiastic sailor that ever hit boot camp." I don't know if she did, but she made it through and completed her hitch.

Boot camp is difficult. So is being switched to a new teaching assignment or even a different school. Life transitions can be tough. It's tempting to bail, to "phone home" and tell God we quit. It's much harder to say—even yell enthusiastically—the prayer of Jesus in the garden.

Father, even when it's extraordinarily difficult, help me do your will. Amen.

JUNE 21
REJOICING IN THE LORD—READ PSALM 118:24 AND PSALM 98:4-9.

It's the first day of summer, the longest day of the year. Those days when I went to school before daybreak and stayed long after sunset seem very far away on this perfect midsummer's day. The mosquitoes and flies have barely started; the heat waves won't arrive in earnest until July and August. The world is still green and new and full of hope.

It's Saturday, and my students are cruising up and down Main Street. Some have hauled a grill, a huge stereo, and some sofas to the parking lot of the Super Foods for a cookout. They call it "couching." Their friends stop by to visit in the soft, summer night. Later on, the cop will stop by just to check on things. Other kids lounge on cars outside the Kwik Stop, or sit on the picnic tables in front of the Sweden Creme. It seems as if everyone just can't get enough of this day, even as it darkens into night.

The passage of time is marked sometimes in small ways. Sometimes I think our students understand this better than we do. The passing of one season into another is not an occasion of great moment, but there they are in the Super Foods parking lot. Bryan has even pulled in his camper.

Lord, thank you for those who celebrate with us even the small passages of life; thank you for friends. Amen.

JUNE 22

DEALING WITH DISCOURAGEMENT—READ JAMES 1:12.

It's summer, but you'd never know it in here! I'm in a folding metal chair in the basement of the Fine Arts Building listening to Professor Spillway orate about persuasive speaking. We're in the experimental theatre; the walls and ceiling are painted black, and the floor is concrete. I've been sitting here for two-and-a-half hours, and I can feel my blood pooling in my legs. I'm cold, cold, cold.

These all-day classes are really a convenient way to earn college credit; two four-day weeks and we pick up three credit hours. But they're really a marathon! There's no kind of classroom furniture ever devised that can be comfortable for an entire day. But it's almost over. At the end of the summer, I'll have completed my master's degree, and I can move up a notch on the pay scale. The coursework really wasn't that difficult; it's been more of an endurance test than anything else.

Sometimes life's passages are like that—not so much difficult as they are boring. What gets us through is often not talent, but persistence. The victory belongs to the stubborn. Maybe that's one of the purposes of classes: to teach us that in spite of the discomforts and boredom of life, we can still win the prize and wear the crown.

Lord, help me keep my eye on the crown—the purpose of my life—rather than on the day-to-day discouragements. Amen.

JUNE 23

OVERWHELMING TRIALS—READ PSALM 143:1-2 AND MATTHEW 16:24.

The rumors flew around school for months: the reason Shannon was absent, was tardy, looked tired, or got sick was that she was pregnant. For months, she had hidden her condition under loose sweats and an oversized jacket, and no one had known. No one had helped her deal with the physical and psychological changes that were taking place in her. Finally, the secret was out. She looked relieved.

But she hadn't taken care of herself. She'd stopped eating to avoid gaining weight. Her mother kicked her out of the house; then three weeks later relented and took her back. The boyfriend father, apparently, was history. Shannon's life became a roller coaster.

Then she was absent again, for a week. We found out she'd gone into labor. Despite medical efforts, she'd delivered a baby boy who'd died within an hour. In only a few short months, this poor fifteen-year-old had experienced more turmoil—more of life's joys and sorrows—than most people three times her age.

Lord, some of these students have crosses to bear that are heavier than I can imagine. Please send them your special help and love. Amen.

JUNE 24
HELPING OUR FELLOW TRAVELERS—
READ LUKE 10:30-37.

Even before the van in front of us had dropped a muffler and edged to the shoulder, I'd noticed it had a school district license plate. It was headed for the same place we were: the state speech contest. Before we'd fully stopped, the two sponsors and half a dozen kids came running with all their gear. Being stranded at the side of a busy interstate can be a frightening experience, especially with a vanload of other people's children.

A few years later, I was the teacher in a van stranded on the shoulder of the interstate with a blown-out tire. My students were the ones in danger. But no sooner had we stopped than our rescuer pulled up behind us. I knew him; his daughter had been competing at the same speech contest we'd just left.

Within minutes, he and two of the boys in the van replaced the bad tire.

How often do we pause to offer a hand to a "stranded traveler"? How much easier it is to rush past than to stop and listen to someone who's lost the way, or who's simply lonely. How much more convenient it is to ignore the people we pass than it is to stop and greet them. How simple it is to treat even our families with scorn.

Lord, help me take time out of my busy life to minister to my fellow travelers on this road of life. Amen.

JUNE 25
BEING THERE FOR EACH OTHER—
READ ECCLESIASTES 4:9-10.

At the county fair, I recognized him immediately; he hadn't changed much in the fifteen years since graduation. He and his wife were watching their children whirl gleefully on the carousel. He greeted me with surprise and expressed amazement that I was still teaching. We small-talked about the weather, the fair, the changes in the high school. Neither of us mentioned the circumstances of our last meeting.

It was outside the church at the funeral of his best friend Cliff, also a former student. The summer after graduation, Cliff had driven his pickup to a well-used campground at a local lake. There he had run a garden hose from the exhaust to the cab, rolled up the windows, and started the motor. I really think he'd hoped someone would find him, but no one did—until too late. I sent the family a folder of his poems he'd left at school, one of which was read at his funeral: "How Hard It Is to Be a Man."

So at the fair, Shane and I didn't talk about that. We didn't discuss how a cool guy like him had embraced an old lady schoolteacher in full light of day in front of everyone in town, how we'd left tears on each other's shoulders for the friend we should have been able to save but didn't.

Lord, help us be there for each other and recognize each other's needs. Amen.

JUNE 26

TRUST IN THE LORD—READ 2 CORINTHIANS 5:6-7.

Our classrooms for the next ten days—three vans and a Toyota 4-Runner—wait in the driveway outside the Administration Building. I recognize only two other teachers. I look at the thirty strangers with whom I'll be traveling, sharing meals, and camping in church basements, tents, or tepees. I look at our gear and wonder how we'll all fit.

I haven't been camping in decades. Will my old bones be able to take ten nights in a bedroll on the self-inflating pad I borrowed from my son? Will I be able to drag this huge bag crammed with all my worldly needs? Will my new hiking boots give me blisters? Will my new yellow windbreaker be warm enough? Taking this summer class, "Lewis and Clark Trails," is beginning to look like a really stupid idea!

I guess this trip is a lot like life. We don't choose our fellow travelers; we can't trust the weather; we're blind to what's beyond the next turn in the road. To embark at all requires faith.

Lord, help me find the faith to walk through life, blind though I am. I place my trust in you. Amen.

JUNE 27

SEEING GOD—READ PSALM 139:7-12.

Our sleeping bags are spread over the floor of the kindergarten Sunday school room of a church somewhere in Montana. One wall has what appear to be random splotches of black on the white background. Dixie says it's the face of Jesus, and I guess it sort of looks like that if I squint. But when we turn out the lights, dozens of glowing eyes appear on the walls!

271

We turn on the lights. Yes, the eyes are there, but hardly noticeable. We wonder what the lesson was? Did a teacher pass out stickers for children to paste on the walls? Wouldn't small children be frightened of all those eyes staring at them in the dark? "It's really spooky," someone says. Another voice quips, "This is a church; they're the eyes of God."

Funny, I muse, that the face of Jesus can be too obvious to see. Funny that the eyes of God upon us are so nearly invisible to us in the light of day, yet so obviously watching over us in our darkest hours of night.

Lord, thank you for watching over us both day and night; teach me to see your face. Amen.

June 28

Proclaiming God's Glory—Read Psalm 19:1-4.

We were too tired to set up the tents, so I'm lying on my back in a sleeping bag somewhere in Montana (or maybe Idaho) looking at millions of stars. This place is almost completely flat and treeless, and there are no lights anywhere— nothing but uninterrupted stars from horizon to horizon all around. I spent the first hour with a SnakeLight around my neck, book in hand, trying to find the familiar constellations: the swan, the eagle. There are just too many stars.

This is something I can't photograph. I wish I had kids with me. I want them to know that countless stars are invisible to us because of earthly lights. I want them to know that countless more are invisible to those without a telescope. And beyond the reach of the telescope? Who knows?

I want to shout, to spread the news! Things we can't see *do* exist! Stars exist, and galaxies and universes. They're out there careening through space, exploding, imploding, changing. And God, though unseen, exists.

I'm a teacher of English and speech; I'm supposed to be good at explaining things. Yet I lie here pinioned to the earth, not quite part of that either, wondering.

Lord, transform me; help me get up and proclaim your majesty, your glory. Amen.

JUNE 29

TRAVELING IN THE SPIRIT—READ EPHESIANS 4:3-5.

For a real travel experience, there's nothing quite like a bus full of students. Every year at play contest time, my drama students pack the hold full of platforms, steps, wooden cubes, and furniture. The small or soft stuff goes inside with us: tool kit, makeup box, props box, video equipment, and costumes. Each student has a large gym bag, a pillow, a blanket, and a sack full of food. We really fill a bus.

Once they gave us a particularly small bus without even an overhead rack for students' bags. There was no hold, so we had to pack the set in a pickup. Students had to sit two to a seat. Everyone was disgruntled as we set out on the four-hour trip. "Sit by someone you like," I advised. "It's going to be a very cozy ride." As it turned out, what I thought would be a nightmare turned into the highlight of the season. They bonded. New people joined drama the next year because they'd heard how much fun everyone had on the bus!

It's difficult to guess where life's travels will take us. Sometimes the stress of it all stretches our patience to the breaking point. But with the right spirit, we can turn even a nightmare into a very cozy ride. The right spirit, of course, is God's.

O Lord, send us your Spirit; guide us through this confusing, stressful maze we call life. Amen.

JUNE 30

LOOK WHAT HE LEFT BEHIND—READ JOHN 4:37-38.

I don't remember her name, but she was showing me through the small private grade school run by our church.

She was also trying to persuade me to teach a Sunday school class. I was resisting. We were a young couple with a baby, and my husband was in a government job. We might be transferred at any moment.

She unlocked a door and turned on the light. "See?" she asked. All I saw was a small library. "We didn't used to have a library," she explained, "until a staff sergeant at the air base got the ball rolling. He's gone now, but look what he left behind."

That epiphany changed my life focus. We put in storm windows and a new shower stall at our rental house; I planted raspberries and apple trees whose fruit we might never enjoy. But we also enjoyed house renovations made by others, apricots and asparagus planted by those who came before us. And what better motto for a teacher? Although we see our students only a few hours five days a week for part of a year, hopefully people will be able to say, "Look what she left behind!"

Lord, thank you for the people who left good things in my path; help me leave behind only that which is good for those who follow me. Amen.

JULY
Renewal

Cathy Howard

JULY 1
RENEWAL IN THE SPIRIT—READ JOHN 3:5-8.

SUMMER IS A TIME OF RENEWAL FOR TEACHERS. THE FUROR OF GET-ting those last exams corrected, averaging the grades, and dealing with disappointed students is all in the dim past. Summer is a time to do mindless work in the garden and yard, to wear grubby clothes, and to sleep more than six hours a night. It's time to travel or take a class. It's time to reconnect with family. In summer, we actually have time to take on a project or pursue a hobby just because we enjoy it.

By the time July rolls around, it's easy for me to get lazy. My planner's not crammed full for the next nine months; there are no bells to raise me out of my torpor. It's easy to forget that this gift of time has its limits. After all, by July the summer is nearly half gone. It would be so easy to waste this opportunity to become not only a better teacher, but also a better person.

In the coming month, we celebrate this season of renewal; we'll explore the many ways the Lord gives us to restore our spirits—not only to help us fall in love with teaching all over again, but especially to renew his Spirit within us again. Though some of the devotions are set within the school year, all point us to life-giving lessons that can help prepare us—mentally and spiritually—for the upcoming school year.

Lord, you restore my soul; you are the source of all that is beautiful and new. Amen.

JULY 2

UGLINESS TRANSFORMED—READ MARK 2:15-17.

There's something so elemental, so basic about digging in the dirt. My enjoyment of gardening takes a sharp dive when the hundred-degree weather sets in; but in early summer, I'm still out there rearranging flower beds and working compost into the vegetable patch. Last year's yard waste moldered and simmered in the weather, sending up a sour, rancid smell when disturbed. Now, all by itself, it's transformed. Under the surface is a black, rich layer of faintly musty compost.

A squeamish person could be really disgusted even thinking about dirt. It's full of crawly things that eat one another, leave waste, and harbor germs. "Wash your hands," we warn our children. "Be sure to get all the dirt off." We were taught that dirt was bad, as were dirty jokes, dirty tricks, and dirty deals. Dirty dishes and dirty laundry should be hidden away to be dealt with by machines. Dirt and mud are anathema to our gleaming floors.

Yet, in nurturing healthy vegetables and beautiful flowers, it's all about that lowly dirt. We can't be too squeamish about the lowly. That unattractive, whiny, snotty-nosed child is God's child; so is her slovenly, rude, ill-tempered mother.

Lord, help me remember that all of us—even the most unappealing people—are in the process of being transformed by your Spirit. Amen.

JULY 3

OFFERING HOSPITALITY—READ MATTHEW 10:40-42.

Years ago when I stayed out of teaching to raise children, one of the ladies in my new congregation persuaded me to visit shut-ins with her. I wasn't sure; I had an eighteen-month-old. What if he cried? What if he needed a nap and got cross? My excuses fell on deaf ears, and there we were on the doorstep of an elderly lady who lived across the street from a large high school.

Immediately it became apparent that I wasn't the important player here. When the woman opened the door, her eyes fastened on my beautiful son. She let us in and asked if he wanted a cookie; so he followed her to the kitchen and reentered with a paper plate of stale Girl Scout cookies. As he offered them to us, she served small glasses of lemonade.

Every day, she could look out and see young people sitting on cars in front of her house, laughing and talking. But she was all alone. She could watch the band practice marching, but the music was outside. Now she had a real visitor, a small angel from God whom she could welcome. All he had to offer was his beauty and his youth. But that was more than enough.

Lord, thank you for the hospitality of others, no matter how small it may seem; thank you especially for those who can offer simply their being. Amen.

JULY 4

LIGHTS IN THE DARKNESS—READ MATTHEW 5:14-16.

To most people, Scottsbluff, Nebraska, seems like a small town. But it's way too big for everybody in town to expect to fit in one place. However, I think they're all here tonight. The entire mall parking lot is filled, as well as the fast food, video rental, and convenience store lots along the strip. Parked cars clog streets for miles. Surely the lots, roads, and stands of the junior college stadium filled up first. Everybody in town has turned out to watch the fireworks display.

It's a beautiful summer night, and the display lives up to expectations. I notice a plane overhead and wonder what "July 4" looks like from above. In the distance, I can see other fireworks displays in towns up and down the valley. From the air, it must look like a sparkling jeweled necklace tossed onto the floor of the Nebraska panhandle. I wonder what it looks like from space.

Oh, to be in that plane! Our earthbound feet so limit our field of vision! We celebrate our single light in the darkness, only dimly aware that there are other lights out there, too.

Lord, remind me that I'm not alone in the dark; help me notice the lights of others and see the big picture from "above." Amen.

JULY 5

BEING OPEN TO CHANGE—READ ACTS 2:1-4.

My Lewis and Clark trip was exciting, but it's good to be home. For me, it was a journey into the past: to a summer job as a newlywed, to where children were born, to where we fished and laughed and camped, to where a husband and father is buried. It wasn't what I expected. Years ago, I lived in all those places, yet I never really saw them at all.

Did I learn something I can take back to my classes? I don't know. I learned that life doesn't hold still, that the world we live in is in a constant state of change. Past joys fade with time; past adventures dull. But pain and sorrows, thank the Lord, are softened. The only constant is the Lord.

What I learned can't be put into lesson plans, but certainly I'll need to know these things. Certainly I'll be given occasion to pass them on to my students. No gift is given for our own use exclusively. My "lesson plan" will be to stay open to whatever opportunities God gives me.

Dear Lord, thank you for change; help me be open each day to the coming of the Spirit in my soul. Amen.

JULY 6

BIRTHDAY CELEBRATIONS—READ ACTS 2:43-47.

Birthdays are a much bigger deal on the grade-school side of our complex. The cafeteria stages birthday parties with decorated cakes every month, and the teachers advertise birthday parties in the teachers' lounge—complete with a potluck lunch and, of course, cake. I've never been particularly interested in celebrating my birthday. All I did, after all, was get born. I'd rather celebrate some special accomplishment. But still, those grade-school teachers do know how to stage a party. One of my students said it best at a high-school writers' conference: "Everything's always better with food."

My children usually had to celebrate their birthdays late because I was out of town for a speech contest, or had to put on a play. But we always celebrated. Last summer, they helped transport my invalid sister two hundred miles to celebrate my mother's ninetieth birthday.

Our school counselor is an example to us all. When we see her roaming the halls wearing two or three novelty necklaces and carrying a basket of lollipops, we know the "birthday stalker" is at it again. Even students deep into hard-core adolescence eagerly await their birthday gifts.

Lord, help me be a better friend to my family, peers, and students by giving and receiving in your name. Amen.

JULY 7
RULES, RULES, RULES—READ MARK 12:28-34.

They're everywhere: the signs with all the rules! Poster groups in the halls announce the five rules each for a formal line, an informal line, a respectful listener. Each classroom displays not only the "five rules of this classroom," but also additional sets of rules posters from the behavior modification sessions the teachers attended a few years ago. Children are instructed in how to ask for help and how to take a compliment.

The student handbook has pages filled with both rules and the penalties for their infractions. The library posts rules for proper library behavior as well as computer use; from the cafeteria walls students learn rules for lunch tickets, orderly lunch lines, proper disposition of used lunch trays, and the recommended amounts of each food group. Even in the rest rooms we are warned to wash our hands with soap and water and to pull a towel with *dos manos*—two hands.

Even though the laws of Moses are many, they've been summarized in only ten commandments. And Jesus managed to boil those down into only two: love God, and love our neighbor. It's all so simple to say, but so difficult to put into practice!

Lord, thank you for reminding us of the purpose—the heart—of all the rules. Help me keep the love of God at the center of my life. Amen.

JULY 8

UNSELFISHNESS—READ MATTHEW 25:34-46.

There must be a big sign on my classroom door that says "Sucker!" and another on my forehead. Selling magazines for the junior class? Stop in here. Light bulbs for the sophomores? Fudge for cheerleading camp? Frozen pizza for the church youth group? Just stop here and ask the "sucker teacher."

The Cub Scouts usually hit me up two or three times, and I owe several kids for the Saint Jude bike-a-thon. I haven't yet swum laps for the heart fund, but I've sponsored many swimmers. My desk drawers and cupboards are full of Girl Scout cookies and Boy Scout popcorn I can't eat because it sticks in my throat. I've even stocked up on canned-good specials from the supermarket so I can give to the church group pantry drive.

Maybe it's my imagination, but I think teachers are suckers for all this stuff because we know more kids than anyone else does. And they always send the cutest little Girl Scouts! How can you say no to those sweet little faces with the big pleading eyes? And how can you refuse adolescents who put aside their habitual surliness to collect food for the poor?

Lord, thank you for the unselfishness of others; please help me follow their lead and be unselfish, too. Amen.

JULY 9

TRUSTING OUR FATHER—READ MATTHEW 7:7-12.

He was so small that the door appeared to be opening itself as he struggled into my classroom after school. "May I help you?" I asked. With hands on his hips, he surveyed the room, his huge blue eyes coming to rest on the sorted coins and bills on my desk. As student council sponsor, I'd been counting the day's receipts from our fundraiser—the lobby juice machine. "I need money," he announced, making no move. "Money for the juice machine."

I caught a glimpse of movement in the hall and heard the stifled laughter of the older kids who had sent him in here. They were waiting to see the embarrassed look on his face when he came out empty-handed, waiting to enjoy his disappointment when he discovered that the only money I gave was change for a dollar when the bill slot wasn't working.

So I explained that the money he saw was payment for the deliveryman. Then I offered him his choice of juice from the closet. He thought, selected fruit punch, and thanked me. We're friends now. On his regular visits, I give him juice; he feeds my class's gerbil and gives me artwork, which I hang on my bulletin board to inspire my students—those older kids who never got to laugh at him.

Father, help me be filled with the absolute faith and trust of a child when I come to you with my needs. Amen.

JULY 10
SITTING IN ANOTHER PERSON'S DESK—
READ JOHN 13:12-17.

What's the best thing about school being out? Close to the top of my list is three months without teacher in-service! The students don't know how good they have it; their classes last only forty-six minutes. Then, they get to stretch out, walk around, get a drink, talk to their friends. Mom can write an excuse if they feel sick or sleep in. Teachers, however, have to listen to a motivational speaker for at least an hour. Each sectional lasts an hour and a half.

Usually we get to choose between exciting topics such as "Meeting the State Standards," "The Reluctant Learner," or "Achievement Tests: What Good Are They?" (Do they really want me to answer that one?) Usually, the classroom is so overcrowded that people stand in the back. The desks are undersized. It's too hot or too cold. The speaker puts transparencies on an overhead or takes thirty minutes getting a PowerPoint to work. Then she reads the slides to us and gives us a handout with the same information.

Is this what school is like for our students? Are they that uncomfortable? Are we that poorly prepared? I'd like to think not, yet. . . .

Lord, help me see the view from the other side of the desk; remind me to treat those unmotivated students with compassion. Amen.

JULY 11
ACCEPTING THE KINDNESS OF OTHERS— READ MARK 14:3-6.

"Your tag is showing," they cluck, tucking the offender into the back of my sweater. "And your earrings don't match!"

"I'm starting a fashion trend," I answer. They give me "the look," and I drop the earrings into my pocket.

Since my youngest daughter left for college last year, these girls in my first-period class have taken over as my fashion monitors. Every day I am scrutinized for loose strings, lint, and mismatches by these miniskirted fashion gurus with tattooed snakes around their necks and arms. I get free advice on eye shadow, skin care, and jewelry from these budding women with pierced tongues, noses, eyebrows, and navels.

When I finally pass inspection, they settle in and begin the lotion ritual. Today we try cucumber, strawberry kiwi, and the ginger apricot one of the girls might wrap for her mom's birthday. I sniff and approve her choice. Soon, the whole room reeks of fruit salad. The bell rings, I thank them, and we're all ready to begin another day.

Lord, help me receive the small kindnesses of others in the tolerant spirit of your love. Amen.

July 12

Lounge Gossip—Read Psalm 15:1-4.

Normally, the teachers' lounge isn't a bad place to be, but sometimes it's alive with the buzz of gossip. Today is one of those days. Did we hear what "Suzy Student" did last night? Well, with a mother like hers, what can you expect? Four children, and each with a different father! And then there's the Snopes kids. ADHD, every one. Probably fetal alcohol and drug syndrome, too. Did we hear what that stupid school board did? And how the principal caved in to them? And on and on.

Sometimes we teachers have to stick together. When those unhappy students tell me I'm the only teacher that won't let them do whatever they want, it's nice to be able to do a reality check with all my allegedly permissive peers. But sometimes lounge talk oversteps the bounds of mutual helpfulness. It becomes gossip that eats away at people's reputations for no constructive reason.

Sometimes small complaints turn into habitual griping: an endless stream of negativism about students, parents, administration, the board, the job in general. It's an easy trap to fall into: seeing only the negatives in life, in people. To find the good is much harder.

Lord, help me avoid the trap of rumors and gossip; help me find the good—no matter how small—in every person. Amen.

July 13

Taking Time to Pray—Read Ezekiel 3:22-24.

I wonder why I didn't start walking to school a long time ago. It's not that far—just a couple of blocks down the street and four more through the tree rows alongside the athletic fields. It's good exercise, but more important, it's good time "away from it all"—time to stop and smell the roses. Well, not roses, really—more like wildflowers named blue flax and fleabane. Some days the grass is wet with dew; some days the snow shows tracks of others who walk here: rabbits, birds, and humans.

But whether it's an eight-minute walk through trees or a forty-minute commute through traffic, the trip to and from school is a gift of time—time to reflect on the day, time to reflect on God, time to listen and to pray.

Walking against the cold wind helps me wake up; maybe it can wake up my soul as well. It pumps my blood and strengthens my legs; maybe it can do the same for my faith. All I need to do is gird myself against the weather and take that first step every morning.

Lord, thank you for the gift of time; help me use it wisely to become closer to you. Amen.

JULY 14
FINDING JOY—READ PSALM 149:1-3.

The drill team doesn't practice here anymore, and I miss their upbeat music echoing in the commons. I even miss having to thread my way through three moving lines of teenage girls when I come to school. How can they have so much vitality at seven o'clock in the morning? About two dozen of them roll out of bed two days a week all year long to practice routines they use only a few times.

They're not sponsored by the school, so maybe that's why they can't use the commons anymore. But I miss them. How many other people are lucky enough to be able to go to work in a place where people dance in the halls? How many other people have a job where they can watch such a celebration of youthful energy—of life?

I'll admit: I sometimes danced a little myself while weaving through the choreography. At the very least, I could tap my toes while grading papers in my classroom nearby. Yes, I miss the drill team. I hope they come back.

Lord, thank you for the gifts of music, youth, and dancing; help me remember how to celebrate, how to dance! Amen.

July 15

DEPENDING ON EACH OTHER—READ ROMANS 15:1-2.

I'm flying! When our community players did *Peter Pan*, the stagehands offered free rides on the flying equipment to anyone in the cast and crew who could make the weight limit. So, a lot of kids and a few of us small adults took our turns at strapping on the harness and being hooked onto the cable.

As former students Frank and Jim manned the ropes, I flew up and down and back and forth across the stage. The view was about the same as what I see when I hang lights. But the sensation of flight was wonderful!

Eventually, they got tired. I had to land. "Weren't you worried?" Frank said with a grin. "I had you for English. Let's see," he rubbed his hands together, "what was my grade?" I smiled back. "I made you stage manager, remember? I trusted you then, and I trust you now."

In the theater, students and I work hand in hand, depending on one another. I hope it's as profound a lesson in life for them as it is for me. Somehow, we all get our chance to "fly."

Lord, thank you for the strong people who help me "fly"; make me strong when it's my turn to help others. Amen.

July 16

BEING GOD'S KID—READ MATTHEW 5:3-12.

It's tough to be a teacher's kid in a small town where there's only one school. All students complain about their teachers, but it's one thing to gripe about your own mom and another thing altogether to listen to other kids gripe about her. My own kids had to learn how to respond to disgruntled students who tried to get back at me by picking on my family—students who said, "I hate your mom." Teachers' kids get dirty looks from fellow students who are sure that teacher parents will favor their own offspring with unearned good grades.

Teachers' kids can't have any secrets; if Mr. Benson makes them spit out their gum, they can be sure he'll tell me at lunch. If my kids were late to school, they knew I wouldn't excuse them. If they decided to skip, they knew they'd be missed instantly. Of course, there were perks: my keys could provide access to the book they forgot to take home; also, they never had to go far to ask for money.

It's tough to be God's kid, too. Sometimes people pick on us because they're mad at God. We can't have any secrets, and even if we try to go AWOL, we're still in God's sight. But the perks are great. We have access to all we need, 24/7. And we don't have to go far to ask for anything.

Lord, thank you for being our loving Father—for keeping us always in your love even when we try to skip out and run away. Amen.

July 17

Prejudging Others—Read Romans 14:1-4.

Suddenly the room is quiet enough to hear the proverbial pin drop. I can't find a folder, and "Loser Lyle" has made a crack about my memory. The class waits expectantly for me to get angry and kick him out. If "Winner Wyatt" had said the same thing, we all would have laughed it off, because Wyatt is a "good kid" and can tease even teachers without consequence.

The class waits. They don't know that Lyle and I had a little chat about his grade. He wants to bring up his grade, and I suggested he attend regularly, do his homework, and not come to class high. So far, he's kept his promise; and right now, he's grinning from ear to ear at me—not at them! He wants my approval, not theirs. So I make a crack about his forgetting homework, and we all laugh, the tension broken.

But in that split second of stunned silence, Lyle taught me that in spite of ourselves, we have prejudices we're blind to—prejudices against the "Loser Lyles," from whom we expect only the worst. And so we usually get it.

Lord, open my eyes; help me find goodness in all your children. Amen.

JULY 18

PROCLAIMING GOD—READ REVELATION 7:9-12.

By their clothes ye shall know them! Boy, can you tell a lot about people by their T-shirts! Justin's wearing a black shirt with an almost psychedelic dragon design on the front and the schedule of a heavy metal band's tour on the back. Enrico, Joe, and Brian show their loyalty to the Broncos, the Royals, and the Cubs; DeeDee's pink shirt proclaims she's a Princess. Walk through the halls and meet Pooh, a white-tailed deer, Phys Ed Dept., Sponge Bob, State Track Meet, and *Midsummer Night's Dream*.

Students seem to have a shirt for every sport, play, musical, or camp in which they've participated. They can get a shirt from every conference, state contest, or activity they attend. Moms and grandmas make memory quilts from all of a graduate's old T's. Of course, nearly everybody in my home state of Nebraska has a wardrobe of Husker shirts.

Truly, our T-shirts show people who we are—a way we proclaim our message to the world. But how do we show the world we belong to God?

Lord, help me proclaim my message openly. Let me not be too shy to show I belong to you, that I'm on your team. Amen.

JULY 19

SECOND CHANCES—READ MATTHEW 18:21-22.

The principal—my boss—thinks Sinead deserves a second chance. For an entire year, she sat in my classroom and devoted herself to entertaining everyone. Highly intelligent, she aced all the tests, but she failed the course because she never did any homework. I thought I'd done all the parent notification things, but apparently there was a little glitch in the reporting system. Sinead was absent at the end of the quarter, and her grade in my class said "Incomplete" on her report card. When I turned in the completed grade, the school didn't notify the parents that she'd failed.

So now, in the middle of the summer, here I am in the principal's office. Mom and Dad have somewhat belatedly decided Sinead should have passed. I agree. She should have. So it goes a little against my grain that I'm supposed to come up with some assignments she can do during the rest of the summer to bring her grade up to passing—assignments I can also correct during the summer.

I'm clearly outnumbered here, and also outranked. So I grit my teeth and come up with some assignments. I guess it's always easier to *ask* for second chances than it is to *give* them.

Thank you, Lord, for the second chances you've given me. Help me be generous enough to give second chances to others. Amen.

JULY 20
BREAD—READ JOHN 6:30-33.

One thing I miss about school is the smell of fresh bread. The impersonal atmosphere of a stainless-steel school kitchen becomes downright cozy when Joyce and her lunch ladies set the dough hooks fwap-fwapping with soft fragrant homemade rolls in the making. Throughout the morning, the delicious aroma of baking dough fills the hallways.

I used to bake bread—the old way, not by tossing ingredients into an appliance and setting the timer. There's something so elemental about setting dough to rise, kneading it, and forming it into loaves with your bare hands. A gift of homemade bread—even a quick bread that doesn't involve much work—sends a message unmatched by any other offering.

Every cuisine I know of has some type of bread as its most basic component, and the ability to make fine bread has been a cook's source of pride for centuries. For the Mexican dinner, tortillas must be rolled by hand and made from scratch with flour or *masa harina;* for the Norwegian buffet, the *lefse* has to be made from newly harvested potatoes.

Bread; we call it the staff of life. Throughout the Bible we read how God nourishes his people with bread, culminating in the Bread of Life—Jesus.

Lord, thank you for the wonderful gift of bread, and for the Bread of Life. Amen.

July 21
Seeing Past the Surface—Read 1 Samuel 16:4-7.

Paula, busily steaming a pair of slacks before putting them on the rack, turns to examine me. I don't normally shop at this store, but they're having a good sale. Besides, it's kind of fun to reconnect with Paula, a former student now in college. She smiles in approval. "It looks great on you," she gushes in her best salesclerk voice. "Besides, it'll go with everything you have." Then she starts naming the various blouses I have that this skirt will match!

"How do you know what I have?" I ask. She looks puzzled. "I took your class, remember?" Day after day, she watched me explain verbs, thesis statements, and Steinbeck. I thought she was learning English, but she'd really been memorizing my wardrobe! Well, to be fair, it is Paula's job to help people renew their tired wardrobes.

But I think of her sometimes on Sunday when I catch my attention wandering to the pastor's haircut, a fellow worshiper's wrinkled jeans, a teenager's skimpy dress. I think of her when I answer that student who comes in every day after school to ask the same questions over and over. Am I seeing what God wants me to see, or am I just looking at the outside? Am I doing what God wants me to do, or just going through the motions?

Lord, help me look past outer appearances; help me learn your true message. Amen.

July 22
Minimum Standards—Read 1 Corinthians 3:1-4.

Yippee! A summer workshop on standards assessment. We have to figure out cutoff scores on the state standards tests

289

given by Educational Service Unit 15. What this means is that we have to say how low the kids can score and still pass the test. People outside of education don't understand why we can't say that everybody has to read at twelfth-grade level to get out of the twelfth grade. I'm not sure I understand, either, but I know that if we did say that, a lot of kids wouldn't graduate.

The trouble with a minimum standard is that it encourages people to aim low and to be satisfied with a mediocre effort. Indeed, how many of our students do the least amount of work possible to pass? But we fear a standard too high can be discouraging to less capable students. Where's the happy medium?

God sets high standards. Casting sin out of our lives is a tall order, especially if that includes *keeping* it out. But God doesn't have a cutoff score. We're always welcomed back if we repent. Still, we look for the minimum. How little time can we spend going to church, reading the Bible, praying, or helping our neighbors and still squeeze past "graduation"? What's the minimum effort we can put forth to meet God's standard?

Lord, help me aim high; help me look past the standards of the world and serve only you. Amen.

July 23

Safe Havens—Read Matthew 10:29-31.

I wonder where Kyle goes in the summer? During the school year, he's always alone in the commons at 6:30 A.M. doing his homework. Sometimes I think our school should serve breakfast; his is usually a candy bar and a soda. There are others like him—even some from primary grades. Do they walk to school on their own, or do their parents drop them off on the way to work?

After school, they hang around in the lobby, sometimes into the evening. They're at all the ball games, getting supper from the concession stand. They show up for Saturday speech contests and Sunday community concerts. Sometimes when the building is closed, they skateboard or play games outside the front door, dodging the barn swallows that build nests under the overhang. Don't they have homes?

I've heard whispered comments about Kyle's "family situation." Once his grandmother came to parent conferences. She said that he'd always liked school, that he'd always felt safe in school. I wonder what "family situations" impel these kids, many of whom profess to hate school, to be here day and night? It's almost as if school were their home. Maybe it is.

Lord, help us make school a safe haven for kids; more important, help their parents make a safe haven for them at their homes. Amen.

JULY 24

SERVICE AND WORK—READ LUKE 10:38-42.

Where *do* they get those brown paper towels that hang from dispensers all over the school? Those are some tough towels! In first grade, my son had a habit of collecting them. Instead of finding frogs and snakes in his pockets, I found brown paper towels. Once I forgot to check until I pulled from the dryer a clean, dry brown paper towel—completely intact! They may not be as absorbent as the expensive brands, and they certainly aren't as decorative, but they are sure tough!

Sometimes I think we teachers have to be like that: impervious to everything. Kids fighting in the hall? No problem; just break it up. Playground duty in the middle of January? Bring your snow boots. Have to drive an activity van at 4 A.M.? Bring coffee. We're good at responsibility. Our lives become defined by our work.

But sometimes, we "brown-paper-towel people" can too easily lose sight of our purpose if all we see is the work. We bury our noses in job after little job, secretly rejoicing in our indispensability but losing sight of the reason for our service. Like Martha, we can overlook the presence of the Lord in our lives.

Lord, help me discern the difference between just working and laboring in your service; help me rejoice in your presence. Amen.

JULY 25

NEW LIFE—READ JOHN 16:21-22.

Shari had her baby; the word is all over school. Everyone was wondering if she'd make it through graduation; the word was her husband's friends had a betting pool on her delivery time. But she walked in with the other seniors and sat through the two-hour ceremony. The next day, she had a baby girl. Even the teachers are happy for her. In January, she married the baby's father, who graduated last year. He works for a local farmer, so their little family will live in the hired man's house. This baby will have a home. Teachers worry about things like that.

Too often the story doesn't turn out happily. A too-young mother has to turn her back on sports, on cheerleading, on the prom, and grow up too soon. A teen father cries out in anguish when he discovers his girlfriend has aborted his child. Parents turn into grandparents, and then back into parents of the babies their children can't raise. Single teen moms go on welfare because they can't afford to work and pay child care. We cluck our tongues at the irresponsibility of it all.

But Shari and her young husband have a new daughter, and both families are rejoicing.

Lord, thank you for the gift of life; let me see in every child a renewal of your Spirit. Amen.

JULY 26

EXPECTATIONS—READ JOHN 9:1-7.

I got talked into helping sponsor a junior-high dance. Little knots of girls busily twist crepe paper streamers, sprinkle glitter on posters, and tape dollar store decorations to the walls of the church basement. On the night of the dance, the blue and purple mood lights are dimmed. The disc jockey dad is trying out some tunes. The refreshments are set, and we chaperones are on duty. The girls wait. Where are the boys? Finally, they edge through the door—all of them at once.

Soon, a mischievous-looking boy comes to the kitchen for more punch. "Don't worry," he grins as he careens out the door, the glass bowl balanced precariously on one hand. A distraught girl comes in for more cookies. "No one wants to dance," she says. The boys only want to jump up and down, and then check to see who has the fastest pulse. "It wasn't supposed to be like this," she wails. I smile inside. It never is.

Sometimes we adults also worry about how things are "supposed to be" according to *our* standards; sometimes God has a different plan that leaves us confused, disappointed, or even angry.

Lord, give me the faith to accept your plan for me, even when it doesn't meet my expectations of what I think it's "supposed to be." Amen.

JULY 27

THE SHEEP OF HIS FLOCK—READ JOHN 10:1-10.

It's county fair time. Many of my students display their 4-H animals, so I pack up the grandkids for a visit to the cattle, poultry, hogs, and sheep. The little lambs in my childhood Bible storybooks were so white and cute and soft looking. When I moved to rural America years ago, the sight of real sheep was a shock! They're dirty and stupid. The 4-H kids have to groom them almost constantly to keep them presentable for judging.

Countless references in the Bible compare us humans to sheep. It's not a flattering comparison. You can look into their eyes and see . . . absolutely nothing! I'm told the ewes have to be shown how to nurse their young, and even then, the poor lambs might be rejected by their mothers. My veterinarian friend says they get all manner of diseases and parasites, and they'll blindly follow one another even into perdition. Truly, it takes a special kind of person to be able to put up with sheep.

With our college degrees and years of experience, it's easy for us to think we're the shepherds instead of the sheep. But encounters with real sheep have given me a deeper understanding of just what the Lord is trying to tell us about our condition, and the depth of his love for us.

Lord, renew in me the spirit of humility. Amen.

293

JULY 28
BEING A POSITIVE INFLUENCE—
READ MATTHEW 18:6-7.

On the midway at the county fair, I heard her call my name. As we traded small talk, I finally recognized her. "Lori?" I asked. "I'm an English teacher now," she said. I never would have guessed. In my class, she was more interested in beauty, fashion, and popularity than in great literature. She was a good student, but I hadn't thought about her since she graduated. Suddenly, she blurted out, "You were my favorite teacher, you know." I hadn't known. I'd had no clue.

It always surprises me when I run across a former student who not only recognizes me after ten or twenty years, but also confides in me a strong emotion held over from high school. Some are still angry because they think I lost their papers or because they got bad grades. Others, like Lori, saw me in a more positive light. It staggers my imagination to think what a powerful influence we must have on these young people with whom we share a classroom day after day.

I hope I can remember each time I walk into the classroom just how impressionable these youngsters are. Unfortunately, there will be some who will latch onto some perceived shortcoming of mine, surround it with resentment, and carry it into their future. Others, I hope, will be able to find something more positive.

Lord, help me bring your peace and love to every student. Amen.

JULY 29

GETTING CREDIT—READ MATTHEW 20:1-6.

How did I get into this? Here I am sitting above the dunk tank at the county fair, waiting for someone to throw a baseball hard enough to trip the lever that will drop me into the water. We're raising money for the Little League program—

we teachers taking our turns on "dunk your favorite teacher" day. So far, I'm lucky; most of my students aren't yet off work from their summer jobs. The only people trying to dunk me are my friends and family.

I'm also lucky because it's hot outside. It actually feels good to be wet. The people who really deserve the credit for raising money for this cause are the ones who have to sit here and shiver in a cold wind on a sunless day. I'm one of those servants who gets the same credit as everybody else, even if I don't deserve as much.

The times I'm on the other side—when I get the largest classes, the most discipline problems, the eighth-period freshman study hall—it's really easy to complain loudly at the unfairness of life. It's easy to forget the times like today at the dunk tank, when my "job" is simply to sit in the sunshine, enjoying my friends and family, just waiting for a refreshing dip.

Lord, when life is unfair, help me look at my own balance sheet, where I'll see many more easy jobs than difficult ones. Amen.

JULY 30

REFRESHING WATERS—READ ISAIAH 12:2-4.

I love to dive into the startlingly cool water of the pool. I breaststroke, sidestroke, backstroke, and crawl back and forth until, exhausted, I pull myself out onto the warm concrete. Cool water! It's one of the best things about summer. After a stint of baking on the beach at the lake, I love to run splashing into the water. I taught all my children to swim, and now I'm teaching my grandchildren. There's something about the weightless sensation of floating—about the velvet pressure on my skin as I stroke through water—that seems almost mystical.

However, for those just learning to swim, entering the water can be frightening indeed. Water can destroy as well as soothe us. What if we become tired far away from shore? What if a storm comes and makes the water rough? Why risk drowning when it would be safer to stay out of the water?

The "waters" of discipleship can also be frightening. Wouldn't it be easier to stay out of the water than live a life of commitment to Christ? What if we don't like being a Christian as much as we thought we would? What if we get tired? Sometimes it's easy to forget that only in Christ can we find true joy.

Lord, help me immerse myself in your life, live joyfully my commitments to you, and help others do the same. Amen.

JULY 31
HEALING—READ PSALM 147:1-3.

I don't recall her name, or why she'd remained so long in my classroom after school. Maybe she was getting help with a vocabulary lesson, or struggling with an essay we'd begun when she was absent. I was helping her with half my mind, the other half being preoccupied with grading papers and preparing tomorrow's lesson plans. "I was absent a lot last year," she confided. I vaguely recalled thinking her spotty attendance was the reason she'd failed and was now repeating my class. "Maybe you noticed I always wear long sleeves," she continued. I hadn't. "Mmmm," my voice replied.

Then she showed me the scars on her wrists. My mind snapped to attention. She'd tried to kill herself last term, and I hadn't noticed! She was OK now, she said. Regular counseling from her pastor had helped her come through her crisis. But she was still ashamed of the scars. What could I say?

I told her how my own children had fallen, failed, and been wounded in spite of my best efforts to protect them. They have scars, too, I told her, both physical and emotional—but only scars, not open wounds. Then words came from somewhere outside me: Our scars are *healed* wounds—proof of survival, badges of the healing power of God.

Lord, thank you for renewing us with the healing power of your love. Amen.